MUSIC THEORY TRANSLATION SERIES, 4
CLAUDE V. PALISCA, EDITOR

The Art of
Strict
Musical Composition

JOHANN PHILIPP KIRNBERGER

Translated by
DAVID BEACH *and* JURGEN THYM
Introduction and Explanatory Notes by
DAVID BEACH

NEW HAVEN AND LONDON
YALE UNIVERSITY PRESS

Designed by James J. Johnson
and set in Monophoto Plantin type by
Asco Trade Typesetting Ltd., Hong Kong.
Printed in the United States of America by
Halliday Lithograph, West Hanover, Mass.

Library of Congress Cataloging in Publication Data

Kirnberger, Johann Philipp, 1721–1783.
  The art of strict musical composition.

  (Music theory translation series, 4)
  Includes index.
  1. Composition (Music) I. Title. II. Series.
MT40. K5713   781.6′1   81–853
ISBN 0–300–02483–5   AACR2

10 9 8 7 6 5 4 3 2 1

Contents

Preface

With this volume the Music Theory Translation Series returns to territory
penetrated by our first, Gasparini's *Practical Harmonist at the Harpsichord*
of 1708. A treatise on accompaniment, to be sure, it teaches as well the
fundamentals of harmonic practice. Gasparini's blinkered vision of chord
progression, shared by his contemporaries, barely spanning a cadential
pattern of a few chords, could not yield a theory of harmonic progression. A
leap to such a modern longitudinal harmonic conception was taken by
Rameau. Now that his *Traité de l'harmonie* of 1722 has become available in
an excellent English translation by Philip Gossett (New York: Dover,
1971), the time is ripe to make accessible to the non-German-reading world
the system of Johann Philipp Kirnberger, whose ideas on harmony were
influenced by Rameau. In choosing from Kirnberger's multivolume work,
Die Kunst des reinen Satzes in der Musik (1771–79), the heart of his theory
of harmonic syntax—all of Volume I (1771) and the first part of Volume II
(1776; omitting the volumes of 1777 and 1779 on double counterpoint)—
we were guided by the objective of this series to make available treatises
that are landmarks in musical thought and not merely pedagogical hand-
books. (A supplement to Kirnberger's major work, published under his
name but actually by Johann Abraham Peter Schulz, *Die wahren Grundsätze zum Gebrauch der Harmonie* [The true principles for the practice of
harmony] in a translation by Beach and Thym has been published separately in *Journal of Music Theory* 23, no. 2 [1979]: 163–225.)

  Kirnberger's central contribution is his theory of harmonic progression
and of the art of constructing harmonic periods, including modulation to
both near and remote keys. Although rooted in the discipline of strict
counterpoint of his teacher, Johann Sebastian Bach, Kirnberger did not fail

to recognize the melodic and harmonic style that he calls *galant*, thereby revealing himself a true child of his age, sensitive to the current preoccupation with periodic phraseology and melodic and motivic construction. He thus lays the groundwork for the later exhaustive study of melody building in the treatise that will be the next volume in this series, a translation by Nancy Kovaleff Baker of the sections on melodic composition from Heinrich Christoph Koch's *Versuch einer Anleitung zur Composition* [Introductory essay on composition] of 1782 to 1793.

As with the other volumes of this series, the translation of Kirnberger has received several close readings and word-for-word comparisons with the German original, not only by this editor but also by a bilingual specialist in the music theory of the eighteenth and nineteenth centuries, Harald Krebs, whom we thank for his many incisive and helpful recommendations. Having as one of the translators a native German speaker and musicologist and as the other a musical theorist whose Ph.D. dissertation at Yale was a study of Kirnberger's theories confers on this volume redoubled authority.

The preparation of this translation, along with several others soon to appear, was supported by a grant from the National Endowment for the Humanities. To the director of its Translation Program, Susan Mango, and her advisors, we are grateful for the encouragement of and confidence in our series. The continuing enthusiastic interest of Edward Tripp, Editor in Chief of the Yale University Press, has been an inspiration to all of us. To Walter Biddle Saul II we owe the elegant autography of the musical examples and to Maura Tantillo the smooth progress of this book's production.

CLAUDE V. PALISCA
Editor, Music Theory Translation Series

Introduction to the Translation

One of the primary theoretical concerns of the eighteenth century was the redefinition of harmony. With the exception of the few works that were limited to the subjects of counterpoint, ornamentation, or performance, hardly a treatise was written during that time which did not deal in some way with the classification of chords and the rules that govern their use. This preoccupation with the vertical dimension in music can be traced, at least in part, to needs arising from the practice of thorough bass. By the turn of the eighteenth century the number of signatures employed, and thus the number of discrete chords identified, had increased to the point where some means of organization was required for the figured-bass method to remain of practical use to musicians. This need led to the development of several different systems of classification, all of which were designed to facilitate learning the growing number of signatures. Probably the most famous, and certainly the most thorough and informative, of the figured-bass treatises was Johann David Heinichen's monumental work *Der Generalbass in der Composition* (Dresden, 1728). Heinichen divided all chords into two categories, those that were composed exclusively of consonant intervals, the triad and sixth chord, and those that contained one or more dissonant intervals; the latter were classified according to the size of the dissonant interval(s) above the bass, in ascending order from seconds to ninths. The matter of chord succession was also considered by Heinichen, first in his exhaustive study of the treatment of dissonance in the theatrical style and immediately following in the chapter on unfigured bass. His rules for determining the figures from an unfigured bass contain the seeds for a theory of chord progression, but this potential was never realized. *Der*

Generalbass in der Composition was the last of the major treatises, at least in Germany, to deal with this important topic.

A vastly different approach to harmony was presented by Jean Philippe Rameau in his several publications, beginning with the *Traité de l'harmonie* (Paris, 1722). Unlike the early figured-bass theorists, whose orientation was practical rather than speculative, Rameau based his theory on the premise that harmony has its roots in acoustical phenomena and mathematical relationships. Throughout his works Rameau strove to provide a scientific explanation and justification for the practice of harmony. During the course of his investigations he presented several concepts that eventually were to have a profound effect on the theory of harmony. Quite ironically it was not the scientific validity but the practical implications of these principles that led to their acceptance. In this respect his definition of chord inversion is of utmost importance. Although Rameau was not the first to describe this phenomenon, he was the first to describe it in the manner that was to become generally accepted. Also, Rameau was the first to propose a theory in which all chords can be related to one of two fundamental harmonies, the perfect triad and the seventh chord, which is given as the source of all dissonant chords. Finally, he proposed a theory of chord progression through his definition of the fundamental bass and the rules that govern its succession. Although the details of Rameau's theories of chord classification and progression were not generally accepted, the ideal they represented became a fundamental ingredient in many subsequent theories of harmony.

The resistance to Rameau's theories in his own country as well as elsewhere was considerable at first. However, it was probably inevitable that his definition of chord inversion and notion of fundamental harmonies should achieve some acceptance, since they provided the possibility for a clearer definition of harmony. Gradually these ideas, often appearing in modified form, gained a foothold in Germany, causing a split in the ranks of the figured-bass theorists. Heinichen, Mattheson, and C. P. E. Bach can be counted among those who rejected Rameau's theories, while his influence is evident to varying degrees in the writings of men such as Sorge, Daube, and Marpurg. The primary reason for rejection is obvious: the principles upon which Rameau's theories and the German tradition of thorough bass were founded are totally at odds. With the exception of Marpurg, who was the chief advocate of Rameau's theories in Germany, those who chose to borrow from Rameau did so without any regard for the premises upon which his ideas were built. These men were interested in the practical application of ideas, and they must have realized that a simplification of existing theories of harmony would most readily be achieved through some sort of synthesis of Rameau's definition of chord inversion and the principles of figured-bass theory. This synthesis was eventually realized in the writings of Johann Philipp Kirnberger (1721–83).

The most complete statement of Kirnberger's theories is contained in *Die Kunst des reinen Satzes in der Musik* (1771–79), the work translated in part here. According to Johann Abraham Peter Schulz, Kirnberger's most accomplished student, the first volume of this work was the direct result of Kirnberger's association with the aesthetician Johann Georg Sulzer.[1] Sulzer had engaged Kirnberger to instruct him in the principles of music theory and to provide him with information for the music articles in his *Allgemeine Theorie der schönen Künste*.[2] In the process of doing so, Kirnberger was forced to organize his ideas more clearly than he might have otherwise.[3] The first fruit of this collaboration was the publication of the first volume of *Die Kunst des reinen Satzes in der Musik* in 1771; the first volume of Sulzer's work (entries *A–I*) followed later in the same year. In 1773 Schulz returned to Berlin after a five-year absence and became involved to an increasing extent in the preparation and, from the letter *S* on, the writing of the music articles for the second volume of Sulzer's encyclopedia, first published in 1774. Meanwhile he became acquainted with Kirnberger's treatise and, for his own benefit, wrote out a summary of the principles of harmony expressed in it. According to Schulz, Kirnberger was pleased with the result and allowed it to be published as an appendix to his own work under the title proposed by Sulzer: *Die wahren Grundsätze zum Gebrauch der Harmonie* (1773). According to Johann Friedrich Reichardt,[4] Schulz was also involved to some extent in the preparation of the second volume of *Die Kunst des reinen Satzes in der Musik*, which was published in three installments. The first of these, published in 1776, is a direct continuation of the material

1. J. A. P. Schulz, "Über die in Sulzers Theorie der schönen Künste unter dem Artikel Verrückung angeführten zwey Beispiele . . . ," *Allgemeine musikalische Zeitung* II (1800), pp. 273–80.
2. Johann Georg Sulzer, *Allgemeine Theorie der schönen Künste* (Leipzig, 1771 and 1774).
3. Kirnberger apparently had considerable difficulty organizing and expressing his ideas clearly in writing, which leads one to speculate whether his work would ever have reached print had it not been for the assistance of Sulzer and later Schulz.
4. J. F. Reichardt, "J. A. P. Schulz," *Allgemeine musikalische Zeitung* III (1801), p. 601.

contained in Volume I, and together they form a complete unit. It is this portion that has been chosen for translation here. The remaining two parts, first published in 1777 and 1779, also form a complete and separate unit; they deal exclusively with double counterpoint and its compositional applications.[5]

Die Kunst des reinen Satzes in der Musik contains considerable information about a wide variety of topics ranging from scales, keys, and modes to tempo, meter, and rhythm. The major portion of the work, however, is devoted to a consideration of harmony and its relationship to melody, counterpoint, and form. First of all, there are several chapters or parts of chapters that deal with chords, their classification and their treatment, and with rules that govern their progression. There are also several chapters that deal with the articulation of larger and smaller formal divisions by means of harmonic cadences, and the relationship of modulation to larger formal design. Finally, it is pertinent to note that even in his discussion of melody and simple counterpoint Kirnberger placed much of the emphasis on their relationship to harmony.

A basic feature of Kirnberger's harmonic theories is his method of relating all chords used in music to two fundamental harmonies, the triad and the essential seventh chord. All other chords are shown to be derived from one of these two by inversion and/or temporal displacement of one or more of their tones. This view leads to the following four categories of chords: (1) the consonant triads and their inversions; (2) the dissonant essential seventh chords and their inversions; (3) chords resulting from the displacement of one or more tones of the consonant triads and their inversions; and (4) chords resulting from the displacement of one or more tones of the seventh chords and their inversions.[6] Related to this system of chord classification is Kirnberger's definition of essential and nonessential dissonance, an important step in the development of harmonic theory. The seventh chords built on all degrees except the leading tone of the scale were considered by Kirnberger to be essential, while chords resulting from rhythmic displacement (suspension) were not. That is, only the former were considered by Kirnberger to be harmonic entities. The differences between these two types of dissonance and their treatment in both the strict and

---

5. A later work, *Grundsätze des Generalbasses* (1781), was written by Kirnberger as an introduction to *Die Kunst des reinen Satzes in der Musik.*

6. These chords are listed in the four tables at the end of chapter 3.

galant styles[7] are discussed in the third, fourth, and fifth chapters of *Die Kunst des reinen Satzes in der Musik* I.

There are many other features of Kirnberger's harmonic theories that warrant comment. Two of these, Kirnberger's dual interpretation of the six-four chord and his use of the fundamental bass, are of special significance to the present discussion. First of all, the fact that Kirnberger identifies both a consonant and a dissonant six-four chord sets him apart from the other theorists of his time. It is also an indication of the different forces that influenced his thinking. The earlier figured-bass theorists like Heinichen and Mattheson, for example, considered all six-four chords to be dissonant because of the dissonant interval of a fourth. On the other hand, Rameau and his followers viewed all such chords as consonant because they are related to consonant triads by inversion. Kirnberger, however, stated that the six-four chord could be either consonant or dissonant, depending upon the context. The six-four chord that occurs at a cadence was considered by him to be dissonant because it is a nonessential chord that displaces the five-three, which normally follows over the same bass note. (Though the reasoning is different, this conclusion is consistent with figured-bass theory.) In additon, Kirnberger stated that the roots of the two chords are the same (the bass), which stands in direct contradiction to Rameau's view that each has a separate root. However, in other circumstances Kirnberger followed Rameau's view that six-four chords are consonant inversions of the perfect chord. Although this dual interpretation of the six-four chord did not meet with approval in Kirnberger's time, it is generally accepted today.

It is clear that Kirnberger owed a lot more to Rameau than he would have cared to admit. With the one exception noted above, he adopted Rameau's definition of chord inversion and, like Rameau, related all chords to two fundamental harmonies, though, of course, in quite a different way. He also borrowed from Rameau the idea of the fundamental bass to indicate his own view of the roots of chords and thus the harmonic organization of a succession of chords. His application of this device to the analysis of his own Fugue in E minor, which was first published at the end of the first volume of

---

7. The relative brevity of Kirnberger's discussion of the treatment of dissonance in the *galant* style is indicative of his conservative attitude toward the art of composition. In the preface to *Die Kunst des reinen Satzes in der Musik* he states his conviction that the basis of composition lies in the observance of the rules of strict composition. The liberties associated with the *galant* style are thus to be understood only in relation to their counterparts in the strict style.

Die Kunst des reinen Satzes in der Musik, is of considerable historical significance; it and the two "analyses" of Schulz[8] rank among the earliest attempts at harmonic analysis.[9] However, it must be pointed out that there is only a superficial similarity between Kirnberger's and Rameau's application of the fundamental bass since there is such a vast difference in their concepts of harmony, or more specifically in their conceptions of the relationship between vertical and linear aspects of harmony. Rameau considered all chords, even those resulting from temporal displacement, as harmonic entities, whereas Kirnberger gave such status only to his two fundamental chords, the triad and the essential seventh chord, and their inversions. Thus, for example, where Rameau would indicate two separate fundamentals for a suspension chord and the harmony supporting its resolution, Kirnberger would indicate only the latter. Furthermore, even though Kirnberger did borrow from Rameau, he did so without accepting the acoustical and mathematical premises upon which Rameau's theories were built. In fact, Kirnberger, whose training and sympathy lay with the German tradition of figured bass, was outspoken in his criticism of Rameau's theories. Thus it is not surprising that he would be reluctant to acknowledge Rameau's influence and would try to minimize his contributions by placing the credit elsewhere, as in the following passage:

> Since Rameau was the first to introduce a written fundamental bass, his countrymen have credited him with its discovery. Some of them are so ignorant that they proclaim with amusing assurance that Rameau was the first to reduce the science of harmony, which before him was most uncertain, to its basic principles, and was the first to show that certain chords are not true fundamental chords, but inversions of others. These people must not know, then, that the science of double counterpoint, which many Italian and German composers have understood far better than Rameau, is by all means based on this recognition of fundamental harmonies, since it is impossible in double counterpoint to compose even one measure without the inversion of chords. Thus what all good composers understood and used daily more than a hundred years before

8. Schulz's analyses of two works by J. S. Bach, the Fugue in B minor from Volume I and the Prelude in A minor from Volume II of *Das wohltemperierte Klavier*, were published at the end of *Die wahren Grundsätze zum Gebrauch der Harmonie* (1773).

9. For further information regarding the significance of these early attempts at harmonic analysis, see David Beach, "The Origins of Harmonic Analysis," *Journal of Music Theory*, vol. 18, no. 2 (1974), pp. 274–306.

Rameau, this wonderful man, this sole lawgiver of music, has discovered first.[10]

That Kirnberger would not only borrow from Rameau without acknowledging his source but, more importantly, that he would then use these ideas in his own way was a source of conflict between Kirnberger and Friedrich Wilhelm Marpurg, the self-appointed defender of Rameau's theories in Germany. In the lengthy appendix to his *Versuch über die musikalische Temperatur* (Breslau, 1776), Marpurg unleashed a bitter attack on Kirnberger's theories, much of which was directed at *Die wahren Grundsätze zum Gebrauch der Harmonie*. The major objects of Marpurg's criticism were Kirnberger's definition of essential and nonessential dissonance,[11] and his use of the fundamental bass.[12] Marpurg, who was an admirer of Bach's music, was also angered by Kirnberger's claim that his and not Rameau's or Marpurg's principles were based on those of J. S. Bach, with whom Kirnberger had studied for a year or two.[13] This prompted Marpurg to call on the authority of C. P. E. Bach to settle the matter once and for all. The result, which is of historical significance, proved disastrous for Marpurg, since Kirnberger was able to reply by publishing the following excerpts from a letter he had received from C. P. E. Bach.

The behavior of Herr Marpurg toward you is detestable.

You can loudly proclaim that mine and my late father's principles are anti-Rameau.[14]

10. From the article "Fundamentalbass" in Sulzer's *Allgemeine Theorie der schönen Künste*. Here Kirnberger is reflecting the observation made years earlier by Heinichen that chord inversion has its origin in double counterpoint. See *Der Generalbass in der Composition*, p. 206, note Z.

11. F. W. Marpurg, *Versuch über die musikalische Temperatur, nebst einem Anhang über den Rameau- und Kirnbergerschen Grundbass* (Breslau, 1776), p. 240.

12. Marpurg spends considerable time showing how Kirnberger's use of the fundamental bass differs from that of Rameau, which eventually led Marpurg, partially through a misinterpretation of Rameau, to characterize Kirnberger's fundamental bass as an "interpolated" bass. For one opinion regarding the fairness of this characterization, see Cecil Power Grant's article, "The Real Relationship between Kirnberger's and Rameau's Concept of the Fundamental Bass," *Journal of Music Theory*, vol. 21, no. 2 (1977), pp. 324–38.

13. Kirnberger studied with Bach in Leipzig between 1739 and 1741. Whether or not Kirnberger studied with him for two full years or for just part of that time is not known.

14. These comments were published at the very end of *Die Kunst des reinen Statzes in der Musik* (volume II, part 3, p. 188).

Kirnberger's admiration for the elder Bach's music is evident through-out his writings. It is clear from the following passage that he had an equally high regard for Bach's method of teaching composition and that this method had a direct influence on his own approach to the subject.

> In all his works Johann Sebastian Bach employs a completely pure style; every piece has a definite unified character. Rhythm, melody, harmony, in short everything that makes a composition really be-autiful he has completely in his power, as witnessed by his written works. His method is the best because he proceeds step by step from the simplest to the most difficult, whereby even the step to fugue itself is no more difficult than any other step. For this reason I consider *the method of Johann Sebastian Bach to be the only and best one.*

> It is regrettable that this great man never wrote anything of a theoretical nature about music and that his teachings have survived only through his students.

> I have sought to reduce the method of the late Joh. Seb. Bach to basic principles and to present his teachings to the best of my ability in my *Kunst des reinen Satzes*.[15]

The context from which these comments are taken is Kirnberger's evaluation of what he considered to be the best of the existing treatises on counterpoint.[16] This must be kept in mind when considering Kirnberger's claim that his treatise is a reflection of Bach's method of teaching.[17] That is, this claim does not imply that all of his ideas (e.g., his classification of chords and theory of essential and nonessential dissonance) are attributable to Bach, but only that he had followed his teacher's method and order of

15. Kirnberger, *Gedanken über die verschiedenen Lehrarten in der Komposition, als Vorbereitung zur Fugenkenntniss* (Berlin, 1782), pp. 4–5.

16. The three treatises discussed briefly by Kirnberger are Berardi's *Documenti armonici* (Bologna, 1687), Bononcini's *Musico prattico* (Bologna, 1688), and Fux's *Gradus ad Parnassum* (Vienna, 1725).

17. The strongest support for this claim comes from Johann Nicolaus Forkel in his biography of Bach, *Über Johann Sebastian Bachs Leben, Kunst und Kunstwerke* (Leipzig, 1802). See *The Bach Reader*, edited by Hans T. David and Arthur Mendel, revised edition (New York, 1966), p. 330. From this passage it would appear as if Forkel was simply paraphrasing Kirnberger rather than substantiating his claim.

presenting materials. A description of Bach's approach to teaching composition was provided by his most famous son, C. P. E. Bach, in a letter to Johann Nicolaus Forkel (dated 13 January 1775).

> In composition he started his pupils right in with what was practical, and omitted all the *dry species* of counterpoint that were given by Fux and others. His pupils had to begin their studies by learning pure four-part thorough bass. From this he went to chorales; first he added the basses to them himself, and they had to invent the alto and tenor. Then he taught them to devise the basses themselves. He particularly insisted on the writing out of the thorough bass in [four real] parts (*Aussetzen der Stimmen im Generalbasse*). In teaching fugues, he began with two-part ones, and so on.

> The realization of a thorough bass and the introduction to chorales are without doubt the best method of studying composition, as far as harmony is concerned.[18]

The basic features of Bach's method of teaching composition, as reported here, are clearly reflected in Kirnberger's writings. *Grudsätze des Generalbasses* (1781) was written expressly for the purpose of providing the beginning student with proper instruction in figured bass and four-part harmony. In *Die Kunst des reinen Satzes in der Musik* the steps to composition lead from the study of four-part harmony to simple counterpoint, and eventually to double counterpoint and fugue. As far as simple counterpoint is concerned, Kirnberger recommends that the student begin with four parts rather than two or three, since it is always easier to deal with complete as opposed to incomplete harmony. And, as was the case with Bach, the art of composition is introduced through the four-part chorale, first note against note and later embellished.

During the latter half of the eighteenth century, counterpoint instruction normally meant the study of species counterpoint as codified by Johann Fux in his *Gradus ad Parnassum*. This approach, which begins with two-part writing, is primarily linear in conception. The vertical dimension is controlled exclusively by intervallic considerations. Thus in recommending that the study of counterpoint begin with four parts to accommodate harmonic considerations, Kirnberger was going against the prevailing practice of treating harmony and counterpoint as separate disciplines. Although

18. See *The Bach Reader*, p. 279.

Kirnberger's recommendation would seem to be a logical corollary to the compositional practice of the time, the idea was ignored. Species counterpoint persisted as the backbone of counterpoint instruction for some time, while so-called Bach counterpoint did not gain favor until well into the nineteenth century.[19] In contrast, Kirnberger's harmonic theories, particularly those noted above, had an immediate impact on musical thought.[20]

In preparing the translation of Volume I and Volume II, part 1, of *Die Kunst des reinen Satzes in der Musik*, the following editions and printings were consulted: the original edition of Volume I (Berlin: C. F. Voss, 1771) and its reprint with a new title page (Berlin and Königsberg: G. J. Decker and G. L. Hartung, 1774); the corrected edition of Volume I (Berlin: H. A. Rottmann, 1776?); the first printing of Volume II, part 1 (Berlin and Königsberg: G. J. Decker and G. L. Hartung, 1776); and the modern reprint of the entire work (Hildesheim: Georg Olms, 1968).[21] The only significant difference between the first and subsequent printings of Volume I was the incorporation of the errata into the text of the Rottmann edition. This change has been adopted in the present translation.

The reader may note certain minor differences between the original version and the following translation, none of which affect the content. One change involves the numbering of the musical examples and tables so that they could be moved if required by the pagination. This in turn has required some liberties in the text, so that references could be made to specific examples or tables. Otherwise every attempt has been made to be faithful to the original. Also certain additions have been made to make the translation

19. See, for example, Ernst Richter's *Lehrbuch des einfachen und doppelten Kontrapunkts* (Leipzig, 1872).

20. The influence of Kirnberger's harmonic theories is most evident in the writings of Augustus Frederic Christopher Kollmann and Daniel Gottlob Türk. For further information regarding Kirnberger's harmonic theories and their influence, see David Beach, *The Harmonic Theories of Johann Philipp Kirnberger; Their Origins and Influences* (Diss., Yale University, 1974), Ann Arbor: University Microfilms (no. 75–1338).

21. The Olms reprint claims to be a photocopy of the Berlin and Königsberg edition of 1776–79. However, the first volume was not printed during that time and thus this reprint is probably a copy of one of the earlier printings (either of 1771 or 1774) with the substitution of the title page belonging to the 1776 printing of Volume II, part 1. The only other difference is the placement of Kirnberger's analysis of his own Fugue in E minor, which appears at the beginning rather than the end of Volume I, where it belongs.

easier to use and more valuable as a research document. A table of contents and an index, which were lacking in the original, have been added. Explanatory notes have been added to clarify certain points or to indicate, for example, the translation of problematic terminology. (The explanatory notes are indicated by lowercase letters, beginning a new series for each chapter; Kirnberger's notes are numbered consecutively throughout each volume, as in the original.) Finally, the bracketed numbers in the text refer to the corresponding page numbers in the modern reprint of the German edition.

There are many individuals who should be mentioned for their assistance in this project. I would especially like to thank the staff of the Sibley Music Library of the Eastman School of Music and the staff of the Music Library at Yale University for their cooperation. I am particularly indebted to Allen Forte for his generosity and trust in lending me his personal copy of the 1771 edition of *Die Kunst des reinen Satzes in der Musik* I. Finally, it should be noted that this project was supported by a Fellowship for Independent Study and Research (National Endowment for the Humanities), 1976–77, during which time the initial stages were completed.

David W. Beach

Rochester
February 1979

Die Kunst

des reinen

Satzes in der Musik

aus sicheren Grundsätzen hergeleitet und mit deutlichen
Beyspielen erläutert

von

Joh. Phil. Kirnberger

Ihrer Königl. Hoheit der Prinzeßin Amalia von Preußen Hof-Musicus.

Berlin,

in Commißion bey Christian Friedrich Voß, 1771.

THE ART
OF
STRICT MUSICAL COMPOSITION,

derived from reliable principles and
illustrated with clear examples

by

JOHANN PHILIPP KIRNBERGER

Court Musician to Her Royal Highness,

Princess Amalia of Prussia

VOLUME I

To Her Royal Highness,
The Most Serene Princess Amalia of Prussia,
Abbess of Quedlinburg,
etc., etc., etc.

MOST SERENE PRINCESS!
MOST GRACIOUS PRINCESS AND LADY!

I may be too bold in placing the VENERABLE NAME OF YOUR ROYAL HIGHNESS at the beginning of this work; yet I hope that I am justified to some degree by the reasons that led me to do so.

I am indebted to YOUR ROYAL HIGHNESS for the material of this work, because I have found it necessary to reflect on all that pertains to composition more rigorously and thoroughly than was my custom in order to satisfy YOUR deep inquiring thoroughness. Above all I am indebted to the great genius of YOUR ROYAL HIGHNESS that has forced me, as it were, to dispel some of the darkness that till now has made the path from harmony to melody so difficult for aspiring composers.

The gracious compensation that YOU have granted me for my services at a time when YOU no longer require them—since YOUR own insights have reached so extraordinarily far—has given me the spare time without which I would never have been able to publish this work.

Thus it is gratitude that leads me to this faux pas, a gratitude that will remain with me forever.

The most humble servant of
YOUR ROYAL HIGHNESS,
Joh. Phil. Kirnberger

Preface

Since it has been my principal occupation for many years to instruct prospective composers in strict composition, my utmost concerns have been, on the one hand, to discover the true principles upon which the rules of harmony are based and, on the other hand, to listen to and study most attentively the works of the greatest harmonists, who are generally considered the foremost masters of the art. The present work has gradually evolved from observations gained by this two-fold effort.

I flatter myself that in this work the true principles of harmony are presented with ease and simplicity; this will facilitate to a considerable extent the study of strict composition. I have aimed for the highest degree of strictness throughout, because I have found that the greatest geniuses of composition have painstakingly sought to attain it. Some will find my prescriptions too strict and think perhaps that I have made the art unnecessarily difficult. But I know from long experience how advantageous it is to familiarize prospective composers with the highest level of strictness. Once they have overcome the difficulties associated with it, they have harmony so well in their grasp that it proves easy for them to extricate themselves from difficulties in which those who have been taught less strictly always remain trapped.

Next, I must also state what I know to be true from experience—that any mistake in the harmony, even when it is not perceptible to untrained ears, is so offensive to those who have a more refined ear that it noticeably spoils compositions that are well-designed in other respects. Such errors are often sensed by the less experienced, even though they do not recognize what has caused the trouble.

I know very well that the greatest masters occasionally deviate from the strict rules, and yet their compositions always sound good. However, they could do this only because they were well-versed in the strictest rules. Only they could have found the way out of harmonies that are composed contrary to the rules without detriment to the euphony. For that reason every responsible teacher of composition will be wary of allowing his apprentices to use all those digressions from the rules that were deliberately employed by the great masters. Beginners would run the risk of stirring up a barbaric cacophony by using harmonies that those great masters have solved most successfully. In fact, strictness cannot be exaggerated with beginners. Once they have mastered it, they will discover on their own where to digress.

I have made it my business to be as complete as possible, and one will come across many important matters in this work about which nothing, or at least nothing adequate, has been written elsewhere. I dare not assert that nothing essential has been omitted or, even less, that I have not erred at all. For that reason I would be grateful if those who notice any mistakes would point them out to me. Nevertheless I believe that the most important matters regarding strict composition can be found in this work.

In another work, which can be considered as the second part of this one, I intend to discuss what is required for a beautiful, pleasing, and forcefully expressive melody. I have already collected the materials needed for that and will soon begin to organize them. If this work finds the approval that several of my friends expect, the other will follow soon after.

Introduction

[1] Since it can be assumed that those who want to profit from this book are already trained in the fundamentals of music, everything that pertains to these elementary studies is omitted here. Most technical terms that are used in music, as well as everything pertaining to the historical knowledge of scales, intervals, notes and their value, and of meter and so forth are known to those who will read this work. Wherever appropriate, however, certain more subtle and not commonly known observations about these different subjects will be cited in footnotes.

This work is not intended merely as a proclamation of the rules of strict composition; wherever possible the reasons that make these rules necessary will be indicated. This will occasionally require an involved discussion of well-known matters, which will be considered superfluous only by those who content themselves with a vague knowledge of the nature of things.

The art of composition, insofar as it is subject to precise rules, seems to depend mainly on the following points.

1. One must know all individual notes that can be used in music, or the scale and modes that arise from them.

2. All intervals that occur in each mode.

3. All chords that occur in each mode.

4. One must know how to create a harmonic period from different chords and how to organize the harmony of a complete composition from such periods.

5. One must know how to compose a smooth melody and how to add one, two, or more parts to it. Also, one must know how to compose one or more parts above a given bass.

[2] 6. One must know how to give an appropriate meter and rhythm to a piece in one or more parts in consideration of its character.

These different points will be discussed in order in this work.

CHAPTER 1

Scales and Temperament

It is known that in olden times the only notes available on the organ were those that are currently designated by the letters C, D, E, F, G, A, H[B], c, d, e, etc. However, in those days the letter H was not yet in use, and this note was designated by the letter B instead.[a] Since the pitches C–c, D–d, etc., are so much alike, it is difficult to hear them as two different notes when they are sounded together; for this reason they were given the same name. Furthermore, in the entire range of useful notes, only seven were considered different enough to warrant a special name.

These notes that have been considered alike because of their great correspondence or complete agreement are those whose string or pipe lengths are related to one another as are the numbers 1, 1/2, 1/4, 1/8, etc. That is, when a stretched string produces a note designated as C, half of this string under the same tension will produce a higher note that the ear accepts as just the same. For this reason they have been designated by the same letter. Notes produced by 1/4, 1/8, 1/16, etc., of the string are likewise considered the same. All these notes have the name C.

Thus only those notes lying between C and c were considered as distinct and therefore given different names. Because there were only six notes employed between C and c, it was found that whichever pipe or string of an instrument was sounded, the eighth one above or below it always produced the same note higher or lower. Thus the intervals C–c, D–d, etc., were given

[a]The English equivalents of the German H and B, that is B and B-flat, will be used throughout, except in the few places where Kirnberger's comments require retention of the original letters.

the name "octave."[1] Similarly the other intervals, C–D, C–E, C–F, etc., were called a second, third, and fourth,[2] depending upon whether the string sounding the higher note was the second, third, or fourth string above the lower one.[b] [3] This is the origin of the current designation of intervals.

Previously each interval was designated according to the number of strings [scale degrees] from the lower to the higher pitch, no matter how great the difference might be. Thus, e was called the tenth from C, g the twelfth, and so forth, depending upon the distance from the fundamental tone. Today this designation is seldom used, because the high notes e, g, b are not considered in relation to the low C, but in relation to its octave, c. Therefore, e is called the third, g the fifth, and b the seventh.[3]

The older composers used this or that note of this scale C, D, E, F, G, A,

1. From the Latin word *octavus*, the eighth.
2. That is, the second, third, fourth tones, etc.
3. Today intervals are designated only up to the ninth, which, as will be shown in the proper place, must not be equated with the second. The tenth is rarely distinguished from the third of the octave; this is done only in cases where the seventh and ninth progress upward by several steps and then return to their original positions before resolving. In this case, the figuring must be done in a natural way, as follows.

7. 8. 9. 10. 11. 10. 9. 8. 7.
5. 6. 7. 8. 9. 8. 7. 6. 5.

Here it can be seen that the ninth leads to the following steps (10, 11, etc.). But if this progression were to be designated as follows,

7. 8. 2. 3. 2. 8. 7.
5. 6. 7. 8. 7. 6. 5.

one could think that 8 leaps to 2, which would be completely unnatural.

Only when speaking of counterpoint can one not dispense with the terms tenth and twelfth, since counterpoint at the tenth is entirely different from counterpoint at the third, and counterpoint at the twelfth cannot be mistaken for that at the fifth.

[b] Here and in subsequent passages Kirnberger describes the steps of the scale as strings (or pipes) of some instrument. Each string (or pipe) represents a different note in the scale being considered. For example, in the old diatonic system the pitch E may be described as the third string (scale degree) of the mode on C and the second string (scale degree) of the mode on D; therefore, it forms an interval of a third above C and that of a second above D, etc. Similarly, in chapter 2 the pitch C-sharp is described both as the major third of A and the second string (note) of the chromatic scale on C. In such a context it is clear that the word *Sayte* has a double meaning—string (of an instrument) and note or degree (of a scale). In order to clarify the meaning while preserving the original terminology, *Sayte* has been translated either or both ways depending upon the context.

B, c, d, e, etc., as the lowest one, and regarded it as the final[c] of their melody.

Thus the quality of the intervals changed whenever a different note was used as the final. Beginning from C, C–D was the second, C–E the third, etc.; but if D were used as the final, D–E was the second, D–F the third, etc. The latter intervals are noticeably different from the former; thus a melody having some other final would necessarily have had a different character. This is the origin of the different modes of old.

[4] To make this all clearer, let us imagine the notes in relation to the lengths of their strings. The old diatonic scale was so constituted that when the length of the string producing the pitch C is designated as 1, the strings of the remaining pitches had to have the lengths as they are indicated here below the names of the notes.[d]

C	D	E	F	G	A	H[B][4]	c	d	e	f	etc.
1	8/9	4/5	3/4	2/3	3/5	8/15	1/2	4/9	2/5	3/8	etc.

Beginning with C as the final, the second is 8/9, the third 4/5, the fourth 3/4, etc. However, with D as the final, the second is 9/10, the third 27/32,[5] etc. In this way each final had its fixed intervals, which were sometimes larger and sometimes smaller than the intervals bearing the same names above some other final.

The differences between the intervals above C and those above A were especially great. The octave A–a contained the following tones.

---

4. What the older theorists designated by B is our H [B-natural] today.

5. Because 8/9 (D) is to 4/5 (E) as 1 is to 9/10, and 8/9 (D) is to 3/4 (F) as 1 is to 27/32.

---

[c]Here Kirnberger uses the word *Grundton*, by which he means the first degree of the scale. In this chapter it will be translated either as "final" or "tonic," depending upon the context. In subsequent chapters it assumes additional meanings, e.g., fundamental (of the overtone series), root or bass note (of a chord), etc.

[d]The string lengths given here by Kirnberger are those of so-called just intonation, yielding pure fifths and fourths (3/2 and 4/3) and pure thirds (5/4 and 6/5). Called by Ptolemy (*Harmonics*, i.15) the syntonic diatonic, it became the standard theoretical tuning through the authority of Gioseffo Zarlino (1517–90), who upheld it as the most natural and rational for polyphonic music in his *Le Istitutioni harmoniche* (Venice, 1558), part II, chapters 39–40. For a brief consideration of this system and Zarlino's defense of it, see Zarlino, *The Art of Counterpoint*, trans. Guy A. Marco and Claude V. Palisca (New Haven, 1968; New York, 1976), pp. xiii–xviii. Although Vincenzo Galilei and others demonstrated the impracticality of this tuning, most writers on musical composition in the seventeenth century continued to treat this division of the monochord as the norm, while recognizing that different instruments used a variety of temperaments.

A	B	c	d	e	f	g	a
3/5	8/15	1/2	4/9	2/5	3/8	1/3	3/10

When the number 1 is assigned to A, this becomes:

A	B	c	d	e	f	g	a
1	8/9	5/6	20/27	2/3	5/8	5/9	1/2

Thus, in this mode, the second, fifth, and octave are the same as in C, but all other intervals are noticeably different, except the fourth 20/27, which is only slightly smaller than the fourth 3/4.

In C the third, sixth, and seventh are major, but in A these intervals are minor. For this reason the mode on C is called the major mode, but that on A the minor mode.

This is the former arrangement of the diatonic scale, whose origin is not fully known. Similarly, one cannot say with any certainty how the older theorists arrived at their different systems or scales. We know only that the diatonic system of the ancient Greeks, which was somewhat different from that given here, can be derived from a series of pure fifths. It is also known that in the eleventh century Guido d'Arezzo modified the old diatonic system somewhat with regard to the position and arrangement of the notes. [5] He established the arrangement and proportions of tones as follows.[e]

G	A	B	C	D	E	F	g	etc.
1	8/9	64/81	3/4	2/3	16/27	9/16	1/2	etc.

In this scale, as in the ancient Greek diatonic scale, all wholetones were the same (8 : 9) and both half tones, E–F and B–C, had the ratio 243 : 256. It is not clear how the later or present system, whose succession and proportions were given above, was derived from this one. (Some claim that it was fully established only by Zarlino, who lived in the sixteenth century.)[f] Yet it

---

[e]The proportions given are those of Pythagorean tuning. In the third chapter of the *Micrologus* (eleventh century) and in other sources, Guido described two distinct methods of dividing the monochord, both of which give these proportions. See *Hucbald, Guido, and John on Music*, trans. Warren Babb, ed. Claude V. Palisca (New Haven and London, 1978), p. 60.

[f]Although Zarlino was responsible for establishing "the modern system," that is, just intonation, as the standard theoretical tuning for vocal music (see note d, above), he was not the first to propose it as the most desirable. This was Lodovico Fogliano in his *Musica theorica* (Venice, 1529).

can be understood how this system resulted from the filling in or division of the larger intervals.[6]

6. On this occasion it is suitable to become acquainted with the method by which the older theorists discovered the larger [*sic*, smaller] intervals by inserting a note between two others. Imagine two notes according to the length of their strings, e.g., those notes that form an octave by the numbers 2 and 1, or 4 and 2, etc. If one now wants to place a note halfway between these two, this can be done in three ways. To clarify this, let us call the first note A, the other C, and the new one, which shall fall between the others, B. Now one could attempt to place the note B halfway between A and C in three ways. (1) In such a way that B would be as much higher than A as it is lower than C, i.e., so that both intervals A–B and B–C would be equal. To do that it is necessary that the number by which the length of the string B is expressed is the mean proportion between A and C. However, since only a few numbers are such that a mean proportion could be found, and also since no interval that is only an octave or smaller has such a number, this method could not be used. (2) One could also take the middle number B so that its difference from A and C would be the same. This is called the arithmetic mean. Thus the mean of 12 and 6 would be 9, since the difference from both is 3. (3) This mean could also be such that the number B differs from A by just as great a fraction as from C. Thus the number is 8, which is smaller than 12 by 1/3 and greater than 6 by 1/3. This is called the harmonic mean. Therefore one adhered to these last two types and called the first the arithmetic division and the other the harmonic division of the interval.

Thus one sought to divide the octave, as the largest interval, and then also the small intervals arithmetically and harmonically. Arithmetic division occurs as follows: The two numbers that express the interval are subtracted, and half this difference is added to the smaller number, giving the arithmetic mean. For example, when the numbers are 12 and 6, their difference is 6, half of which is 3. This added to 6 gives 9 as the arithmetic mean.

The harmonic mean is found as follows: The two numbers of the interval are multiplied, and then the result is multiplied by 2; this number is then divided by the sum of the two numbers. Thus when the numbers are 12 and 6, these numbers are multiplied and the resultant number (72) doubled. This makes 144, which is then divided by the sum of 12 and 6, or by 18. The quotient 8 is the harmonic mean between 12 and 6, and is smaller than 12 by 4 or 1/3 of 12 and greater than 6 by 2 or 1/3 of 6.

The older theorists divided all intervals harmonically or arithmetically in this way. Both divisions produce new smaller intervals; in fact, both produce the same ones, but with this difference: with harmonic division the more perfect interval is situated below (i.e., between the lowest note and the new one) and the less perfect above; the reverse is true for arithmetic division. For example, harmonic division of the octave 12 : 6 produces the note 8, which forms a fifth in relation to 12 and a fourth in relation to 6. Arithmetic division produces 9 as the new note, which forms a fourth in relation to 12 and a fifth in relation to 6. From this it is understood what the older

[6] Harmonic division of the octave $1 : 1/2$ (C–c) produces the fifth $(2/3)$, or G, and above it the fourth G–c $(2/3 : 1/2,$ or $3/4)$. Harmonic division of the fifth produces the major third $(4/5)$, or E, and above it the minor third E–G $(4/5 : 2/3,$ or $5/6)$. Further division of the major third produces the large whole tone $(8/9)$, or D, and above it the small one, D–E $(8/9 : 4/5,$ or $9/10)$. [7] This procedure produced the notes C, D, E, G, c in the proportions used today. Arithmetic division of the octave gave the note F $(3/4)$, and harmonic division of the fifth F–c gave the major third above F, that is A $(3/5)$. Finally, G, the first note produced by division of the octave, was also given its major third $(8/13)$, or B, thus completing the system.

The difficulty with this arrangement of the scale was that the note B could not be used as a final because it lacked a fifth, the interval B–F $(8/15 : 3/8,$ or $45/64)$ being of no use whatsoever in this capacity. Furthermore, the note F did not have a fourth, because the interal F–H[B][7] not only sounds bad but is also difficult to sing. Because it is made up of three whole tones, this interval was called the tritone; its proportion is $3/4$ to $8/15$, or $32/45$. To remedy this deficiency, past theorists have inserted between A and B a note that forms a pure fourth with F and a pure fifth with its octave.

(*Footnote 6 continued*)

theorists intended to say when they represented the harmonic division of the octave in this way: [musical staff example], and the arithmetic in this way: [musical staff example] .

Harmonic division of the fifth $(15 : 12 : 10)$ produces the major third at the bottom and the minor third above it.

Harmonic division of the major third $(45 : 40 : 36)$ produces the large whole tone $40/45$ or $8/9$ at the bottom and the small one $36/40$ or $9/10$ above it.

The fifth and fourth were found in this way by division of the octave, the major and minor third by division of the fifth, and the major second, or large whole tone, and small whole tone by division of the major third.

Next it was noticed that the distance between the major third and the fourth gives the minor second, or large half tone $15/16$, and that this subtracted from the large whole tone gives the small half tone $128/135$.

It is worth noting here in passing that the keyboard makers are wrong when they take the ratio $24/25$, which is the difference between the major and minor third, as the small half tone. It should really be $128/135$; but because this division is somewhat difficult, it is reasonable to use $18/19$ or $19/20$ instead. The former can be used in place of $128/135$ for the linking of D-sharp and E, F and F-sharp, G-sharp and A, and B-flat and B, and the latter in place of $243/256$ for the linking of C and C-sharp, D and D-sharp, and G and G-sharp. The proportion $15/16$ can be used to connect C-sharp and D, E and F, F-sharp and G, A and B-flat, and B and C.

7. When speaking of the old scale, it must be remembered that B is the same as H [B-natural] today.

[8] Thus the length of the string for this note would have to be 9/16. This note was also given the name B [B-flat], but to distinguish it from the original B, or 8/15, it was called the soft or round b. The old B, or today's H [B-natural], was called hard or square.

In this diatonic scale the steps between consecutive notes are of three types. Those from C to D, F to G, and A to B are 8/9; this interval is called a large whole tone. The steps D–E and G–A are only 9/10; this interval is called a small whole tone. The steps E–F and B–c are 15/16, and this is called a half tone.

Still one further observation can be made regarding this scale. If C is taken as the final and all the notes of the scale C to c are sounded in succession, one notices upon arriving at the note B that it anticipates and to some extent awakens a desire to hear the following note c. The same happens when one begins on F and has arrived at e. But if one goes from D to d, the seventh note (c) does not at all suggest the following d.

This observation, which everyone can make very easily, demonstrated to the older composers[8] that the major seventh C–B, or F–e, has a power to make the half step directly above it perceptible in advance; for this reason they called this note the leading tone,[g] and thereby intimated that it announces the half tone above it as the tonic. Soon they saw that music would gain if each final had this advantage. Thus it may have happened that by seeking to provide such a leading tone to the remaining four notes (D, E, G, and A), the half steps were inserted between C and D, D and E, F and G, and G and A. This appears to be the origin of today's scale, in which the inserted notes have been given the names C-sharp, D-sharp, F-sharp, and G-sharp. However, these same notes could also be introduced for other reasons.[9]

8. Here this word [*Alten*] does not refer to the ancient Greeks, from whose music ours developed through various transformations, but to the composers of the sixteenth and even part of the seventeenth century, who did not yet have our current scale consisting of twelve tones.

9. Yet it appears that the cited origin of the new half steps C-sharp, D-sharp, F-sharp, and G-sharp is the most natural. It is particularly obvious to the ear that the descant cadence from the leading tone to the tonic is much more perfect than the cadence from the minor third of the dominant to the tonic, with which the older composers had to be content in the minor modes. Thus it may indeed be that these new tones were introduced by speculating how cadences in minor keys were to be made more perfect.

---

[g] In the early chapters of this work, Kirnberger uses the Latin term *subsemitonium modi* to describe the half step below the tonic; it has been translated throughout as "leading tone." Later, he switches to the German word *Leitton*, sometimes with the French term *note sensible* in parentheses to clarify its meaning as an ascending rather than a descending leading tone.

[9] If one wanted to make these tones exactly the same distance from the notes a half step above them, as E is from F, or B from C, the length of the strings would have to have the proportions given here.

C♯	D♯	F♯	G♯
128/135	64/75	32/45	16/25

It could also be surmised that those who first sought to introduce these four new tones tuned them by ear as close as possible to these proportions so that C-sharp was the leading tone of D, D-sharp of E, and so forth. Yet it must have been noticed soon afterward that a precise proportion does not matter here. These notes can be somewhat higher or lower without weakening their quality of anticipating the tonic directly above.

This situation was very advantageous in that it allowed these new half steps to have a double use. Without damaging their primary function as leading tones, they could be raised or lowered somewhat, and thus it was also possible to use them as fifths, thirds, or fourths of other keys. This increased the number of tonics, and thus music could be given more diversity.

Thus it was found that when the F-sharp string was given the length 32/45 it was not only the leading tone of G but also the pure fifth of B and the pure major third of D. This happy observation led composers to investigate how the other three half tones (C-sharp, D-sharp, and G-sharp) could also be adjusted to this double or triple use.

Reports of the various attempts to accomplish this have not come down to us. We know only that they have finally led to the twenty-four different scales in use today, because each of the twelve notes of the octave could be made the tonic and each of these could support a major as well as a minor mode. It may have happened in the following way.

[10] In the prior diatonic scale, a few notes, like C and F, had their pure fifths and major thirds. Others, like A and E, had only minor thirds in addition to pure fifths. But D had neither a pure fifth nor a pure minor third, and lacked a major third completely.

B was without a fifth, and thus it was possible to play major or minor modes in tune in only a few keys.

The observation that B had acquired a fifth and D a major third by the introduction of F-sharp gave composers the idea that it would perhaps be possible to give each string [note] a major and minor third, and a fifth. The four new tones C-sharp, D-sharp, F-sharp, and G-sharp, tuned in such a way that they could be used as leading tones of the principal notes above them, already gave hope to the possibility of such a new system of music. The mere thought of it found so much approval that countless attempts were then made to bring the system to perfection.

Thus one sought to tune the four semitones C-sharp, D-sharp, F-sharp, and G-sharp in such a way that each note of the chromatic scale C, C-sharp, D, D-sharp, E, F, F-sharp, G, G-sharp, A, B-flat, B had a fifth, major third, and minor third.

It was soon noticed that this is possible only if the intervals could be made a bit larger or smaller on occasion. If, for example, D-sharp was adjusted so that it was exactly the pure minor third of C, it could not at the same time be the pure fifth of G-sharp. Nevertheless it was found that a means could be devised for adjusting these new tones so that the intervals would still be tolerable, even though not entirely pure. This was called *tempering* the system.

Every organ builder and instrument maker did his best to find a *temperament* that involved the least inconveniences. And that is still the way things are today.

After countless temperaments were devised, a few theorists thought that the simplest means of solving the matter was to separate the notes C, C-sharp, D, D-sharp, etc., equally from one another. Thus the octave was divided into twelve equal parts, where each was approximately a half-step; this was called *equal temperament*. Many considered this to be very advantageous because each step of the chromatic scale had a major and minor third in addition to its fourth, fifth, and sixth, all so nearly in tune that the ear scarcely noticed the difference from absolute purity.

[11] Consequently it is possible in this temperament to play with almost complete purity in all the major and minor keys that exist in the chromatic system.

However, more careful consideration soon leads to serious doubts about this temperament.

First of all, it is impossible to tune this temperament without a monochord or something that takes its place. Consonant intervals can be tuned pure by the ear alone, but the dissonant ones cannot be found precisely.

Second, the diversity of keys is eliminated by equal temperament. It leaves only two characters, since on the one hand all major keys and on the other all minor keys are exactly the same.

Thus nothing was really gained by the twenty-four scales; on the contrary, a great deal was lost. As was mentioned above, the simple diatonic scale as used by the older composers produced various modes, each quite distinct in character. Of these modes, the ones best suited for expression could always be chosen. Equal temperament eliminates this and allows the composer only the choice between the major and the minor mode.

These reasons are important enough to abandon a temperament that has so many drawbacks.[h]

To be good, a temperament must be easy to tune, it must not harm the diversity of keys, and finally it must produce intervals that correspond wherever possible to those resulting from pure melodic progressions.

One finds, for example, that entirely pure melodic progressions in two parts produce various tempered or not quite pure harmonic thirds.

Consider example 1.1. Leaps of fourths and fifths occur in both voices. As was said, these cannot be sung other than pure. [12] Thus, when both voices arrive at their last notes, they form a third that is not pure. If c^2 is

---

[h] Although Kirnberger states various objections to equal temperament here, he had at one time shown considerable interest in the subject. In 1760 he published a short work, *Construction der gleichschwebenden Temperatur* (Berlin), in which he demonstrated how to determine equal temperament by means of geometric construction. Methods using arithmetic divisions are not precise, Kirnberger tells us, although the approximations they produce are so close that the ear cannot perceive the difference. Proportions resulting from geometric construction, however, are exact, and thus please the mind as well as the ear. This statement is rather unusual for Kirnberger, who was normally more interested in practical application than theoretical abstraction.

In "Von der Temperatur," published at the end of the final part of this work, Kirnberger informs us of an earlier "discovery," first reported in the preface to the fourth collection of his *Clavierübungen* (Berlin, 1766) and later in the preface to his *Vermischte Musicalien* (Berlin, 1769). This discovery is the tempered fifth whose ratio (10935 : 16384) is almost exactly 1/12 of a comma smaller than the pure fifth. Kirnberger arrived at this ratio in the process of developing his own temperament. The method by which he arrived at this figure was to take seven pure fifths in succession plus one pure major third. This gives the tempered fourth 8192 : 10935, which is larger than the pure fourth by 1/12 of a comma; its inversion is the tempered fifth 10935 : 16384. According to Kirnberger, he showed this discovery to the mathematician Leonhard Euler (1707–83) in 1766, and remarked to him that this tempered fifth could be used to determine all ratios of equal temperament. This idea was subsequently developed by Johann Heinrich Lambert (1728–77) and published in the *Memoires de l'académie royale des sciences et belle lettres* (Berlin, 1774), pp. 64ff.

Lambert's method of determining the fifth 10935 : 16384, which indeed does bear a remarkable resemblance to Kirnberger's, was reported by Friedrich Wilhelm Marpurg in his *Versuch über die musikalische Temperatur*. (He later translated Lambert's essay into German and published it with commentary in his *Historisch-kritische Beyträge zur Aufnahme der Musik*, vol. 5, part 6 [Berlin, 1778], pp. 417–50.) Marpurg praised Lambert's method and pointed out that its deviations from exact equal temperament never exceed .00001. Another advantage of this method is that it does not require a monochord. Marpurg, who supported equal temperament and was violently opposed to Kirnberger's views on temperament as well as on harmony, was only too eager to point out that this feature of Lambert's method invalidated one of Kirnberger's objections to equal temperament.

EXAMPLE 1.1

expressed as 1, the g¹ in the upper voice is a pure fourth lower (4/3), from which the pure fifth d² is 6/9.[i] In the lower voice, c² (1) falls a fifth to f¹; consequently, f¹ is 3/2. From there it ascends a pure fourth (9/8).[j] Thus here b-flat¹ to d² is in the ratio as 9/8 is to 8/9 or as 1 is to 64/81. Although the third b-flat¹–d² (64/81) is a comma (80/81) larger than the pure third (4/5), it is not to be discarded for that reason. First of all, it is more important that the larger intervals (fourths and fifths), from which this third arises, be pure than for the latter to be pure and the former impure. Second, it is impossible to temper these fourths and fifths in singing so that the third b-flat–d comes out pure.

EXAMPLE 1.2

But if the two voices were to progress as in example 1.2, C and e would be the pure major third; g in the lower voice against the last e in the upper voice forms the pure sixth (3/5), whereas in the preceding example f in the lower voice against d in the upper one forms a sixth that is 16/27. Thus progressions by pure intervals result in thirds that are sometimes larger and sometimes smaller.

---

[i] The modern designation of pitch, where middle c is represented by c¹, will be used throughout. Thus, where Kirnberger wrote c̿, as was the practice of his time, this will be notated as c².

[j] The pure fourth from f¹ to b-flat¹ is, of course, 3/4. What Kirnberger means is that b-flat¹ forms the interval 9/8 in relation to the pitch c².

What was stated here parenthetically—that it is more important to have the large rather than the small intervals pure—deserves further explanation. It is known that octaves do not tolerate the slightest tempering but must be completely pure because they sound very bad if they are even a little too large or too small. The reason for this is obvious. Because they are of one kind, the comparison is so simple that the slightest difference is noticeable. As we know from experience, fifths can be somewhat smaller without becoming offensive, since the comparison between 2 and 3 is not as simple as that between 1 and 2. Therefore the defect is not as easily perceived with the fifth. [13] For this very reason, thirds tolerate still greater deviation from purity before becoming unpleasant, since the ratio 4 : 5, or 5 : 6, is even more difficult to comprehend than 2 : 3; consequently, the deviations from purity are less noticeable. This agrees completely with perception, even that of the greatest masters. They unanimously agree that fifths are tolerable when smaller by no more than a half comma, or 1/160, from the true proportion 2/3. However, major thirds can be larger by a whole comma,[k] or 1/80, and minor thirds smaller by the same.

Because one must take as much care as possible to make fourths and fifths pure, the impure thirds that necessarily result are to be accepted without hesitation.

It was demonstrated above how the third 64/81 comes about. Since this third is unavoidable, still another, which is expressed by 405/512 and is somewhat smaller than the former, is also necessary. It results from the difference between the pure major third (4/5) and the largest third (64/81) to the octave. If the interval b-flat^1–d^2 is 64/81 by necessity, as we have seen, but d^1–f-sharp^1 is the pure major third, then f-sharp^1 with b-flat^1 must form the interval 405/512.

After these introductory suggestions, one will without doubt consider the temperament that is to be given below as the best possible.[l] It has the following essential qualities: (1) it is easy to tune; (2) the principal intervals, the fourths and fifths, are either perfect or so pure that the difference cannot be heard, as is to be shown shortly; and, finally, (3) it contains no other

[k] According to Kirnberger, J. S. Bach required that all major thirds be tuned sharp on his clavier. This claim was reported by Marpurg on page 213 of his *Versuch über die musikalische Temperatur.*

[l] The temperament proposed here by Kirnberger is a modification of Pythagorean tuning, with the syntonic comma divided arithmetically between the fifths D–A and A–E. As Kirnberger points out, all other fifths are pure except for F-sharp–C-sharp, which is only about 1/10 [1/12] of a comma smaller than pure. This temperament differs only slightly from two earlier

ones proposed by Kirnberger in the prefaces to the fourth collection of his *Clavierübungen* (1766) and his *Vermischte Musikalien* (1769). A detailed account of these temperaments is contained in the twenty-third chapter of Marpurg's *Versuch über die musikalische Temperatur*. There Marpurg gives the following numerical values for the first of these temperaments, below which the ratio of each note has been added.

C	C♯	D	D♯	E	F	F♯
7776	8192	8748	9216	9720	10368	10935
1 : 1	256 : 243	9 : 8	32 : 27	5 : 4	4 : 3	45 : 32

G	G♯	A	B♭	B	C
11664	12288	12960	13824	14580	15552
3 : 2	128 : 81	5 : 3	16 : 9	15 : 8	2 : 1

The method by which Kirnberger arrived at this temperament was as follows: Tune seven successive pure fifths beginning from C-sharp. Then tune the tempered fifth from D by taking the pure major third above F. Finally, tune three more pure fifths from this A, which completes the system. This method can be diagrammed as follows.

C♯ – G♯ – D♯ – B♭ – F – C – G – D   (7 pure fifths)
$\downarrow$
F – A   (1 pure major third)
$\downarrow$
A – E – B – F♯   (3 pure fifths)

The result of this method is that all fifths are pure except for F-sharp–c-sharp and D–A. The first of these has a ratio of 10935 : 16384, which is almost exactly 1/12 of a comma smaller than pure. According to Kirnberger, this important discovery was used by Lambert as the basis for his method of determining the ratios of equal temperament. (See note h, above.) The fifth D–A (8748 : 12960), however, is 1/80 (a full comma) smaller than pure, which was too great a difference even for Kirnberger. For this reason he then divided the difference between the fifths D–A and A–e, giving the value 13041 to A. This is the second tuning mentioned by Marpurg. It differs from the first only by this one note, A, which now has the ratio 161 : 96 instead of 5 : 3 in relation to C. The only difference between this temperament and the one given by Kirnberger in *Die Kunst des reinen Satzes in der Musik* is a different division of the comma between the fifths D–A and A–e. In the latter, A is given the ratio 270 : 161 instead of 161 : 96.

As is well known, Kirnberger's views on temperament were not universally accepted during his day. In his *Versuch über die musikalische Temperatur*, particularly in the twenty-third chapter, Marpurg attacked these views vigorously. This was a major reason for the controversy that developed between these two men. However, Kirnberger's ideas did find some support during his own lifetime and for several years thereafter. In his *Gedanken über die Temperatur des Herrn Kirnberger* (Berlin and Leipzig, 1775), G. F. Tempelhof stated flatly that the temperament given by Kirnberger in *Die Kunst des reinen Satzes in der Musik* is correct since it "has all the properties that are required of a good and useful temperament." The criteria used by Tempelhof were almost the same as those given by Kirnberger. Several years later Kirnberger's position was supported by Heinrich Christoph Koch in his *Musikalisches Lexikon* (Frankfurt, 1802). On page 1501 of that work, Koch observed that the majority of younger theorists preferred Kirnberger's unequal temperament to equal temperament because it preserved the character of the different keys. Finally, it should be noted that Daniel Gottlob Türk gave Kirnberger's temperament as the model of unequal temperament in his *Clavier-schule* (Leipzig and Halle, 1789), pp. 381ff. As was his habit, Türk did not take a stand on the issue but simply reported on two different types of temperament, equal and unequal.

thirds than those that are either completely pure or that arise by necessity from pure fifths and fourths. In this temperament, the pitches have the following proportions.

C	C♯	D	D♯	E	F	F♯	G	G♯	A	B♭	B
1	243/256	8/9	27/32	4/5	3/4	32/45	2/3	81/128	161/270	9/16	8/15

In this scale all tones of the pure diatonic scale have been retained except for the note A, which, instead of being 3/5 or 162/270, is 161/270, and thus is 1/162, or a half comma, larger here so that it can be used as the fifth of D. This fifth, D–A, and consequently also the fifth A–e, is only a half comma smaller than the completely pure fifth 2/3. Except for these two fifths, all others are completely pure. No matter how refined the ear may be, it is impossible for it to hear that the fifth F-sharp–C-sharp is 1/10 of a comma less than pure. Since all fifths except two are pure, the same is true of the fourths.

[14] The major thirds are of four types: (1) completely pure (C–E, D–F-sharp, G–B); (2) others of 64/81, which are a comma too large; next, (3) those that are less than a comma too large, like those of 405/512; and, (4) those that come even closer to being completely pure, like F–A (128/161), which is not noticeably different from 4/5, and A–c-sharp (13041/16384), which is just as unnoticeable in its difference from 405/512.

There are even more of the minor thirds that deviate from purity. However, the difference never exceeds a comma, and consequently they are all tolerable.

Finally, the proposed temperament has the advantage above all others that it can be tuned simply by using pure fifths and a single major third (4/5), as can be seen in example 1.3.

EXAMPLE 1.3

After one has tuned the notes in this way up to the F-sharp at (a), it is quite easy to determine the a that is still missing by making the fifth d–a at (b) just as small as the fifth a–e¹. This will not cause the slightest difficulty for anyone who has a little experience at tuning. Above all, this temperament is commendable because it is simple to tune.

CHAPTER 2

Intervals

As was mentioned previously, the older theorists calculated intervals according to the diatonic steps. Thus there were seven intervals above each final in the span of an octave, since there were seven diatonic steps from any note to its octave. Intervals greater than the octave were always designated by the number of steps from the lowest note. Thus the second and the third of the octave were called the ninth and the tenth, and so forth for all remaining notes within the range of the former system. Today this manner of counting has mostly been abandoned, intervals above the octave now being given the same names as those in the first octave; i.e., the tenth is a third, the eleventh a fourth, etc. Only in certain special cases are intervals in the second octave indicated by the figures 9, 10, 11, etc.; an example of this was given in footnote 3. [15] The ninth in particular retains its name when it is treated differently from the second in a harmonic context, as will be seen later on. These intervals kept the same names for each final, but they differed greatly in their actual size and sound. The interval C–D was called a second as were the intervals D–E and E–F, even though they differ in size.

Table 2.1 is inserted here to enable the reader to see at a glance the actual size of the intervals as they were used by the older theorists in their different modes.

In looking at this table, it is apparent that no two modes were exactly the same. The modes on C and F differ with respect to two intervals—the fourth, which in C is 3/4 but in F is 32/45, and the sixth, which in C is 3/5 but in F is 16/27 and therefore larger by a comma. [16] Thus the diatonic scale produced six different modes.[10] The seventh one, on B, was totally rejected because its fifth, 45/64, could not be used. The quality of the intervals is shown in the table. The seconds have three sizes: 8/9, 9/10, and 15/16. The

TABLE 2.1. Intervals in the Old Modes.

	I	II	III	IV	V	VI	VII	VIII
C	1 C	$\frac{8}{9}$ D	$\frac{4}{5}$ E	$\frac{3}{4}$ F	$\frac{2}{3}$ G	$\frac{3}{5}$ A	$\frac{8}{15}$ B	$\frac{1}{2}$ c
D	1 D	$\frac{9}{10}$ E	$\frac{27}{32}$ F	$\frac{3}{4}$ G	$\frac{27}{40}$ A	$\frac{3}{5}$ B	$\frac{9}{16}$ c	$\frac{1}{2}$ d
E	1 E	$\frac{15}{16}$ F	$\frac{5}{6}$ G	$\frac{3}{4}$ A	$\frac{2}{3}$ B	$\frac{5}{8}$ c	$\frac{5}{9}$ d	$\frac{1}{2}$ e
F	1 F	$\frac{8}{9}$ G	$\frac{4}{5}$ A	$\frac{32}{45}$ B	$\frac{2}{3}$ c	$\frac{16}{27}$ d	$\frac{8}{15}$ e	$\frac{1}{2}$ f
G	1 G	$\frac{9}{10}$ A	$\frac{4}{5}$ B	$\frac{3}{4}$ c	$\frac{2}{3}$ d	$\frac{3}{5}$ e	$\frac{9}{16}$ f	$\frac{1}{2}$ g
A	1 A	$\frac{8}{9}$ B	$\frac{5}{6}$ c	$\frac{20}{27}$ d	$\frac{2}{3}$ e	$\frac{5}{8}$ f	$\frac{5}{9}$ g	$\frac{1}{2}$ a
B	1 B	$\frac{15}{16}$ c	$\frac{5}{6}$ d	$\frac{3}{4}$ e	$\frac{45}{64}$ f	$\frac{5}{8}$ g	$\frac{9}{16}$ a	$\frac{1}{2}$ b

first two, which differ only by a comma, were considered identical and called major seconds; the other was called a minor second.

Likewise there were three types of thirds: the major (4/5) and the [two] minor ones (5/6 and 27/32); the latter, which is only a comma smaller than 5/6, was still considered a minor third. Thus there were only two thirds, the major and the minor. The fourths were all identical except for the one on F (the actual tritone) and the one on A, which is too large by a comma.

10. In passing, we may mention the names of the ancient modes. The mode on C was called Ionian; on D, Dorian; on E, Phrygian; on F, Lydian; on G, Mixolydian; and on A, Aeolian. Each of these six modes was treated in two ways, called authentic and plagal. The range of the authentic type was from the final up to its octave, but that of the plagal was from the fourth below the final up to its fifth. For example, in C, or the Ionian mode:

This resulted in a total of twelve modes. If the modern scale were to be treated in this way—authentic and plagal types for both the major and minor modes on each note—this would result in forty-eight different modes.

These first three types of intervals determine the others, since by inversion fourths become fifths, thirds become sixths, and seconds become sevenths.[11]

Thus all fifths were pure except for the one on D. There were two kinds of sixths, major (3/5) and minor (5/8), and also two kinds of sevenths, major (8/15) and minor (9/16).

[17] Thus all intervals are of the size mentioned here; they are designated simply by name, or by adding the labels "major" or "minor." The major second is 8/9 or smaller than that by a comma; the minor second is 15/16. The major third is 4/5 or slightly larger (but never by more than a comma). However, there is only one type of fourth, 3/4; it cannot be larger by a comma without losing its character. The same applies to the fifth. For this reason the interval F–B (32/45) has not been called a fourth, but the tritone, and its inversion, B–f (45/64), has been called the false fifth.

This may suffice regarding the structure of the old scale. By adding four new tones (C-sharp, D-sharp, F-sharp, and G-sharp), music has assumed a completely different character. (1) Instead of having seven intervals within an octave, each key now has twelve. (2) Instead of having only one mode for each final, in which all intervals are precisely determined, there are now two modes for each, the major and the minor. That is, previously the final C had only a major third and a minor [sic, major] sixth; now it also has a minor third and a major [sic, minor] sixth. While one could only play in C major before, now one can also play in C minor. (3) In addition to the diatonic intervals, both modes (major as well as minor) also have chromatic ones, i.e., a minor second [sic, augmented prime] C-sharp, an augmented fourth F-sharp, etc. This has led to a much greater variety in melody and harmony.

In the old diatonic system, progressions were completely determined; that is, from C one could only progress by a major second (C–D), or by a major third (C–E), etc. However, today one has the choice of progressing from any note by a minor, major, or augmented second, by a minor or major third, etc. As we shall see later on, this has the advantage of allowing one to modulate more quickly into other keys. In addition, the diminished and

---

11. Here the term inversion means the transposition of the higher note of an interval down by an octave. If the note c¹ in the third a–c¹ is put an octave lower, the result is the sixth c–a. The second c–d becomes the seventh D–c by inversion. The inversion of intervals can be expressed numerically by inverting the fraction and doubling the denominator. The inversion of the minor third (5/6) is 6/10 or 3/5, the major sixth; and the inversion of the major third (4/5) is 5/8, the minor sixth.

EXAMPLE 2.1

augmented intervals provide a convenient means of expressing the different types of passions.

[18] Today it is also possible to take smaller steps in succession by inserting chromatic notes between the diatonic ones, as in example 2.1. This procedure frequently gives melody the greatest power of expression. These small chromatic steps are augmented *primes* (F–F-sharp, G–G-sharp, etc.) or diminished *primes* (B–B-flat, etc.); they should really be 24/25,[12] but in our system are 243/250, and thus are always notably smaller than the smallest diatonic progression, 15/16 (E–F).

It is possible to get even smaller progressions, called *enharmonic*, by deceiving the ear. To understand this, we must keep in mind that each note in the current system represents more than one tone, even though it never changes pitch or height. For example, our second string [note] represents the major third from A, in which case it is considered as a raised C and called C-sharp; at the same time, it represents the minor third of B-flat, and is considered as a lowered D and called D-flat. In the first case its string length would have to be 12/25;[13] but in the other, 15/32.[14] These tones differ by 125/128, which is the smallest enharmonic interval,[15] and is called the enharmonic *comma*.[16]

[19] Even though the same string [note] is used for C-sharp and D-flat, its connection with other notes causes the ear to consider it lower when used

12. That is, c-sharp, as the pure major third of A, should be 12/25, and thus should form an interval of 24/25 in relation to C, or 1/2. In our temperament we have raised it to 243/256, since otherwise the minor second C-sharp–D would have been 25/27, which would be too close to the major second.

13. See the preceding note.

14. B-flat is 9/16, since the minor third is in the ratio 5 : 6, as 45 : 96 or 15 : 32 is to 1.

15. 12/25 ÷ 15/32 = 1 : 376/384, or 125/128.

16. It is often said that the notes C-sharp and D-flat, G-sharp and A-flat, etc., differ by a comma. However, this is not correct, since the term "comma" means the small interval 80/81. The comma 80/81 is much smaller than the enharmonic comma 125/128. The former never occurs as the difference between enharmonic and chromatic notes, like C-sharp and D-flat, but is always the difference between two intervals of the same name, such as the two major thirds 4/5 and 64/81, or the minor thirds 5/6 and 27/32.

EXAMPLE 2.2

as C-sharp and higher when used as D-flat.[a] The same also applies to other strings [notes].

This is the origin of enharmonic progressions, the finest and most minute that exist in today's music. See example 2.2. Even though enharmonic intervals do not actually exist in our system, they can be made audible by the correct treatment of harmony, as will be shown in the course of this work. It is a known fact, and every ear perceives it, that such enharmonic changes create the most pleasant harmonic effects.

Melody would, of course, gain even more if we actually had enharmonic tones in our system. In this case, singers would become accustomed to singing the smallest enharmonic intervals correctly from childhood on, and the ear of the listener would become accustomed to understanding them. This would mean that the expression of passions could be intensified greatly in many a case.

That this is not mere speculation is evident from the fact that the enharmonic genus alone was used by the greatest ancient composers for a long time, and that eminent Greek writers have confirmed that this genus was considered the most perfect.[17]

Two tables [tables 2.2 and 2.3] are added here to provide a clear grasp of the keys in use today.

The first contains the diatonic intervals for all twelve keys, both major and minor. The proportions are based on the temperament given in the preceding chapter.[b]

17. See Plutarch on music, chapter 17. [See *Plutarque, De la musique*, Texte, traduction, commentaire . . . par François Lasserre (Lausanne, 1954).]

[a]In just intonation, the sharps are actually lower than their flatted enharmonic equivalents. However, in current practice the opposite is normally true. That is, where there is a choice, C-sharp is usually sung or played higher than D-flat.

[b]The proportions given here by Kirnberger are actually based on the second of two temperaments mentioned in the fourth collection of his *Clavierübungen*. (See note 1 in chapter 1 for further information.) In this temperament the interval C–A has the ratio 96 : 161, whereas the temperament given in the preceding chapter of this work specifies the ratio 161 : 270 for this interval. Otherwise the two temperaments are identical.

The information contained in these two tables corresponds to that given in the article "Intervall" in Sulzer's *Allgemeine Theorie der schönen Künste*.

TABLE 2.2. All Current Diatonic Scales.

Intervals: I	II	III	IV	V	VI	VII	VIII
C major	D $\frac{8}{9}$	E $\frac{4}{5}$	F $\frac{3}{4}$	G $\frac{2}{3}$	A $\frac{96}{161}$	B $\frac{8}{15}$	c $\frac{1}{2}$
C minor	D $\frac{8}{9}$	E♭ $\frac{27}{32}$	F $\frac{3}{4}$	G $\frac{2}{3}$	A♭ $\frac{81}{128}$	B♭ $\frac{9}{16}$	c $\frac{1}{2}$
C♯, D♭ major	D♯, E♭ $\frac{8}{9}$	E♯, F $\frac{64}{81}$	F♯, G♭ $\frac{8192}{10935}$	G♯, A♭ $\frac{2}{3}$	A♯, B♭ $\frac{16}{27}$	B♯, c $\frac{128}{243}$	c♯, d♭ $\frac{1}{2}$
C♯ minor	D♯ $\frac{8}{9}$	E $\frac{1024}{1215}$	F♯ $\frac{8192}{10935}$	G♯ $\frac{2}{3}$	A $\frac{8192}{13041}$	B $\frac{2048}{3645}$	c♯ $\frac{1}{2}$
D major	E $\frac{9}{10}$	F♯ $\frac{4}{5}$	G $\frac{3}{4}$	A $\frac{108}{161}$	B $\frac{3}{5}$	c♯ $\frac{2187}{4096}$	d $\frac{1}{2}$
D minor	E $\frac{9}{10}$	F $\frac{27}{32}$	G $\frac{3}{4}$	A $\frac{108}{161}$	B♭ $\frac{81}{128}$	c $\frac{9}{16}$	d $\frac{1}{2}$
E♭ major	F $\frac{8}{9}$	G $\frac{64}{81}$	A♭ $\frac{3}{4}$	B♭ $\frac{2}{3}$	c $\frac{16}{27}$	d $\frac{128}{243}$	e♭ $\frac{1}{2}$
D♯, E♭ minor	E♯, F $\frac{8}{9}$	F♯, G♭ $\frac{1024}{1215}$	G♯, A♭ $\frac{3}{4}$	A♯, B♭ $\frac{2}{3}$	B, c♭ $\frac{256}{405}$	c♯, d♭ $\frac{9}{16}$	d♯, e♭ $\frac{1}{2}$
E major	F♯ $\frac{8}{9}$	G♯ $\frac{405}{512}$	A $\frac{120}{161}$	B $\frac{2}{3}$	c♯ $\frac{1315}{2048}$	d♯ $\frac{135}{256}$	e $\frac{1}{2}$
E minor	F♯ $\frac{8}{9}$	G $\frac{5}{6}$	A $\frac{120^\star}{161}$	B $\frac{2}{3}$	c $\frac{5}{8}$	d $\frac{5}{9}$	e $\frac{1}{2}$
F major	G $\frac{8}{9}$	A $\frac{128}{161}$	B♭ $\frac{3}{4}$	c $\frac{2}{3}$	d $\frac{16}{27}$	e $\frac{8}{15}$	f $\frac{1}{2}$
F minor	G $\frac{8}{9}$	A♭ $\frac{27}{32}$	B♭ $\frac{3}{4}$	c $\frac{2}{3}$	d♭ $\frac{81}{128}$	e♭ $\frac{9}{16}$	f $\frac{1}{2}$
F♯, G♭ major	G♯, A♭ $\frac{}{3645}$	A♯, b♭ $\frac{}{405}$	$\frac{}{3}$	♭ $\frac{}{10935}$	♭ $\frac{}{1215}$	$\frac{}{135}$	♯ $\frac{}{1}$

TABLE 2.2. (*continued*)

F♯ minor	G♯ $\frac{3645}{4096}$	A $\frac{135}{161}$	B $\frac{3}{4}$	c♯ $\frac{10935}{16384}$	d $\frac{5}{8}$	e $\frac{9}{16}$	f♯ $\frac{1}{2}$
G major	A $\frac{144}{161}$	B $\frac{4}{5}$	c $\frac{3}{4}$	d $\frac{2}{3}$	e $\frac{3}{5}$	f♯ $\frac{8}{15}$	g $\frac{1}{2}$
G minor	A $\frac{144}{161}$	B♭ $\frac{27}{32}$	c $\frac{3}{4}$	d $\frac{2}{3}$	e♭ $\frac{81}{128}$	f $\frac{9}{16}$	g $\frac{1}{2}$
A♭ major	B♭ $\frac{8}{9}$	c $\frac{64}{81}$	d♭ $\frac{3}{4}$	e♭ $\frac{2}{3}$	f $\frac{16}{27}$	g $\frac{128}{243}$	a♭ $\frac{1}{2}$
G♯, A♭ minor	A♯, B♭ $\frac{8}{9}$	B, c♭ $\frac{1024}{1215}$	c♯, d♭ $\frac{3}{4}$	d♯, e♭ $\frac{2}{3}$	e, f♭ $\frac{256}{405}$	f♯, g♭ $\frac{2048}{3645}$	g♯, a♭ $\frac{1}{2}$
A major	B $\frac{161}{180}$	c♯ $\frac{13041}{16384}$	d $\frac{161}{216}$	e $\frac{161}{240}$	f♯ $\frac{161}{270}$	g♯ $\frac{4347}{8192}$	a $\frac{1}{2}$
A minor	B $\frac{161}{180}$	c $\frac{161}{192}$	d $\frac{161}{216}$	e $\frac{161}{240}$	f $\frac{161}{256}$	g $\frac{161}{288}$	a $\frac{1}{2}$
B♭ major	c $\frac{8}{9}$	d $\frac{64}{81}$	e♭ $\frac{3}{4}$	f $\frac{2}{3}$	g $\frac{16}{27}$	a $\frac{256}{483}$	b♭ $\frac{1}{2}$
A♯, B♭ minor	B♯, c $\frac{8}{9}$	c♯, d♭ $\frac{27}{32}$	d♯, e♭ $\frac{3}{4}$	e♯, f $\frac{2}{3}$	f♯, g♭ $\frac{256}{405}$	g♯, a♭ $\frac{9}{16}$	a♯, b♭ $\frac{1}{2}$
B major	c♯ $\frac{3645}{4096}$	d♯ $\frac{405}{512}$	e $\frac{3}{4}$	f♯ $\frac{2}{3}$	g♯ $\frac{1215}{2048}$	a♯ $\frac{135}{256}$	b $\frac{1}{2}$
B minor	c♯ $\frac{3645}{4096}$	d $\frac{5}{6}$	e $\frac{3}{4}$	f♯ $\frac{2}{3}$	g $\frac{5}{8}$	a $\frac{90}{161}$	b $\frac{1}{2}$

* Incorrectly identified by Kirnberger as $\frac{161}{216}$.

TABLE 2.3. The Diatonic and Chromatic Intervals for Each Tonic.

I	II min.	II maj.	III min.	III maj.	IV	IV maj. Tritone	V	VI min.	VI maj.	VII min.	VII maj.	VIII
C 1	C#* $\frac{243}{256}$	D* $\frac{8}{9}$	D#* $\frac{27}{32}$	E $\frac{4}{5}$	F $\frac{3}{4}$	F# $\frac{32}{45}$	G $\frac{2}{3}$	G#* $\frac{81}{128}$	A $\frac{96}{161}$	B♭ $\frac{9^\star}{16}$	B $\frac{8}{15}$	c $\frac{1}{2}$
C# 1	D $\frac{2048}{2187}$	D#* $\frac{8^\star}{9}$	E $\frac{1024^\star}{1215}$	F $\frac{64^\star}{81}$	F# $\frac{8192}{10935}$	G $\frac{512^\star}{729}$	G# $\frac{2}{3}$	A $\frac{8192^\star}{13041}$	B♭ $\frac{16^\star}{27}$	B $\frac{2048^\star}{3645}$	c $\frac{128^\star}{243}$	c# $\frac{1}{2}$
D 1	D#* $\frac{243}{256}$	E $\frac{9}{10}$	F $\frac{27^\star}{32}$	F# $\frac{4}{5}$	G $\frac{3}{4}$	G# $\frac{729^\star}{1024}$	A $\frac{108}{161}$	B♭ $\frac{81^\star}{128}$	B $\frac{3}{5}$	c $\frac{9^\star}{16}$	c# $\frac{2187}{4096}$	d $\frac{1}{2}$
D# 1	E $\frac{243}{256}$	F $\frac{8^\star}{9}$	F# $\frac{1024^\star}{1215}$	G $\frac{64^\star}{81}$	G# $\frac{3}{4}$	A $\frac{1024}{1449}$	B♭ $\frac{2}{3}$	B $\frac{256^\star}{405}$	c $\frac{16^\star}{27}$	c# $\frac{9^\star}{16}$	d $\frac{128^\star}{243}$	d# $\frac{1}{2}$
E 1	F $\frac{15}{16}$	F# $\frac{8^\star}{9}$	G $\frac{5}{6}$	G# $\frac{405^\star}{512}$	A $\frac{120}{161}$	B♭ $\frac{45^\star}{64}$	B $\frac{2}{3}$	c $\frac{5}{8}$	c# $\frac{1215^\star}{2048}$	d $\frac{5}{9}$	d# $\frac{135^\star}{256}$	e $\frac{1}{2}$
F 1	F# $\frac{128^\star}{135}$	G $\frac{8^\star}{9}$	G# $\frac{27^\star}{32}$	A $\frac{128}{161}$	B♭ $\frac{3}{4}$	B $\frac{32}{45}$	c $\frac{2}{3}$	c# $\frac{81^\star}{128}$	d $\frac{16^\star}{27}$	d# $\frac{9^\star}{16}$	e $\frac{8}{15}$	f $\frac{1}{2}$
F# 1	G $\frac{15}{16}$	G# $\frac{3645^\star}{4096}$	A $\frac{135^\star}{161}$	B♭ $\frac{405^\star}{512}$	B $\frac{3}{4}$	c $\frac{45^\star}{64}$	c# $\frac{10935}{16384}$	d $\frac{5}{8}$	d# $\frac{1215^\star}{2048}$	e $\frac{9^\star}{16}$	f $\frac{135^\star}{256}$	f# $\frac{1}{2}$
G 1	G#* $\frac{243}{256}$	A $\frac{144}{161}$	B♭ $\frac{27^\star}{32}$	B $\frac{4}{5}$	c $\frac{3}{4}$	c# $\frac{729^\star}{1024}$	d $\frac{2}{3}$	d# $\frac{81^\star}{128}$	e $\frac{3}{5}$	f $\frac{9^\star}{16}$	f# $\frac{8}{15}$	g $\frac{1}{2}$

TABLE 2.3. (*continued*)

	I aug. ★	III dim. ★	II aug. ★	IV dim. ★		V false ★		V aug. ★	VII dim. ★	VI aug. ★	VIII dim.	
G#/1	A $\frac{4096}{4347}$★	B♭ $\frac{8}{9}$★	B $\frac{1024}{1215}$★	c $\frac{64}{81}$★	c# $\frac{3}{4}$	d $\frac{512}{729}$★	d# $\frac{2}{3}$	e $\frac{256}{405}$★	f $\frac{16}{27}$	f# $\frac{2048}{3645}$★	g $\frac{128}{243}$★	g# $\frac{1}{2}$
A/1	B♭ $\frac{483}{512}$	B $\frac{161}{180}$★	c $\frac{161}{192}$	c# $\frac{13041}{16384}$★	d $\frac{161}{216}$	d# $\frac{1449}{2048}$★	e $\frac{161}{240}$	f $\frac{161}{256}$	f# $\frac{161}{270}$★	g $\frac{161}{288}$	g# $\frac{4347}{8192}$★	a $\frac{1}{2}$
B♭/1	B $\frac{128}{135}$★	c $\frac{8}{9}$★	c# $\frac{27}{32}$	d $\frac{64}{81}$★	d# $\frac{3}{4}$	e $\frac{32}{45}$	f $\frac{2}{3}$	f# $\frac{256}{405}$★	g $\frac{16}{27}$★	g# $\frac{9}{16}$★	a $\frac{256}{483}$	b♭ $\frac{1}{2}$
B/1	c $\frac{15}{16}$	c# $\frac{3645}{4096}$★	d $\frac{5}{6}$	d# $\frac{405}{512}$★	e $\frac{3}{4}$	f $\frac{45}{64}$★	f# $\frac{2}{3}$	g $\frac{5}{8}$	g# $\frac{1215}{2048}$★	a $\frac{90}{161}$★	b♭ $\frac{135}{256}$★	b $\frac{1}{2}$

The purpose of this table is (1) to show at a glance which keys come closest to complete diatonic purity. It is well known that C major is the model for pure major keys, and A minor for pure minor keys. In comparing all major keys in the table with C major, and all minor keys with A minor, one discovers which differ more or less from the models. [20] For example, one sees that G major differs with respect to just one note, namely the second, from complete purity.

The purpose of this table is also (2) to show which key would be most suitable in cases where a composition has to be transposed to a different key. One can see immediately that a piece in C major cannot be transposed to D-sharp or F-sharp major without altering its character, since these keys differ considerably from C major.

Although music today is always played in one of the keys listed in the preceding table, one is not completely bound to diatonic intervals, but also can use chromatic intervals on occasions where they produce a good effect. That is, although the natural or diatonic second in C major is D, the minor second [sic, augmented prime] C-sharp, or the augmented second D-sharp, can be used occasionally. The same is true of other intervals.[18]

The purpose of the second table [table 2.3] is to show size of the diatonic and chromatic intervals for each of the twelve steps of our current scale. But it is necessary for us to examine these intervals somewhat more closely.

The table shows that most of the intervals contained in the same column

---

18. This is not the place to explain in which cases composers may replace the diatonic intervals with chromatic ones. It is sufficient to say to the beginner that it happens, and sometimes must happen. The reasons for this procedure will be explained clearly in the course of this work.

To say something introductory about this, one can conceive of the origin and use of the augmented prime in this way: Suppose one wants to modulate from C major to G major by using the chord of the major third and seventh on the second degree of the scale, but finds it necessary to use these chords

in inversion. This results in the following chords,

which creates a progression by an augmented prime.

have two names. [21] For example, II min., i.e., the minor second, is written above the second column, and I Aug., or the *augmented prime*, is written below it. The same is true of most of the other columns. This matter can be explained as follows.

1. Intervals appearing in the second column are of two types, augmented primes (C-sharp–C, D-sharp–D, etc.) and minor seconds (D–C-sharp, F–E, etc.). However, augmented primes are sometimes used as seconds (C-sharp instead of D-flat), and thus are placed in the same column. Those intervals best suited to be used as augmented primes are marked with an asterisk so that they can be identified immediately.

2. The same is true of the other columns. The intervals contained in the third column are sometimes used as major seconds and sometimes as *false thirds*;[19] the latter are marked with an asterisk. The same applies to all remaining columns with two designations.

Since it is important for the precise treatment of harmony to know each interval by its correct name and proper proportions, we are going to examine them in greater detail here.

1. The *augmented prime* is produced when a note within a progression is raised by a sharp (for example, C to C-sharp, D to D-sharp, etc.) for harmonic reasons.[20] [22] The true proportion of this interval ought to be 24/25, but in our system it is 243/256[21] or 128/135 (F–F-sharp). This produces the *diminished octave* by inversion.

2. The *minor second* is really the large semitone, such as the small diatonic interval E–F, and its pure ratio is 15/16. In inversion it becomes the *major seventh*.

3. As can be seen from the diatonic scale, the *major second*, or the

19. This false [diminished] third, like the false fifth, is dissonant, although the augmented sixth resulting from its inversion is sometimes used as a consonance. This sixth results from the second inversion of the seventh chord that contains this false third, as is shown in this example. In the first chord, D-sharp and F form a false third, which in inversion becomes an augmented sixth.

20. See note 18, above.
21. See note 6, above.

diatonic whole tone, has two proportions, the large (8/9) and the small (9/10). In inversion it becomes the [minor] *seventh*.

4. The *augmented second* is produced when the major second is raised by a sharp for harmonic reasons. It really ought to be 64/75 or 108/125, depending on whether the half tone 24/25 is added to 8/9 or 9/10. This proportion is approximated in our system by 27/32. In inversion it becomes the *diminished seventh*.

5. The *false third* is occasionally produced where the major instead of the minor third is used above the root for harmonic reasons,[22] and this third forms such a diminished third with the fifth of the chord.[23] Its proper proportion would be 225/256, since that interval remains when the pure major third (4/5) is subtracted from the false fifth (B–f), which is 45/64 (as shown in the table). Our system gives 8/9 instead. In inversion it becomes the *augmented sixth*.

6. The pure *minor third* is 5/6. In inversion it becomes the *major sixth* (3/5).

7. The pure *major third* is 4/5. In our system it also appears as 405/512 and 64/81. In inversion it becomes the *minor sixth* (5/8, or 256/495, or 81/128).

[23] 8. The *diminished fourth* should really be 25/32. It is produced when the pure major third (4/5) is subtracted from the pure minor sixth (5/8). If the pure major third (G-sharp) were to be added above E (which is 4/5 in relation to C), the result would be 16/25; this tone [G-sharp] would form the diminished fourth, or 25/32, in relation to C (1/2). Instead, 64/81 can be used. In inversion it becomes the *augmented fifth*.

9. The pure *perfect fourth*, also simply called the fourth, is 3/4. In inversion it becomes the *perfect fifth*.

10. The *augmented fourth*, also called the *tritone*, has its origin in the old diatonic scale. Its proportion is 32/45. In inversion it becomes the *false fifth*.

These are all the intervals used in today's music. Their use will be demonstrated in detail in the course of this work.

Intervals are considered either melodically, when notes are sounded in succession, or harmonically, when both notes are sounded together.

Melodic intervals are either complex or simple, but harmonic intervals are either consonant or dissonant. Experience has confirmed that the con-

---

22. Namely, in the diminished triad, which will be discussed in the following chapter.

23. See note 6, above.

sonant intervals are without a doubt also the simplest in succession. For this reason it is necessary to become acquainted with the intervals according to their degree of consonance or dissonance.

There have been many attempts to discover the natural basis of consonance and dissonance. Most philosophers maintain that the most consonant intervals are those whose ratios are easiest to understand, and indeed this coincides with experience. Two strings of equal length, thickness, and tension merge so perfectly into one note when sounded together that they are indistinguishable. Thus the unison is the most perfect consonance.

The ratio of equality (1 : 1) is also easiest to comprehend, just as it is easiest for the eye to discover the equality between two adjacent lines. Next to the unison, every ear perceives the greatest agreement in the octave. One, indeed, perceives two tones, but they are so similar that it is difficult for the ear to distinguish them; one hears two pitches, but not two different notes. The strings—or, if one prefers, the frequencies of both tones—have the ratio 1 : 2, the most intelligible after 1 : 1.

After the octave, there is no more agreeable interval than the fifth, whose ratio is 2 : 3; then comes the fourth, whose ratio is 3 : 4, and the major third, whose ratio is 4 : 5.

Thus experience teaches us that the most harmonious intervals are those that can be expressed by the simplest ratios. The more complex the ratios become, the less harmonious are the intervals. Everyone feels that there is no harmony or consonance in the major second. Its ratio is 8 : 9, which is as difficult to perceive as it is for the eye to discover that of two adjacent lines one is longer than the other by a ninth. [24] The closer the tones are to one another, the more dissonant they are. Everyone feels that the minor second (15/16) is much more dissonant than the major second (8/9). The minor third (5/6) is universally considered as a consonance, while the major second (8/9) is always considered as a dissonance. Since one also finds that this minor third can be made noticeably smaller without losing its consonant nature, it follows that the ratio 6 : 7 is the last one that can be comprehended by the ear. Since 8/9 is already difficult, but 5/6 can still be made smaller, this leaves the two proportions 6/7 and 7/8 between the clearly perceived consonances and dissonances. The first is somewhat more difficult to perceive than 5/6, the other somewhat easier than 8/9. Since 5/6 is still strongly consonant (because the minor third can still be made smaller), but 8/9 is certainly already dissonant, the proportion 7/8 appears to be the dividing point between the consonances and the dissonances.

To be sure, the interval 6/7, which could be called a diminished third, cannot be found on our organ or clavier; however, it is produced by trumpets. It is well known that trumpet and horn players generally believe that their instruments, when new, produce the tones b-flat[1] and a[2] too low and f[2] too high. Only a few know that these notes are not faulty, but real natural pitches. It can be demonstrated that each pure string or bell produces its octave, twelfth, tenth, and seventh in addition to its actual fundamental. That is, in addition to the fundamental (1), each produces the pitches represented by the proportions 1/2, 1/3, 1/4, 1/5, 1/6, 1/7, etc., all of which determine the pure sound. These same notes are produced separately by trumpets and horns in this very order. Thus the note b-flat, which is considered too low by horn players, is really the note represented by 1/7; f, by 1/11; and a, by 1/13.[24]

[25] Since the thirds are the smallest consonant intervals, the sixths resulting from their inversion are the largest. Consequently there are only four types of consonant intervals besides the octave and unison within the compass of an octave: thirds, fourths, fifths, and sixths. Actually there are only two, since sixths are inverted thirds and fifths are inverted fourths. However, it must be remembered that not all thirds, fourths, fifths, and sixths are considered to be consonant intervals. Since the names of intervals are taken from the steps of the scale, there are some intervals that are called thirds, fourths, or fifths, even though they are not really those intervals and even though they are not consonant. Occasionally the interval C–c-sharp is called an augmented octave; C–F-sharp, an augmented fourth; and C–G-sharp, an augmented fifth—the first because it is placed on the eighth step above C, and the others because they are placed on the fourth and fifth steps, respectively. We would like to state the true ratios of all consonant intervals

---

24. Thus there would be good reason to include at least 1/7 in our system. When transposed down to the first octave, this note is in the ratio 4:7 to the fundamental. For the fundamental C, it would fall between A (3/5) and B (8/15); we shall label it "I." It is really consonant, and this chord

$$C \; - \; E \; - \; G \; - \; I$$
$$4 \quad\; 5 \quad\; 6 \quad\; 7$$

is not a dissonant seventh chord, but a four-part chord. This is evident from the fact that in certain cases the best harmonists treat the minor seventh as well as the augmented sixth as consonances, examples of which are well known. The reason for this lies without doubt in the fact that these intervals sound like 4:7. In fact, the augmented sixth (128/225) is only 1/225 larger than 4/7, which is not perceptible; and the minor seventh is only 1/64 larger than 4/7.

here so that one is not led astray by names into considering dissonant intervals as consonant.

Consonant intervals are:

the minor third (5/6) – major sixth (3/5)
the major third (4/5) – minor sixth (5/8)
the fourth (3/4)   –   fifth (2/3).

The interval 4/7 could be added to this if the tone proposed in the preceding footnote were introduced.[c]

These intervals are completely pure when they have the ratios given here. However, experience teaches us that these intervals do not lost their consonant character to any noticeable extent when their ratios differ somewhat. Fourths can be raised and fifths lowered by half a comma, or 1/160. Major thirds can be raised and minor sixths lowered by as much as a whole comma, or 1/80, as was shown in greater detail above.[25]

All other intervals of the scale are thus dissonant. In order that both the consonant and dissonant intervals may be surveyed at a glance, we add the following two tables here.[d]

25. See above, pp. 21 and 22.

---

[c]Although Kirnberger was the first to give a special designation (the letter I) to the natural seventh (4 : 7), he was not the first theorist of the eighteenth century to suggest that it be included among the consonances. In his *Tentamen novae theoriae musicae* (St. Petersburg, 1739), Leonhard Euler states that the natural seventh is to be considered as a primary consonance because of its simple ratio. Giuseppe Tartini, in the fifth chapter of his *Trattato di musica* (Padua, 1754), also describes this interval as a consonance. For this reason, says Tartini, the seventh chord on the dominant is a consonant chord and its seventh does not require preparation.

The natural origin of the seventh is also discussed by Georg Andreas Sorge in his *Vorgemach der musikalischen Composition* (Lobenstein, 1745–47). Sorge, however, considers it to be the original dissonance, and thus the mother of all remaining dissonances. He goes on to explain that the seventh above the dominant is treated like a quasi consonance in that it does not require preparation. Sorge's description of the natural origin and treatment of the dominant seventh chord was reflected some hundred years later in François-Joseph Fétis's *Traité complet de la théorie et de la pratique de l'harmonie* (Brussels, 1844).

[d]No new tables are given at this point. Possibly Kirnberger is referring to tables 2.2 and 2.3, which specify the string lengths of the diatonic and chromatic intervals for each tonic. These ratios also provide information about the relative consonance or dissonance of each interval possible within his tuning system.

CHAPTER 3

Chords

[26] In today's music every melody is accompanied by harmonies that are suitable to it. Even in compositions that have only a single melody, as in arias, one hears additional notes that accompany this melody in an appropriate manner. A sound that is composed of several notes is called a chord; thus, every composition consists of a succession of chords.

In older times chords were always composed entirely of consonant intervals or of notes that combined to form an agreeable sound. Gradually it became apparent that under certain conditions it would also be possible to employ dissonant intervals in chords, thereby frequently giving the melody a coherence and charm not possible with consonances alone. For this reason more and more chords have been assimilated into music.

A chord is consonant if it consists of intervals [*sic*, notes] that are consonant not only in relation to the bass note but also amongst themselves; it is dissonant if one or more notes are dissonant either in relation to the bass or in relation to some other note.

Therefore it is possible to construct a chord containing only consonant intervals in just three ways:

    1. the bass note and its third, fifth, and octave.
    2. the bass note and its third, sixth, and octave.
    3. the bass note and its fourth, sixth, and octave.

Continuation beyond the octave would simply result in repetition of the same intervals.

Thus the most complete consonant chord consists of only three notes in addition to the bass note: the third, fifth, and octave; or the third, sixth, and octave; or the fourth, sixth, and octave. The first is called the *perfect triad* because it is the most harmonious; the second is called the *sixth chord*, and the last a *six-four chord*.

40

[27] These three consonant chords are really just three different representations of one and the same chord, the perfect triad, as is clearly evident from example 3.1.

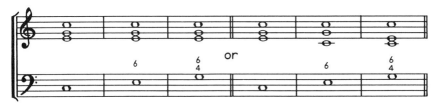

EXAMPLE 3.1

These three chords contain the same notes, except that in each a different note is placed in the bass. In the first, the actual root of the chord is in the bass; in the next, its third; and in the last, its fifth. For this reason the last two chords are called inversions of the triad; that is, the sixth chord is its first inversion and the six-four chord its second inversion. Therefore every consonant chord is either a triad or one of its inversions.

It is likely that music existed long before dissonance came into use. Since dissonances impair the harmony and are troublesome to the ear, those who first used them must have had exceptional reasons for preferring an imperfect to a perfect harmony.

Simply the notion of making harmony somewhat more exciting on occasion or of arousing the listener's desire for this excitement may have been the reason for allowing the harmony to be sounded incomplete directly above the bass note, and the missing note to be reinstated immediately thereafter to the listener's even greater satisfaction. [28] To grasp this clearly, suppose that in example 3.2 the intention was to follow the perfect triad on C (a) by the chord on D. Here one could easily come upon the idea of extending a note of the preceding chord, such as e, over the new bass note D, so that the desire for a more perfect harmony would be aroused by the

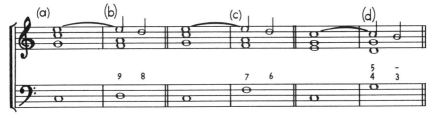

EXAMPLE 3.2

resulting dissonance. This harmony follows immediately thereafter when the dissonance e, as the ninth above the bass, proceeds to the octave. One could proceed in the same way from the seventh to the sixth, as at (c), and from the fourth to the third, as at (d). One finds in fact that this makes the sensation of harmony somewhat more charming.

Following the success of this initial experiment—substituting a dissonance for a required consonance directly over the bass note, which could proceed to that consonance, or *resolve*—one was struck by the idea of delaying two consonances, as in example 3.3. At (a) both the ninth and the fourth are held over the bass note D before proceeding to the octave and third. But at (b) the ninth and the seventh are held over F and at (c) the sixth and the fourth are held over G before resolving respectively to the octave and sixth, and to the fifth and third.

EXAMPLE 3.3

This appears to be the origin of a category of dissonances that can be regarded as *suspensions*. They are dissonant notes which momentarily displace consonances and which proceed to their nearest consonances over the same bass note.

It has generally been noted that these dissonances would be too harsh if they were introduced suddenly, and that they could be used only if they were already present in the preceding harmony, so that they could be extended for a while into the new harmony. [29] It would sound harsh and unpleasant if these two chords were to be sounded as in example 3.4, where the ninth and fourth enter freely. These notes definitely should have been contained in the preceding chord. They become agreeable only when they

EXAMPLE 3.4

form a close association between the two chords, and, so to speak, allow them to flow into one another.

This has given rise to the rule that [the notes forming] these dissonances must always be contained in the preceding chord and must be held over. This is called their *preparation*.

Since they are mere suspensions, it is also clear that by their nature they must proceed to the consonances whose places they have taken. This is called their *resolution*.

Just as one or more notes in the upper voices are held over as suspensions of the following chords in the examples quoted above, the bass note can also be held over as a displacement of the following one. [See example 3.5.]

EXAMPLE 3.5

Here the intention was to follow the C chord by the G chord in first inversion, that is by the sixth chord on B. The harmony of the upper voices is part of this chord; however, the bass note C, rather than moving directly to the B, has been held over from the preceding chord, thus changing the sixth into a fifth and the third into a second. These intervals assume their natural positions again as soon as the suspension is resolved to the correct bass note. [30] This type of suspension is somewhat harsher than the previous ones.

It is clear from these examples that dissonances of this sort could almost always be omitted without resulting in an error or an ambiguity.[26]

26. They simply serve to delay for a moment the real harmony, which could be introduced directly without these delays. Yet they occasionally serve to correct forbidden progressions which would occur between the upper voices, as is clear from this example. Here the omission of the $\frac{9}{7}$ suspension would result in fifths between the soprano and tenor voices. However, forbidden progressions between an upper

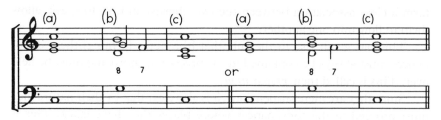

EXAMPLE 3.6

Since these suspensions are not necessary, we prefer to call them *nonessential dissonances.*

In addition to these dissonances there are others that can be called *necessary* or essential. They do not displace consonances, to which they immediately resolve, but maintain their own positions. Their origin can be demonstrated in the following way. [See example 3.6.]

[31] Suppose one starts out to modulate[27] in the key of C major,[a] and

---

(*Footnote 26 continued*)

voice and the bass are not improved by such suspensions. Thus this octave progression

could not be improved in this way:

From this one can make the rule that progressions between the highest voice and the bass never become faulty by the omission of suspensions, provided that they are correct in other respects.

27. Exactly what is meant by playing in a key and by digressing to another key will be explained in detail later on. Those beginners who do not know this can look it up in the chapter on modulation [chapter 7].

---

[a]Here Kirnberger seems to be using the term "modulation" in a very special way, that is, to specify change *within* a key, not change of key. The phrase he uses is "... *in dem* Ton C dur zu moduliren." He does not mean modulation to or from C major, but change within that key. Thus the change (or modulation) from a major triad on C to one on G is, in itself, ambiguous, since it does not define a key center.

consequently has played the perfect triad on C, as at (a); then one goes to G in the bass, as at (b), where the intention is to use the consonant triad again. At this point the trained ear is unsure to which key this harmony (b) belongs, since it can be the harmony on the fifth of C, the key in which one is modulating, as well as the tonic triad of G. Consequently it would be possible to stop at this chord as if at a cadence.

If it is the intention of the player not to cadence on this chord but to return to the C chord, he must play with this chord on G a note that belongs to the key of C and leads back to it. A simple means of accomplishing this becomes evident, namely that of adding the seventh, f, to the consonant triad. In this way it becomes clear that the harmony at (b) belongs to the key of C major and not G major, because in the latter the proper leading tone is f-sharp, not f. Furthermore, this dissonance must lead to a subsequent chord which will resolve it. From this it is evident that the seventh added to the triad clearly defines a previously vague modulation and prepares the ear for the next harmony. In such a case this dissonance is more or less necessary and cannot, like the previously discussed suspensions, be omitted. Otherwise an ambiguity would result, which is always an error. Thus this seventh is an essential dissonance; it does not replace the sixth or the octave, but has its own place. Yet, like the suspensions, it is dissonant, especially when the octave is sounded with it, but less so when the octave is omitted.

[32] For this reason the ear does not tolerate the free introduction of the seventh; it also must be prepared. This can be accomplished in two ways: either the seventh results from a note in the upper voices that is extened into the next harmony, as at (a), or it is introduced above a stationary bass, as at (b). [See example 3.7.]

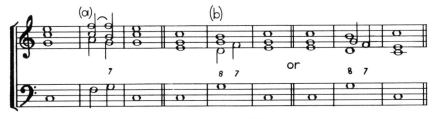

EXAMPLE 3.7

These, then, are the two types of dissonance and the situations in which they can be used.[b] Both types can appear in many different guises, and thus a

---

[b] One of Kirnberger's most important contributions to harmonic theory is his definition of essential and nonessential dissonance. This distinction, which is only outlined here, is explained in greater detail in chapter 4.

large number of dissonant chords is generated. One must know them all, since sometimes this form and sometimes that one is preferable.

The seventh chord, like the triad, has different inversions, and each inversion has a new shape, as can be seen from example 3.8. At (a) it is in its original form, and for this reason is properly called a seventh chord. At (b) the third of the chord is in the bass, whereby the seventh has been changed into the fifth and the octave into the sixth; in this form it is called a six-five chord. [33] At (c) the fifth of the chord is in the bass, whereby the former seventh, octave, and third have become the third, fourth, and sixth, respectively; thus this chord is called the six-four-three chord. At (d) the seventh itself is in the bass, whereby the octave, third, and fifth have become the second, fourth, and sixth, respectively.

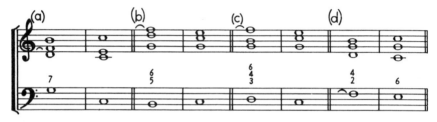

EXAMPLE 3.8

Thus there are altogether four types of chords used in music: (1) the consonant, (2) the dissonant with an essential dissonance, (3) the dissonant with one or more nonessential dissonances, and (4) those resulting from a mixture of types 2 and 3, where nonessential and essential dissonances are combined. The triad with its inversions belong to the first type, the seventh chord with its inversions belong to the next, the suspensions of the consonant chords belong to the third, and the suspensions of the [essential] dissonant chords belong to the fourth.

To become acquainted with all chords used in our current system, one need only proceed in the following way.

(1) Find all triads in the system and take their inversions. In this way all consonant chords are obtained. (2) Add the seventh to every type of triad, and also take all their inversions. In this way all chords of the second type are obtained. (3) If all possible suspensions of each chord in both of the preceding classes are taken, all nonessential dissonant chords of the third and fourth types are obtained. In order that this process be illustrated by clear examples, we have constructed tables 3.1–3.4, in which all chords contained in the C major and A minor scales are listed.

TABLE 3.1. Consonant Chords in Their Various Forms.[c]

THE MAJOR TRIAD.

(a) The triad.

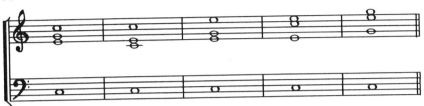

(b) The first inversion of the triad, or the sixth chord.

(c) The second inversion of the triad, or the consonant six-four chord.

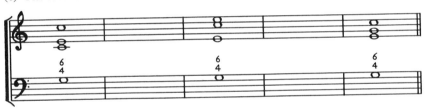

[c]Here it should be noted that Kirnberger includes the diminished triad and its inversions among the consonant chords. Although most theorists of the eighteenth century stated that this chord is dissonant, there were precedents for considering it as a consonance, or at least a quasi consonance. In his *Kleine General-Bass-Schule* (Hamburg, 1735), p. 180, Johann Mattheson states that the diminished triad can be used as a quasi consonance, and lists it among the principal chords [*Hauptaccorde*]. This opinion was stated again a few years later by Georg Andreas Sorge in his *Vorgemach der musikalischen Composition*, pp. 18–19.

For Kirnberger, the justification for considering the diminished triad as consonant lies in his tuning system. (See chapter 1.) He makes a distinction between the false fifth (45 : 64), which is a dissonance and whose inversion is the tritone (23 : 45), and the small fifth, which is larger than the false fifth by 1/64. In the articles "Falsch" and "Verminderter Dreyklang" in Sulzer's *Allgemeine Theorie der schönen Künste*, Kirnberger explains that the closer the proportion is to 5/7, the more usable is the small fifth as a consonance in the diminished triad. However, it should be noted that the relative consonance or dissonance of this interval above scale degree 2 in the minor mode (or scale degree 7 in the major mode) varies from key to key in Kirnberger's temperament.

THE MINOR TRIAD.

(a) The triad.

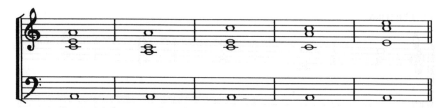

(b) The first inversion of the triad, or the sixth chord.

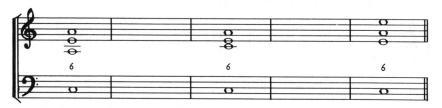

(c) The second inversion of the triad, or the consonant six-four chord.

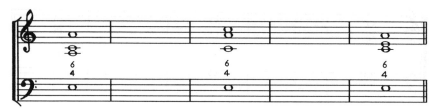

THE DIMINISHED TRIAD.

(a) The triad.

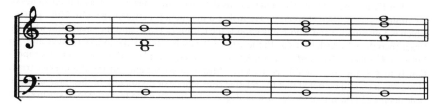

(b) The first inversion of the triad, or the sixth chord.

(c) The second inversion of the triad, or the consonant six-four chord.

TABLE 3.2. The Essential Seventh Chord and Its Inversion.[d]

The minor seventh with the major third and perfect fifth.	The minor seventh with the minor third and perfect fifth.	The major seventh with the major third and perfect fifth.	The minor seventh with the minor third and small fifth.	The minor seventh with the major third and small fifth.

(a) The seventh chord.

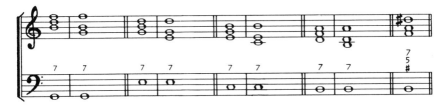

  [d] An unusual feature of this table is the inclusion of the seventh chord B–d-sharp–f–a. In its second inversion this chord forms what is now known as the French augmented sixth chord. However, it is not mentioned elsewhere in Kirnberger's writings as one of the essential dissonant seventh chords. Possibly it was included at this point for the sake of completeness, or because it was mentioned by other theorists. In his *Vorgemach der musikalischen Composition* and *Compendium Harmonicum* (Lobenstein, 1760), Sorge explains this chord as arising from the addition of the minor seventh to the *Triade manca*. He goes on to say that it is most

TABLE 3.2.(*continued*)

The minor seventh with the major third and perfect fifth.	The minor seventh with the minor third and perfect fifth.	The major seventh with the major third and perfect fifth.	The minor seventh with the minor third and small fifth.	The minor seventh with the major third and small fifth.

(b) The first inversion of the seventh chord, or the six-five chord.

(c) The second inversion of the seventh chord, or the six-four-three chord.

(d) The third inversion of the seventh chord, or the chord of the second.

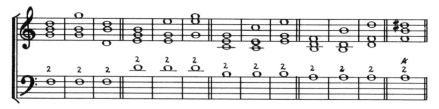

(*Footnote d continued*)
frequently used with the f in the bass. This chord is also mentioned by Marpurg in his *Handbuch bey dem Generalbass und der Composition* (Berlin, 1755) under the heading of simple dissonant seventh chords. It is formed by adding a third to the chord B–d-sharp–f, which is one of the unessential [*uneigentlich*] triads.

It should also be noted that another of the chords listed in this table, B–d–f–a, is later designated by Kirnberger as an unauthentic seventh chord when it progresses to the triad on C. In that case the seventh is considered as a nonessential dissonance displacing the sixth, and thus the real root of the chord is G. Unauthentic seventh chords are discussed in chapter 4 of this work. (See note g in that chapter.)

TABLE 3.3. Consonant Chords with One or More Nonessential Dissonances as Suspensions.

(a) The triad with its suspensions.

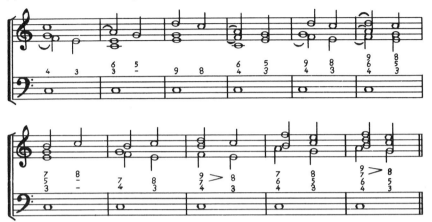

(b) The sixth chord with its suspensions.

(c) The consonant six-four chord with its suspensions.

(d) The consonant chord with the suspension in the bass.

TABLE 3.4. The Seventh Chord and Its Inversions with One or More Nonessential Dissonances [as] Suspensions.

(a) The seventh chord with suspensions.

(b) The six-five chord with suspensions.

(c) The six-four-three chord with its suspensions.

(d) The chord of the second with its suspensions.

(e) The essential dissonant chord with suspensions in the bass.

CHAPTER 4

Observations Concerning the Nature and Use of Chords and Some of Their Intervals

I. THE TRIAD

[34] There are three types of triads: the major (a), the minor (b), and the diminished (c). [See example 4.1.]

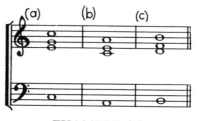

EXAMPLE 4.1

The first, which consists of a major third, perfect fifth, and octave, is the most perfect harmony possible. And since the most perfect harmony is also the most soothing, older composers ended their compositions with this triad, even when the compositions were written in a minor key. But today one no longer hesitates to close with the minor or small triad. Compositions written in major keys are usually begun with major triads and those written in minor keys with minor triads, since the mode of a composition is firmly established from the very beginning by these harmonies.

Because of this power to establish the key, the third, fifth, and octave of the scale were called the essential steps (*chordae essentiales*). Thus, in general, the most important statements of the perfect triad in a major or minor key occur at the beginning and at the end of a composition, or of its major sections, since in the beginning it determines the key and at the end produces the feeling of repose by its perfection.

However, the diminished triad, which will be discussed in more detail later on, is not suitable either at the beginning of a composition, since it does not establish a key, or at the end, since it is not perfect enough.

[35] The triad need not contain all three of its consonances. Either its octave or its fifth can be omitted and, instead, one of its other intervals doubled.

Since neither ascending nor descending parallel fifths and octaves are permitted, as will be demonstrated elsewhere, one is occasionally forced to double the fifth in order to avoid this error. Thus the triad can be found in the forms shown in example 4.2.

EXAMPLE 4.2

It is important to recognize the circumstances under which the third, fifth, or octave must or can be doubled in lieu of an omitted interval. It will be very useful if we state the most essential rules regarding this matter.

The major third above the *tonic* and *subdominant*[28] can be doubled. However, the third above the dominant cannot be doubled; since it is the leading tone of the key one is in and awakens a longing for the tonic, it absolutely must move up to that note whenever it is heard. If the leading tone were doubled, both would have to resolve upward, and this would result in forbidden octaves, as can be seen in example 4.3.

[36] For just this reason the major third above the tonic cannot be doubled when the bass ascends four steps to the following harmony or descends five steps to the triad. For example, if one wanted to double the

28. We make use of these words for the sake of conciseness, and want to clarify their meaning for those who are not accustomed to them. The tonic is the note from which the composition proceeds; thus, for example, in C major or C minor the note C is the tonic. The dominant is always the fifth degree above the tonic; thus in C major or minor it is the note G. The subdominant is the fourth degree; thus the note F in C major or minor. The mediant is the third degree, the submediant the sixth.

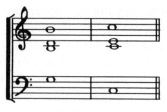

EXAMPLE 4.3

third above the tonic C and from there go to F, octaves would again result, as
shown in example 4.4.

EXAMPLE 4.4

The feeling that the leading tone must resolve upward is most distinct
when one sings the major scale from below. As soon as the seventh degree is
reached, one can neither go back nor go anywhere else than to the octave a
half step above. [See example 4.5.]

EXAMPLE 4.5

The incidental major third that is designated by a sharp over the bass
note cannot be doubled either, since it usually represents the leading tone of
a key to which one wants to modulate, as can be seen in example 4.6. At (a) it
is the leading tone of G; at (b), of A; and at (c), of C.

EXAMPLE 4.6

[37] Otherwise all major thirds (when they are not leading tones of a key) and, in general, all minor thirds can be doubled in order to avoid forbidden fifths and octaves. [See example 4.7.]

EXAMPLE 4.7

The following example [example 4.8] by the elder Bach, where the leading tone is doubled at (a), ought not be taken as the rule by prospective composers. This great man deviated from the rules here for the sake of obtaining a beautiful melody in all parts, and yet was able to avoid octaves.

EXAMPLE 4.8

There are cases where the major third appears to be doubled contrary to the given rule. This occurs in situations where one has already digressed to another key, and thus where the major third is no longer the leading tone, as can be seen in example 4.9. Here the major third of the third chord (on G) can be doubled because the key is no longer C major, but G major.

EXAMPLE 4.9

Likewise, the third above the dominant in the minor mode cannot be doubled.

A composition can neither begin nor end with the diminished triad because of its imperfect fifth. Therefore this triad is used only to connect other chords. [38] In a major key it is built on the seventh degree of the scale, and in the minor on the second degree. Moreover, like both preceding triads, it can appear in numerous forms, as shown in example 4.10.

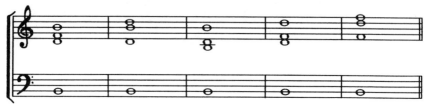

EXAMPLE 4.10

The only possible progression for the diminished triad is upward by four steps. In a major key it leads upward by four steps to the minor triad, but in a minor key it leads to the major triad or to its inversions, that is, down by a third, or up by a half step, or down by a whole step to a sixth chord.[a] [See example 4.11.]

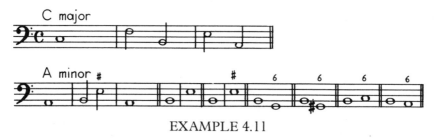

EXAMPLE 4.11

[a] Kirnberger's rule that a diminished triad can only progress upward by four steps applies only when both chords are in root position. Furthermore, as indicated in example 4.11, Kirnberger allows the diminished triad in a minor key to progress in various ways to certain minor as well as major triads and their inversions.

The reason that Kirnberger does not include the progression from the leading tone triad to the tonic triad in this discussion becomes clear later in this chapter. This triad is considered as an incomplete six-five chord, and thus its root is a third below that of the diminished triad.

When the small fifth occurs in the diminished triad, it is consonant and does not have to resolve down by step, as shown in example 4.12.[b]

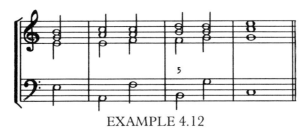

EXAMPLE 4.12

[39] Some theorists list other triads beyond those mentioned. But all chords in which the major third is greater than 64/81 and the minor third smaller than 6/7 (or, on our clavier, smaller than 27/32), and likewise those in which the fifth is greater than 2/3 and the diminished fifth smaller than 5/7 (or, on our clavier, smaller than 32/45), not only are not consonant but completely useless.

If one generates thirds, fifths, and the like by the number of steps on the staff, one lapses into errors that can result in all kinds of disharmonies. Who could tolerate the triads shown at (A) in example 4.13, for instance? Or the following seventh chords at (B), which are based on equally sound reasoning?

EXAMPLE 4.13

[b] See note c in chapter 3.

Consonances can be demonstrated only on the basis of the simple ratio of vibrations or by division of the monochord, not by the number of lines and spaces of a notational system.[c]

II. OBSERVATIONS CONCERNING THE SIXTH CHORD

A. The sixth chord that arises from the major triad

Next to the perfect triad, this sixth chord is used most frequently. It is seldom used at the beginning and never at the end of a composition.

[40] It can be formed in three ways: One can take with the sixth another sixth and a third, as at (a) in example 4.14; or, instead of two sixths, two

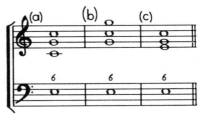

EXAMPLE 4.14

[c]Although Kirnberger does not specify names here, it is likely that his comments are directed against Friedrich Wilhelm Marpurg and some of the absurdities inherent in the "combined Rameau-Marpurg system." This system is described by Marpurg in the article "Untersuchung der Sorgischen Lehre von der Entstehung der dissonirenden Sätze," *Historisch-Kritische Beyträge zur Aufnahme der Musik*, vol. 5, part 2, pp. 131–84. There Marpurg informs us that his system is a compromise (a middle system) between two others: the complete system, in which any and all combinations of notes, intervals, and chords are possible; and the Rameau system, which contains only the "best" intervals and chords, and thus, in Marpurg's opinion, is too selective. The groundwork for a complete theoretical system, says Marpurg, is contained in F. W. Riedt's *Versuch über die musikalische Intervallen* (Berlin, 1753). Examination of that work reveals that Riedt identifies fifty-two discrete intervals within the span of an octave containing twenty-one notes (the diatonic-chromatic-enharmonic scale). Included in these is a triply diminished fifth and a triply augmented fourth! Extension of this mode of thinking would lead to the kind of absurdities given by Kirnberger in example 4.13. However, in Marpurg's defense, it should be pointed out that he does not go quite so far as did Riedt. His compromise system, which is also based on the twenty-one–note scale, does not include all possible intervals and chords, but only those within the scope of a given key and its five neighboring keys. Chords that arise from the mixture of two or more keys (e.g., b–d–sharp–f or d-sharp–f–a) are labeled "fantastisch." Although there are numerous such chords possible within the system, Marpurg describes only a few.

thirds with one sixth (b); or, with the sixth, the octave and third (c). By means of a judicious choice among these three modifications it becomes possible to avoid a large number of faulty progressions.

But there are also situations where the chord of the sixth and the octave cannot be used.

1. It cannot be used when it is built on the leading-tone of the key to which it leads, because this results in octaves, as can be seen at (d) in example 4.15. Since the bass note B must go to C, its octave b—if it were used with the sixth—would also have to go to c.

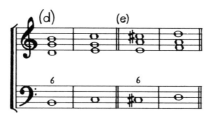

EXAMPLE 4.15

2. The octave of the bass is to be avoided even more assiduously when the bass note is already raised by an accidental, as at (e). In this way the major third would be doubled, which is not permitted. The bass note c-sharp is the major third of A; if c-sharp were also to be used in the chord, this major third would be doubled.

Therefore this sixth chord built on the leading tone has two sixths and a minor third in place of the octave, as at (f) in example 4.16; or, in the same situation, the third is doubled in place of the octave, as at (g).

EXAMPLE 4.16

[41] This is also the case with the sixth chord built on the raised sixth scale degree in the minor mode. Because of the harshness of the accidental note that lies outside of the key, the octave is to be omitted and, instead, the

sixth or third doubled. However, there are instances where one is obliged to use the octave in order to avoid fifths and octaves, and other forbidden progressions, or sometimes also because of what follows.

At (a) in example 4.17, the octave is used, but at (b) the progression is better. At (c) the doubling of the sixth is incorrect, since it entails a forbidden leap of an augmented fourth from g-sharp to d.

EXAMPLE 4.17

At (d) one is compelled, because of what follows, to use the octave in order to prepare the seventh above g-sharp.

It remains to be noted that when the fifth scale degree with the major third in a minor mode ascends to the major sixth, one cannot go back from there, but must continue through the leading tone to the octave, as at (a) above. However, when the fifth ascends in the same manner to the minor sixth, it cannot continue up to the octave either through the minor seventh, as at (a) in example 4.18, or through the major seventh, as at (b). At (b) the progression would involve a forbidden augmented second, and thus is not permitted. However, this can be used in inversion as a diminished seventh in contrary motion, as at (c).

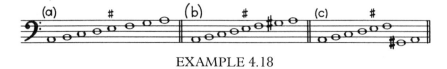

EXAMPLE 4.18

But this is true only when this leading tone actually progresses up by a half step, not when it leads to some other note. Thus the octave in the sixth chord at (a) in example 4.19 is harmless; here the bass note B is no longer the leading tone, but the third scale degree of G.

EXAMPLE 4.19

This is precisely the case with the sixth chord at (b) in example 4.20, where the octave is absolutely necessary with the sixth because of the resolution of the ninth. Here the bass note B is no longer the leading tone of the key, as it was shortly before at (a), but the mediant or third of G.

EXAMPLE 4.20

3. For the same reason the octave can never be used with the sixth when the sixth chord ascends by a half step to a triad, as in example 4.21. [42] Here every bass note with a 6 above it is the leading tone of the note following it.

[43] 4. In such progressions of the bass, as at (a) in example 4.22, the octave cannot be used with the sixth, because it would either result in octaves with the following chord, as at (b), or fifths, as at (c). If the chord at (a) were to be followed by the first inversion of the G chord, then the octave above A would be necessary with the sixth, as will be shown immediately below.

If the problematic situation should arise that the octave must be used with the sixth in such passages, then two voices must be made to move to the fifth of the following chord, as in example 4.23.

EXAMPLE 4.21

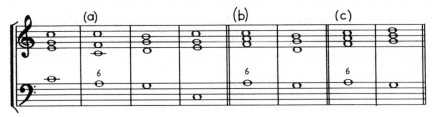

EXAMPLE 4.22

EXAMPLE 4.23

5. Just as the octave had to be avoided in the preceding situations, there are also cases where the octave must be used in sixth chords. This is true when a sixth chord leads to a triad a minor third above it, as in example 4.24 at (a).

EXAMPLE 4.24

If the sixth had been doubled here, as at (b), hidden fifths would result, as can be seen at (c).

[44] The octave is also necessary with the sixth when the bass ascends from this chord, as at (a) in example 4.25. Forbidden octaves would arise if either the sixth or the third were doubled, because the third or sixth above the following note B would also have to be doubled, as was shown in example 4.24 at (b). If the sixth above B were to be doubled in the same register, direct fifths would result.

EXAMPLE 4.25

Finally, we note here that this chord of the minor sixth and minor third, which arises from the major triad, is situated on the third, sixth, and seventh degrees of the scale.

B. *The sixth chord that arises from the small or minor triad*

In this sixth chord, as in the one that arises from the major triad, the sixth or third may be doubled, or the octave added to the sixth, whenever one or the other procedure becomes necessary to avoid forbidden octaves and fifths. Since most of the remarks made about the preceding sixth chord also apply to this one, they need not be repeated here.

However, it should be noted in particular (as has already been done with the preceding sixth chord) that the progression from this sixth chord to a triad must be approached with caution in order to avoid octaves or fifths. Example 4.26 can serve as a model. [45] At (a) a forbidden progression is avoided by having both the octave and the sixth of the first chord descend to the fifth of the following one. If the chord were to proceed as at (b), the unfavorable progression of an augmented second from f to g-sharp would occur. In the preceding case the third above the bass could also be doubled, as at (a) in example 4.27. If the sixth were to be doubled, as at (b), one of the upper voices would form hidden fifths with the bass.

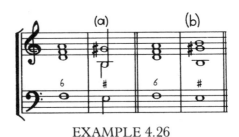

EXAMPLE 4.26

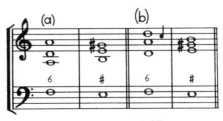

EXAMPLE 4.27

C. The sixth chord that arises from the diminished triad

The first inversion of the diminished triad produces a special sixth chord, whose third or sixth can be doubled, as was the case with both preceding sixth chords. [See example 4.28.]

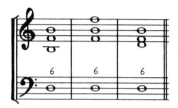

EXAMPLE 4.28

This chord can have no other progression than the following:
1. Up by a step to a minor or a major triad, as at (a) and (b) in example 4.29, [46] or to the first inversion of the triad, as at (c).

EXAMPLE 4.29

29. Both these chords can also occur as follows,

2. Down by a whole step to a sixth chord, as at (d), or to its fundamental chord, as at (e).

[47] Furthermore, as has already been noted, the sixth of this chord can be doubled without hesitation, as in example 4.30, because it is not to be considered here as the leading tone of the key.

EXAMPLE 4.30

It was mentioned just above that this sixth chord must lead either up by a step to a triad or down by a whole step to a sixth chord. However, there are situations that appear to contradict this rule, namely, where this chord of the major sixth leads up by step to a sixth chord or down by step to a triad, as in example 4.31. However, the chord marked with an asterisk must not be confused with our sixth chord that arises from inversion of the diminished triad; it has its origin in the seventh chord, as will be shown below in the remarks about that chord.

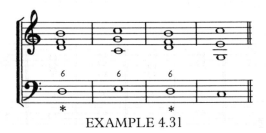

EXAMPLE 4.31

(*Footnote 29 continued*)
and their minor thirds can be doubled; the finest composers do this without hesitation. We mention this because some believe that the diminished fifth of the fundamental chord, namely b–f, is not a consonance. Were this the case, it could not be doubled in the first inversion, as in our example, but would have to be resolved as a dissonance.

D. A few special observations concerning sixth chords and their use

The following remains to be mentioned regarding the doubling of the sixth and the third in all three types of sixth chord.

1. The doubled intervals can either be separated by an octave or be stated on the same degree, as can be seen in example 4.32.

EXAMPLE 4.32

[48] 2. An interval delayed by a suspension, for example, the sixth that is delayed by a fifth or a seventh, or the third that is delayed by a second or a fourth, cannot be doubled. Thus the sixth is doubled when the third is delayed, and conversely the third is doubled when the sixth is delayed, as in example 4.33.

EXAMPLE 4.33

3. Neither the sixth nor the third can be doubled twice in succession when a bass figured by 6 ascends or descends by step, because octaves and forbidden fifths would result, as at (a) in example 4.34. The third can be

EXAMPLE 4.34

doubled after the doubling of the sixth, as at (b), and the sixth after the third, as at (c).

[49] The sixth chord is used instead of the triad when the bass progresses up or down by step; otherwise octaves would result. [See example 4.35.]

EXAMPLE 4.35

An important advantage of the sixth chord is that it can be used to prolong periods whenever desired in order to avoid having too many short phrases in succession, as will be shown later in the sixth chapter.

In this succession of ascending and descending sixth chords, the chords are even more closely connected if suspensions are used, as in example 4.36.

EXAMPLE 4.36

It is necessary to make a clear distinction between the sixth about which we have been speaking and a different sixth, which is a displacement of the fifth of a triad. The latter sixth is related to the fifth, as the ninth is to the octave at (a) in example 4.37, and is easy to distinguish from the sixth of the actual consonant sixth chord. Also, like the other suspensions, it never occurs on the upbeat.

EXAMPLE 4.37

[50] The sixth chord cannot be used to end a composition for many voices. Although this can occur in works for two voices, called *bicinia*, the triad is to be preferred at the close, since the unison or octave normally occurs there.

III. OBSERVATIONS CONCERNING THE CONSONANT SIX-FOUR CHORD

This chord is the least perfect of the consonant chords and thus cannot be used either to begin or to end a composition. Otherwise it has all the properties of a consonant chord; that is, the fourth as well as the sixth can be doubled, both can be introduced without preparation, and neither requires a specific progression or resolution, as do dissonances. This can be seen in example 4.38.

EXAMPLE 4.38

This six-four chord occurs at (a) and (b); in both cases the root is C. At (c) the fourth and the sixth are dissonant suspensions, and the root is G. In the first two, C is heard as the root, but at (c) only G is heard as the root. Here the fourth and the sixth are perceived as dissonant suspensions that delay the third and fifth of the root.[30]

[51] This consonant six-four chord can occur on weak as well as strong beats, but the other, like all suspensions, always falls on a strong beat. [See example 4.39.]

30. These are the true principles according to which the consonant fourth, which occurs in the second inversion of the triad, can be distinguished from the dissonant one, which is a suspension. There are still composers who are afraid to use the six-four chord as a consonance. Those who are not persuaded by the arguments given here might easily be convinced by the authority of many great men. However, we choose to cite only the following:

(Footnote 30 continued)

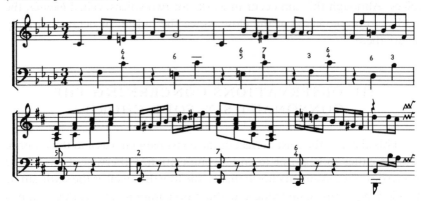

In the fourth measure of both examples there is a six-four chord which, were it dissonant, would have to have an entirely different progression than it has; here neither the fourth nor the sixth is resolved. Thus [in the second example] it is recognized as the second inversion of the F-sharp chord. No one would take either the fourth or the sixth to be suspensions of the third and fifth, since the F-sharp chord of the first measure is retained by the ear until the B chord is reached, as though the bass were as follows:

It is evident from the following passage that one could even begin with the consonant six-four chord in the middle of a composition. However, beginners are advised not to try this; only first-rate composers may take such liberties.

That this six-four chord is the second inversion of the F-sharp triad is evident from the preceding four-two chord, which arises from the seventh chord on C-sharp and which must then resolve to F-sharp.

After the four-two chord one expects to hear the triad on F-sharp or the sixth chord on A, whereby this six-four chord can be justified. It is not possible to begin either a composition or one of its sections with the sixth and fourth without such a means of making the following note sensible.

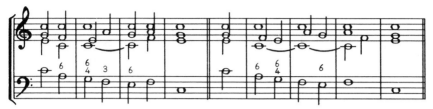

EXAMPLE 4.39

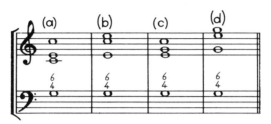

EXAMPLE 4.40

[52] It can appear in various forms: Either with two fourths and a sixth, as at (a) in example 4.40; or with one fourth and two sixths, as at (b); or with a fourth, sixth, and octave, as at (c); or with two octaves and a sixth, as at (d).

[53] When it is used with a sixth and two octaves but no fourth in a four-part texture, or with a sixth and an octave but no fourth in a three-part texture, this is done to preserve good melodic writing, for the sake of which the harmony must occasionally suffer a little.[31]

If the fourth were used at (a) in example 4.41, forbidden fifths would result between the soprano and tenor voices, no matter how they are arranged, as can be seen at (c). [54] At (b) the sixth chord is authentic; its root is E, as is shown in the fundamental bass.[32]

The minor third, which is the minor seventh from the root, can be

31. In both these cases where the fourth is omitted, care must be taken not to figure the bass with 6 like the ordinary sixth chord to which the third belongs; it is better to figure it with $\frac{8}{6}$ in order to distinguish the two. In a four-part accompaniment the fourth must also be stated; in both these cases, the fundamental chords would thus be entirely different. One should consult what Mr. Bach has to say about this in the second part of his work, *Die wahre Art das Clavier zu spielen* [Berlin, 1762].

32. The fundamental bass, which is given here on the bottom staff, contains the true roots of the various chords, or the bass notes as they would be if the chords were always used in their original form, that is, without inversion.

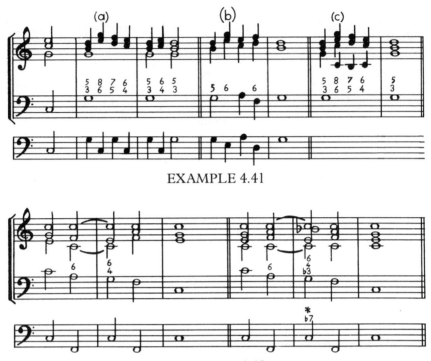

EXAMPLE 4.41

EXAMPLE 4.42

added to this chord when the [fundamental] bass progresses up by four steps to the triad, as can be seen in example 4.42 at the asterisk.

This is one characteristic of the consonant six-four chord, for this third cannot be added to the dissonant one. Another characteristic is that the fifth cannot be used in place of the sixth, as can be done with the dissonant six-four chord. Both types are clearly represented in example 4.43. [55] At (a)

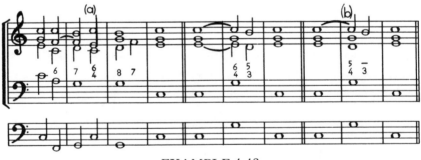

EXAMPLE 4.43

there is no way that the fifth above the bass can be used with the fourth or sixth, as happens at (b), where the fourth is merely a suspension and dissonant.

When there are more than three voices, it is good to add the minor third to the consonant six-four chord whenever possible, because thirds are generally indispensable in nearly every chord. This is the origin of the six-four-three chord that is built on the second degree of the scale. The fourth as well as the sixth remain consonant; only the third, as the minor seventh from the root, is dissonant. [See example 4.44.]

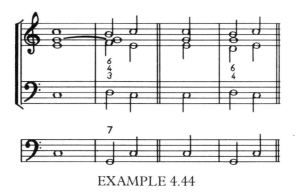

EXAMPLE 4.44

[56] In compositions for three voices, the fourth and sixth can be used without the third, as in example 4.45.

EXAMPLE 4.45

Yet this chord is not consonant enough to produce a feeling of rest and cannot be used at the close or end of a period. It must always be followed by other chords. Thus the phrase shown in example 4.46 is totally wrong; here

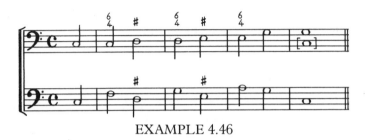

EXAMPLE 4.46

there are cadences[33] at the first half of the second, third, and fifth measures, as can be seen from the fundamental bass.[d]

It was mentioned just above that the fifth cannot be used with the consonant six-four chord. However, there are examples by some composers who have retained the fifth in place of the sixth. To demonstrate this we include example 4.47, but leave it to the best masters of the art to decide if it

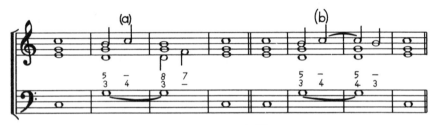

EXAMPLE 4.47

is correct. [57] The fourth at (a) must be resolved like every nonessential dissonance; it is objectionable because it occurs on the upbeat. When it is used as a preparation for a following nonessential fourth, as at (b), it is incorrect because it forms a seventh in relation to the fifth above the bass.

These comments also apply to the inversions of these chords. If the first

33. See the sixth chapter [Harmonic Periods and Cadences], where it is shown how the root progression by ascending fourth produces a cadence.

---

[d]Kirnberger's comments do not fit the example as it is given. If we assume that he has counted the incomplete measure at the beginning as measure one, then by his definition there are cadences on the first half of the second, third, fourth, and fifth measures. Also, the last measure of the figured bass does not correspond with the fundamental bass; either the bass note should be C, or in conformity with the established pattern, the figures $\frac{6}{4}$ have been omitted above the bass note G.

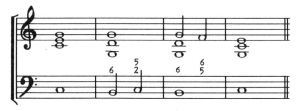

EXAMPLE 4.48

four measures were to be written as in example 4.48, the progression from the second to the third measure would sound very bad.

When the tempo is fast, the fourth may occur in this manner; but it is considered as passing and is not indicated in the figured bass. [See example 4.49.]

EXAMPLE 4.49

[58] Good harmonists avoid writing two successive six-four chords with the fourths in the upper voice, as in example 4.50.

EXAMPLE 4.50

However, when the root or even the third of the six-four chord was heard previously in the lowest voice, this progression can be used without hesitation because the root is retained by the ear, as in example 4.51.

The C on the first quarter [of the measure] is retained by the ear, and the chord on the second quarter is perceived as a sixth chord on C.

EXAMPLE 4.51

An example where even three fourths follow one another in the highest
voice is given in example 4.52.

EXAMPLE 4.52

The chord at (a) sounds like a sixth chord because of the preceding d.
The chord at (b) is thus the first to sound like a six-four chord. [59] However,
the chord at (c) is not a consonant six-four chord, but a chord of the second,
that is the third inversion of the seventh chord on E.[34]

The consonant six-four chord that arises from inversion of the diminished triad merits a special comment because of the similarity between its
large fourth and the tritone; despite this similarity, the former is very
different from the latter in effect. Example 4.53 will clarify this.

EXAMPLE 4.53

At (a) the true tritone, F–b, occurs; this chord, which is the third
inversion of the seventh chord on G, must lead to a C chord in its first

34. In figured bass it is completely wrong to figure this chord with $\frac{6}{4}$; the second
must also be indicated.

inversion. However, the six-four chord at (b) arises from the second inversion of the diminished triad; as was mentioned above, this chord can also contain the minor third in addition to the fourth, as is the case here. Even though the lowest note is F and the highest b, as before, the interval F–b is not the tritone here, but the large fourth that does not have to move up by a half step.

This very distinction also applies to melodic progression. The melody cannot proceed as at (c), where the real tritone occurs. But at (d), where the first inversion of the diminished triad occurs, the progressions mentioned above can be used without hesitation.[35]

IV. OBSERVATIONS CONCERNING THE SEVENTH CHORD

A. The authentic seventh, which is an essential dissonance

[60] As was mentioned in the preceding chapter, the seventh is added to the triad on the dominant of the given key whenever the intention is to return from this harmony to the tonic.[36] Thus this seventh has a double effect: (1) it prevents the dominant harmony from being heard as a place of

35. On this occasion it is important to note that the perception of harmony sometimes can make the most difficult progressions in singing easy and the very easy ones impossible. Thus the leap from f to b at (d) in example 4.53 is easy, since B is felt as the root of the sixth chord arising from the diminished triad. However, in the following passage, the progression of the top voice would be impossible to sing because the ear has already accepted B-flat as the root, which is totally contrary to the b.

36. Since this seventh is added to the dominant triad, it can be distinguished from other sevenths that are entirely different from it in origin. These others will be discussed in greater detail below.

rest; and (2) it leads back to the tonic harmony in a natural way by means of its required resolution.[e]

To understand fully what is said here about the use and treatment of the seventh, one must become acquainted with the contents of the subsequent chapter on cadences [chapter 6].

The first and most important effect of the seventh is that it destroys the feeling of repose or of closure which would otherwise be present, as in example 4.54. [61] Each of the notes marked here with a seventh would be felt by the ear as a resting point or close if this dissonance were removed. Thus the seventh can disrupt the feeling of rest.

EXAMPLE 4.54

When it is used for this purpose, it must be employed where a close would otherwise occur, that is, on the dominant or tonic of the key.

Its second effect is to lead the ear from the chord to which it is affixed to another, as a dominant to its tonic, and to come to rest there. Thus the root of this seventh chord will normally move up by four steps or down by five, since these are the two progressions from a dominant to the tonic, as can be seen in example 4.55.

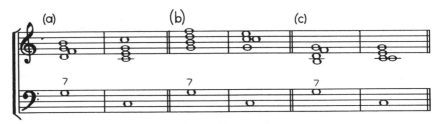

EXAMPLE 4.55

[e] In the article "Dissonanz" in Sulzer's *Allgemeine Theorie der schönen Künste*, Kirnberger indicates that d'Alembert (*Elémens de musique théorique et pratique* [Paris, 1752]) is the source of his opinion concerning the essential characteristics of this chord.

In a subsequent work, *Grundsätze des Generalbasses* (Berlin, 1781), Kirnberger explains that the seventh chord on the dominant originated from a passing dissonance. Rather than go directly from g to e, for example, singers would add the passing note f:

g   f   e.
G   C

To bring about the feeling of complete rest when closing from the dominant to the tonic by means of the seventh, the major third of the dominant seventh chord must be in the top voice, where it leads to the octave of the subsequent chord;[37] this can be seen at (a) in example 4.55. To make the feeling of rest less complete, the seventh chord could be arranged so that the third or fifth of the following chord would be in the top voice; this can be seen at (b) and (c).

[62] It has already been stated that the dominant seventh chord normally progresses up four steps or down five; however, it also leads up a single step to the triad. [See example 4.56.] But this situation is entirely different

EXAMPLE 4.56

(*Footnote e continued*)

Sorge also explained the seventh as arising from the passing motion 8–7 (see his *Vorgemach der musikalischen Composition*, p. 362).

37. It is worth noting here that the dominant seventh chord always has a major third, even if it were not natural to the mode. Thus in C minor the dominant seventh chord would also have the major third, as here:

The reason for this is obvious. Since this major third is the leading tone of the tonic for which one is aiming, it arouses the longing for that tonic. This is also the case with the inversions of the seventh chord, as here:

If one should find somewhere that a good harmonist has used the minor third on the dominant, this is a certain sign that he intends to abandon that key, as here:

Here the minor third of the second chord suggests that the harmony is going to G minor.

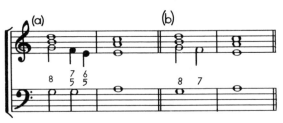

EXAMPLE 4.57

because this seventh is actually the ninth above the real root, which does not resolve until the following chord, as can be seen in example 4.57. Suppose in the passage at (a) that the G chord is followed by the E chord with the ninth and seventh, but in its first inversion, and that the note f, as the ninth from the root, leads immediately to the consonance e. [63] If this resolution of the ninth is delayed until the following measure, the progression at (b) results. At (b) the G chord on the second part of the measure is really the seventh chord on E with a suspended ninth. Consequently the progression to A is not from G, as it appears, but from E. It can be taken as a general rule that every essential seventh is followed by a bass progression by ascending fourth or descending fifth to a triad, unless an inversion of this chord is used.

There is another apparent seventh chord whose bass also progresses up by step; it is really a six-five chord whose sixth is delayed by the seventh, a nonessential dissonance, as in example 4.58.

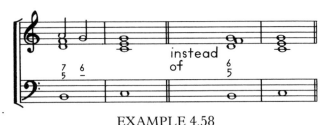

EXAMPLE 4.58

The seventh is normally combined with the third and fifth; but to avoid forbidden fifths, the octave can be used instead of the fifth. That is, instead of the progression at (A) in example 4.59, where forbidden fifths occur, these three measures could be written as at (B).

[64] The seventh chord always contains two intervals that tell us to which key the harmony must lead. These are the seventh itself, which

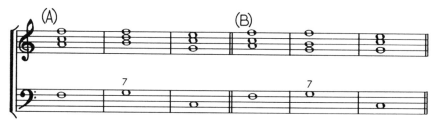

EXAMPLE 4.59

resolves to the third of the key, and the major third, which is the leading tone
and ascends to the tonic in the next harmony.

The seventh is either minor or major. The minor seventh occurs: (1)
with the major triad on the dominant, and leads to a close on the tonic, as can
be seen at (a), (b), and (c) in example 4.55; (2) with the minor triads on scale
degrees two, three, and six, which lead to closes on the fifth, sixth, and
second degrees of the scale, as at (a), (b), and (c) in example 4.60. The minor
seventh also occurs (3) with the diminished triad. This happens only on the
leading tone of the principal key, which then becomes the dominant of the
note that follows it, as can be seen at (d).

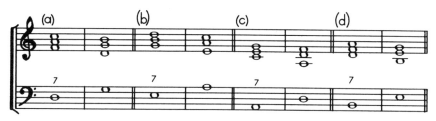

EXAMPLE 4.60

The major seventh occurs with the major triads on the tonic and
subdominant of the principal key. In the latter case it proceeds to the
diminished triad on the leading tone and thus cannot lead to a proper close.
[See example 4.61.]

EXAMPLE 4.61

[65] There is no triad to which the diminished seventh could be added as an essential dissonance. This seventh will be discussed in connection with enharmonic modulation [chapter 8], where it will be reduced to its true fundamental harmony.

The essential seventh can be prepared and resolved in many ways, as can be seen in example 4.62.

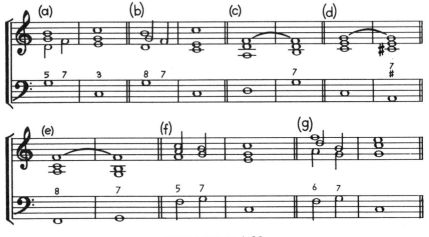

EXAMPLE 4.62

At (a) and (b) the sevenths are introduced on the weak part of the measure over a stationary bass; at (a) it is introduced by the fifth and at (b) by the octave. However, at (c) the third, at (d) the fifth, and at (e), (f), and (g) the octave are sustained from the accented part of the bass and become sevenths when a new root enters on the weak part.[f] [66] In all these cases this seventh resolves on the downbeat of the following measure to the third of the root.

However, when the seventh does not resolve to the tonic triad of the key to which it leads, but goes to its first inversion, the seventh resolves to the octave.

This resolution of the seventh is forbidden to all beginners by the masters of composition, because it leads to hidden octaves. Yet one finds that good harmonists allow the seventh to resolve to the octave by inverting

[f] By "accented part of the bass" [*gute Zeit des Basses*], Kirnberger apparently means accented beat or measure. See example 4.62.

the root in the chord of resolution; however, this always happens in so-called *contrary motion*, about which more will be said in the course of this work.

B. The unauthentic seventh, which is not an essential dissonance but which arises from an inversion

It was mentioned previously that the bass of a true seventh chord must progress up by four steps or down by five. Whenever there is a seventh chord that does not progress in this manner, it is a sign that the seventh is not the essential dissonant seventh but a different interval that has become a seventh through inversion. Such chords shall be considered here. Examples of these unauthentic sevenths are given in example 4.63, where the origin of the seventh can be seen from the fundamental bass at the bottom.[g]

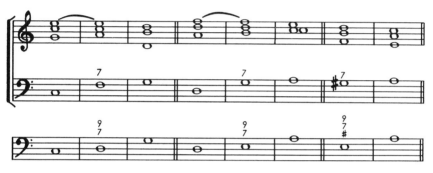

EXAMPLE 4.63

[67] In the first case the seventh on F is actually the ninth above the real root D, which has its own seventh and therefore progresses up by four steps. The unusual feature of this case is that the ninth does not resolve until the following measure. (See above, p. 82.) The other two examples of the unauthentic seventh are to be understood in just this way. The bass of such unauthentic sevenths naturally progresses up by a second, which is the

---

[g]The unauthentic [*uneigentlich*; *unächt*] seventh is the third type of seventh to be discussed by Kirnberger. The first is the essential seventh, and the second the nonessential seventh. The unauthentic seventh is also a nonessential dissonance but, unlike the nonessential seventh, its resolution is delayed until the following harmony. Thus it appears as if it were an essential dissonance, but it is not; instead, it arises from the displacement of the sixth in the six-five chord, which is the first inversion of the essential seventh chord. The seventh chords built on the leading tone of the major and minor modes, for example, fall into this category.

fourth from the real root of these seventh chords. But the situation in example 4.64 is really to be considered as if the first inversion of the E chord were to be sounded in passing before the true E chord is resolved.

EXAMPLE 4.64

V. OBSERVATIONS CONCERNING THE FIRST INVERSION OF THE SEVENTH CHORD, OR THE SIX-FIVE CHORD

Since this chord is really the seventh chord on the dominant of the following note (but with the major third instead of the root in the bass), it is, of course, formed above the leading tone of the key. The fifth of this chord is the dissonance, and the actual root is always three tones below the bass note.

(*Footnote g continued*)

The following table is added to clarify Kirnberger's conception of the unauthentic seventh chord and its inversions, and the relationship of each to the essential seventh chord.

	Unauthentic*		Essential
	7 or 7	in place of	7 6 $\left(\begin{smallmatrix}6\\5\end{smallmatrix}\right)$
	5		5 –
Inversions			
(a) 1st	6	in place of	6 –
	5		5 4 $\left(\begin{smallmatrix}4\\3\end{smallmatrix}\right)$
			3 –
(b) 2nd	4	in place of	6 –
	3		4 – $\left(\begin{smallmatrix}4\\2\end{smallmatrix}\text{ or 2}\right)$
			3 2
(c) 3rd	4	in place of	6 7
	2		4 5 (bass suspension)
			2 3

*The source chord, $\frac{9}{7}$, occurs in place of the essential seventh chord $\frac{9\ 8}{7\ -}$ (7).

That is, the seventh from G becomes the fifth from B, and since the seventh chord on G leads to C, its inversion, or the six-five chord on B, also leads to C. [See example 4.65.]

EXAMPLE 4.65

[68] Just as there is an unauthentic seventh chord, there is also an unauthentic six-five chord, which likewise is an inversion of a seventh chord with its ninth. Because of the inversion that occurs in the bass, the ninth does not proceed to the octave, as is shown in example 4.66. The true fundamental bass is given on the lowest staff.

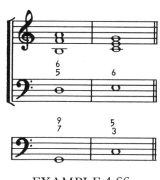

EXAMPLE 4.66

The unauthentic six-five chord is really a six-four-three chord, in which the fifth, as the ninth from the fundamental bass, stands in place of the fourth.

VI. OBSERVATIONS CONCERNING THE SECOND INVERSION OF THE TRUE SEVENTH CHORD, OR THE SIX-FOUR-THREE CHORD

This chord arises when the fifth instead of the root of the authentic seventh chord on the dominant of the key is placed in the bass. As a result of this inversion, the seventh becomes the third (which in this chord is the dissonance), the octave becomes the fourth, and the third becomes the sixth. Because the fifth of the dominant is the second degree of the key, this chord is always placed on that scale degree and thus leads to the tonic, which is a whole tone below the bass note of this chord, as is shown in example 4.67.

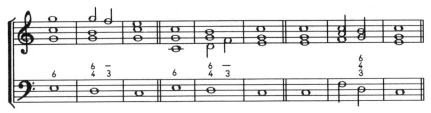

EXAMPLE 4.67

[69] Here it can immediately be seen how the third of this chord is both prepared and resolved. In the first two cases the bass is stationary and the dissonant third is introduced from the preceding consonant six-four chord by one of the two sixths or the octave. But in the third case this third is held over from the preceding harmony while the bass changes.

Occasionally a situation occurs where this chord lacks the fourth, and where the third progresses up by step and becomes the third above the following bass note, as in example 4.68 at (a).

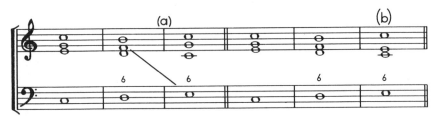

EXAMPLE 4.68

The reason for this irregular resolution lies in the fact that if the dissonant third at (a) had been allowed to resolve downward, the following sixth chord would not have had a third, as can be seen at (b); yet the third is absolutely indispensable in every chord. It could almost be said that the resolution occurs in the bass as a result of inversion.

When a composition is written for only two or three voices and thus one or two of the intervals belonging to the complete chord are omitted, care must be taken not to confuse the chord of the major sixth, which is the first inversion of the diminished triad, with the six-four-three chord, which is the second inversion of the minor [sic, major] triad.[h] [70] In the latter case, the major sixth progresses upward and the minor third downward, as can be seen in example 4.69 at (a); the bass, however, can progress either down by step to the triad or up by step to the sixth chord. However, in the former case the bass progresses up by step to the triad, as at (b), and the minor third can be doubled. Example 4.69, where the fundamental bass clearly demonstrates the origin of both types of chords, will clarify this further. At (c) and (d) the chords appear as they would be if the harmony were complete. The fourth should occur along with the sixth at (c); but at (d) the fifth, as the seventh from the root, should be present.

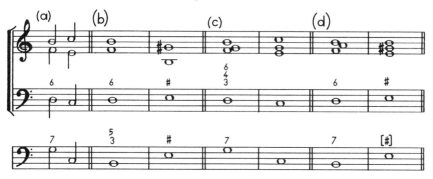

EXAMPLE 4.69

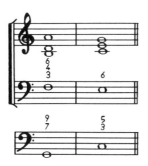

EXAMPLE 4.70

[h] Here one should keep in mind that Kirnberger had indicated earlier in the chapter that the six-four-three chord on scale degree two has its origin in the consonant six-four, to which the minor third, as the dissonant seventh from the root, can be added. Possibly this is the reason he calls it the second inversion of the triad, rather than of the essential seventh chord.

The unauthentic six-four-three chord arises from the chord of the second with the ninth above the fundamental bass suspended, as can be seen from example 4.70.

The chord on F is the third inversion of the seventh chord on G, and the a in the highest voice is the ninth from the root.

VII. OBSERVATIONS CONCERNING THE THIRD INVERSION OF THE SEVENTH CHORD, OR THE SIX-FOUR-TWO CHORD, WHICH IS ALSO SIMPLY CALLED THE CHORD OF THE SECOND

[71] This chord arises when the seventh from the dominant appears in the bass as a result of inversion. This produces the following changes: (1) the chord occurs on the subdominant; (2) the octave becomes the second, the third becomes the fourth, and the fifth becomes the sixth; (3) the authentic dissonance is in the bass and must resolve down by step to the sixth chord, as can be seen [from the opening progression] in example 4.71.

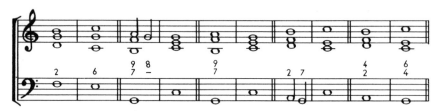

EXAMPLE 4.71

VIII. OBSERVATIONS CONCERNING NONESSENTIAL DISSONANCES, OR SUSPENSIONS, AND THEIR NATURE, USE, PREPARATION, AND RESOLUTION

As can be seen in the third table of chords [table 3.3], these dissonances are the second, fourth, sixth, seventh, and ninth; each of these intervals is dissonant when it is sounded on a strong beat in place of the consonance a step below it, to which it then leads.

Thus when the second is used in place of the unison, the fourth in place of the third, the sixth in place of the fifth, the seventh in place of the sixth, and the ninth in place of the octave, these suspensions always occur on a strong beat and are held over from the preceding harmony, which is placed on a weak beat. These suspensions then resolve down by step to the notes they displaced, as can be seen clearly for each chord contained in table 3.3.

Although any consonant note contained in a chord on a weak beat can be held over as a displacement of a consonance in the next chord (as long as it lies only one step above this consonance), it is most important to become acquainted with the use and treatment of the fourth and ninth. [72] The remaining suspensions either arise from these two through chord inversion, as is clear enough from table 3.4, or they require just the same treatment as these two main suspensions in every detail.

The nature and effect of these dissonances lies in the fact that they connect different measures or parts of measures so that the components of the harmonic progression, or the chords, are more closely linked with one another. Without this connection the harmonic progression would be somewhat similar to verses in which every word is a poetic foot; such verses are universally considered to be inferior. Therefore it is also a principal rule in poetry to place the division of feet in the middle of the word wherever possible.

In addition to this effect, suspensions can act as a powerful stimulus to the ear because of their dissonant quality, and can even awaken, where required, a noticeable feeling of unrest. Thus they contribute to the perfection of the steady flow of music as well as to its expression or power. The ninth is more intense than the fourth in both these respects, since by its nature it is very dissonant against the octave, while the fourth is dissonant only insofar as it disrupts the sensation of the beautiful harmony of the triad, which contains the third and fifth. Only under these circumstances is the fourth really dissonant; when it is not heard in relation to the tonic, which always evokes the feeling of the triad, but in relation to the dominant, it sounds very consonant.[38]

38. This is the proper way to distinguish between the consonant and the dissonant fourth, about which so much has been disputed. As long as one plays in a certain established key, for example in C, the ear continuously accepts the scale of this key; that is, the ear very much has the feeling of the tonic C, its third, and its fifth. Thus when the note F occurs in one of the upper voices, it is the dissonant fourth that displaces the third. But if c is heard as the fourth of the tonic triad in second inversion, that is above the bass note G, it is no longer dissonant.

The dissonances must always occur on the strong beat of the measure and must resolve on the weak beat.[39] In this way they are distinguished from the essential dissonance, the seventh, and those dissonances that arise from inversion of the seventh chord, which usually occur on a weak beat and resolve on the strong beat.

[73] Both the ninth and the fourth can be prepared by various consonances as well as by dissonances. Example 4.72 includes nearly all the ways to prepare the fourth.

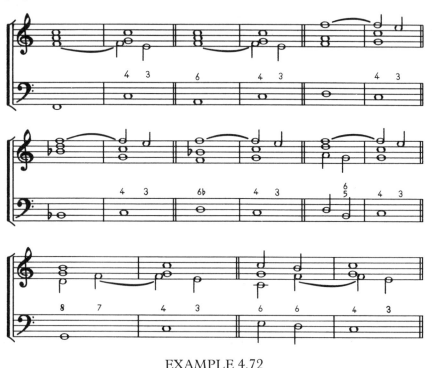

EXAMPLE 4.72

[74] The ninth is also prepared in many ways, as can be seen from example 4.73.[40] Only the octave is not well suited as a preparation of the

---

39. The exceptions to this rule will be discussed below.

40. It appears that a note could be a ninth as well as a second because of their equal distance from the bass; but this is caused by an imperfection in our way of figuring intervals. Consider the following example. The note f in the top voice in the second and third measures is the same distance from the bass; the first is designated

ninth, since a forbidden octave progression results from its resolution. [See example 4.74.] [75] Nevertheless, as shall be demonstrated, even strict harmonists have used this preparation and have avoided the octave progression by not resolving the dissonance over the same bass note, but over a new root. Examples of this will be cited later on.

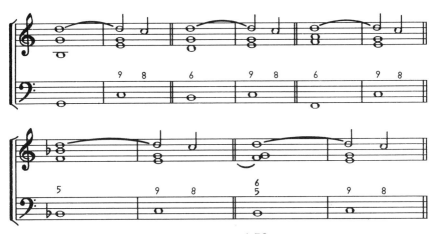

EXAMPLE 4.73

EXAMPLE 4.74

by 2, and the other by 9. The first time, the bass note E is an inverted seventh from F, and thus f is a second from the bass note, which leads down by step so that f becomes the third. However, in the other case, the high f is really the dissonance that displaces the octave; hence it is the ninth.

The nonessential dissonances of the second [ninth] and the seventh arise from the fourth and the ninth by the familiar process of chord inversion, where the third or fifth of the chord, rather than its root, is placed in the bass. That is, the fourth becomes the second in the first inversion of the triad, and it becomes the seventh in its second inversion; but the ninth becomes the seventh in the first inversion of the triad, as can be seen in example 4.75. The fourth can be transferred to the bass by inversion, whereupon the fifth of the triad becomes the second above the bass. But, in spite of that, the real dissonance is in the bass and it resolves down by step. An example of this can be seen at (d) in table 3.3.

EXAMPLE 4.75

EXAMPLE 4.76

The ninth cannot be inverted as in example 4.76.

[76] From what was said at the beginning of these remarks, it follows that the most natural treatment of suspensions is to resolve them to their consonances over the same bass note, as happened in all the examples cited above. But this is not always observed: the bass can be changed without waiting for the resolution as long as it is done in such a way that the resolved suspension is consonant with the new bass note. Example 4.77 clarifies this.

But one must be careful to guard against hidden fifths, which would result if the fourth were to be resolved to the fifth above the bass, as in example 4.78 [77] The fourth, which is a suspension of the third, resolves naturally to it. But when the fourth resolves over a new bass note, the

EXAMPLE 4.77

EXAMPLE 4.78

interval is changed. When the bass ascends three steps, the fourth goes to the octave; when the bass ascends five steps or descends four, it goes to the sixth.

[Example 4.79 shows some ninths that are not resolved over the same bass note.] As shown in example 4.80, the ninth can also be prepared by the

EXAMPLE 4.79

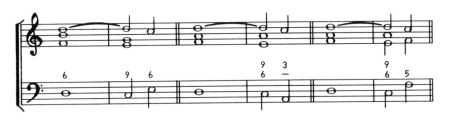

EXAMPLE 4.80

octave; otherwise this would not be tolerable, because forbidden octave-progressions would necessarily result from the resolution, as was demonstrated shortly above. It is also possible to resolve the ninth on the downbeat of the following measure, as in example 4.81.

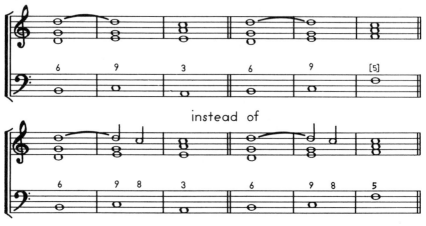

EXAMPLE 4.81

[78] By means of the above-mentioned inversion of the bass, the ninth is not always resolved to the octave, as it naturally should be; it resolves to the sixth when the bass ascends three steps, to the third when the bass descends three steps, and to the fifth when the bass ascends four steps or descends five, which is rare.

Both these dissonances, the fourth and the ninth, are major or minor, depending upon the mode; but they are treated the same in both cases. The fourth can even be augmented, and, contrary to the customary fashion of augmented dissonances,[41] can resolve down to the third. This happens in conjunction with the second inversion of the diminished triad. In this case the large fourth can even be doubled. This fourth, which is formed by the fifth and the octave of the diminished triad, should be called the large fourth to distinguish it from the tritone, since in this case it can resolve downward as a displacement of the third.

It was demonstrated above that the fourth as well as the ninth can become the seventh through inversion of the bass; therefore this seventh is a displacement of the sixth, and it must be distinguished from the other

41. The reason why augmented dissonances resolve upward is given below in the chapter on sudden digressions [chapter 8].

seventh, which is an essential dissonance. Usually it is easy to distinguish the seventh that is merely a suspension from the essential seventh, because the former never falls on a weak beat while the latter normally does. But when the essential seventh falls on a strong beat, as it sometimes does, it is more difficult to distinguish from the suspension. A characteristic of the seventh that is a suspension is that it does not occur with the fifth, because its resolution would produce a new dissonance in the six-five chord.

Furthermore, the essential seventh can be recognized by the fact that it cannot be resolved over the same bass note, since its resolution down by step is not suitable to the rest of the harmony; thus this resolution can only be considered as a passing note, as in example 4.82. [79] However, the unauthentic seventh that arises from the ninth is always compatible with the other notes when it is resolved over the same bass note, as in examples 4.83 and 4.84. In the first, the seventh results from inversion of the ninth chord

EXAMPLE 4.82

EXAMPLE 4.83

EXAMPLE 4.84

and resolves to the sixth over the same bass note. But in the second it results from inversion of the preceding nine-seven chord, and the resolution of the unauthentic seventh produces the six-five chord.

[80] It can also be noted that the bass moves up by step even when the nonessential seventh does not resolve until the following harmony, while the resolution of the essential seventh is accompanied by a bass motion up by four steps or down by five.

Both the major and the minor seventh occur as essential dissonances and as suspensions; only the diminished seventh is always a nonessential dissonance.

CHAPTER 5

The Free Treatment of Dissonant Chords in the Lighter Style

Observance of the rules given in the preceding chapter is absolutely necessary when the composition has a serious character or when, as is commonly said, it is written in the strict style. However, an extraordinary number of exceptions and deviations from these rules are permitted when writing in the free or lighter style.

In the strict style every chord, and almost every note in the vocal parts, is stressed; fewer decorations of the melody, or fewer passing notes that are not indicated in the figures, occur. However, in the freer or lighter style some chords are skipped over and thus have less emphasis. The melody is mixed with numerous passing notes that are considered as decorations of the main notes. The strict style gives a grave character to the melody, all of whose steps are emphasized and progress directly without any secondary motion or decorative mannerisms. But the light style entails a free and decorative character, in which all kinds of ornaments or even leaps occur before the next step is taken.

The strict style is used mainly in church music, whose content is always serious or solemn. But the other is particularly appropriate to the theatre and to concerts, where one is more concerned with the amusement of the listener than the awakening of more serious or solemn feelings. For this reason it is commonly called the *galant style*, and in this style various decorative excesses and numerous deviations from the rules are permitted.

[81] Exceptions to the rules given above, which are taken by the best and most established harmonists when writing in the free style, shall, then, be stated here as fully as possible.[a]

---

[a] Additional information about the treatment of dissonance in the lighter style is scattered throughout subsequent chapters.

I.   The following are the most general deviations of the free style from the rules given in the preceding chapter.

1. In the strict style all dissonances are prepared by preceding consonances and are resolved downward to the next step. The freer style permits the introduction of an unprepared dissonance, the omission of resolution, and resolution of dissonance in another voice. Examples of these will follow.

2. In the strict style the dissonance is never longer than the consonance by which it was prepared; in the free style the dissonance is sometimes much longer. In this case the dissonance is not tied over, but is sounded again on the downbeat.

3. In the strict style a dissonance may not be repeated, but must progress immediately to a consonance; this is not always observed in the free style.

4. Irregular passing notes are avoided in strict composition, but occur frequently in the light style.[42]

5. The so-called false progressions by augmented intervals are avoided in strict composition, but occur frequently in the light style.[43]

[82] 6. In the truly strict style even the consonant six-four chord is somewhat questionable and is used only when the five-four chord follows it above the same bass note, as in example 5.1. In strict composition the consonant six-four chord can never progress to a triad whose bass note is a step higher or lower. Thus example 5.2 would be completely wrong.

EXAMPLE 5.1

42. The passing note is irregular when the second rather than the first note of the accented beat is part of the harmony; the opposite is true of the regular passing note.

43. Composers long ago did not permit even the major sixth; but today this is not observed, even in the strictest style. The major sixth must be avoided in a voice part only when it is contrary to the preceding or following harmony and thus difficult to sing. (See note 35.) But this is true of every other interval as well.

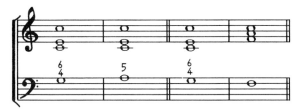

EXAMPLE 5.2

II.   The free treatment of the essential seventh chord is also to be examined closely with regard to the resolution of dissonance.

In the preceding chapter it was shown in detail how the dissonance in the seventh chord and in all its inversions should be resolved, and how the notes in the various voices progress in connection with the resolution. In the freer style one can deviate from this in various ways.[b]

1. Sometimes it happens that the resolution does not occur in the same voice as the dissonance, but in a different voice. For instance, the progression at (A) in example 5.3, which is composed according to the strict rules, can occur as at (B) as a result of its free treatment. [83] By means of an exchange in the second half of the measure, the dissonance is taken by the bass and then resolved down by step. In this way the resolution proceeds from the upper to the lower voice. This also happens with the inversions of the seventh chord, as can be seen in example 5.4. [84] Instead of the seventh chord of the preceding example, its first inversion is used here at (a); in spite of this change, the resolution can occur in the bass, as it did before. At (b) the resolution is taken in the bass, while the third above the bass is in the highest voice. Thus it appears to some extent as if the previous seventh had resolved

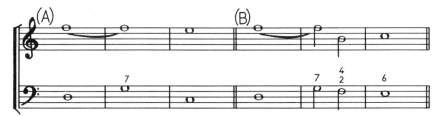

EXAMPLE 5.3

[b] Kirnberger's discussion of the resolution of the essential seventh in the *galant* style was undoubtedly influenced by Heinichen's description of the resolution of dissonance in the theatrical style (*Der Generalbass in der Composition* [Dresden, 1728], pp. 585–724). Heinichen's treatment of the ·subject, which is far more extensive than Kirnberger's, is valuable as a description of then-current musical practice.

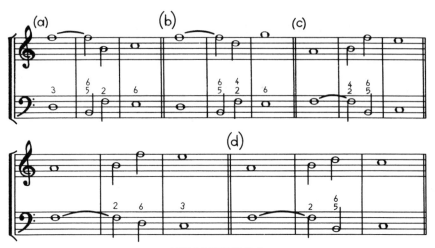

EXAMPLE 5.4

upward; but, as was said, the true resolution occurs in the bass. At (c) and (d) there are a few instances involving inversion of the seventh chord in which the resolution is transferred to the highest voice rather than to the bass, where it would normally occur.

2. Instead of holding the seventh chord for its full duration, all its inversions can be stated in succession. Thus the progression at (a) in example 5.4 can occur as at (e) in example 5.5; and the one at (c) can occur as at (f).

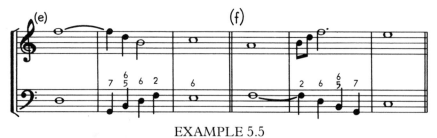

EXAMPLE 5.5

This exchange or transfer of dissonance into another voice applies only to the essential dissonance;[c] the nonessential dissonances, or suspensions,

[c]In chapters 6 and 11 Kirnberger indicates that the essential seventh can also resolve directly to another voice. Both types of resolution, transfer of the dissonance before resolution and transfer of the resolution itself, were discussed by Heinichen, op. cit., who used the term "inversion" [*Verwechslung*] rather than "exchange" [*Vertauschung*] or "transfer" [*Versetzung*] to describe this phenomenon.

do not permit it, as can easily be seen from the nature of both types of dissonance. By its nature a suspension must be situated directly adjacent to the note that it displaces. However, the seventh, which exists simply to define the key, produces this effect no matter whether it occurs high or low. Thus when one encounters a fourth that is transferred, it is not the displacement of the third, but the fourth that occurs in the third inversion of the seventh chord, as in example 5.6.

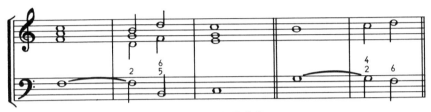

EXAMPLE 5.6

[85] 3. The resolution of the seventh can even be omitted; that is, the consonant chord that results from the resolution can be omitted, and another dissonant chord, whose dissonance would have been prepared by the omitted chord, can follow immediately after it. Thus, instead of the progression shown at (A) in example 5.7, the one at (B) can be used by omitting the consonant chord marked with an asterisk.

From such instances—where two dissonant chords follow one another

EXAMPLE 5.7

EXAMPLE 5.8

directly as a result of omission—other types of progressions arise as a result of inversion, as shown in example 5.8.

[86] 4. In the free style the resolution of the seventh can be omitted when the seventh is formed between a stationary note in an upper voice and a passing note in the bass that leads from a triad to its sixth chord, or vice versa.[d] [See example 5.9.]

EXAMPLE 5.9

In the strict style the notes marked with an asterisk would be passing notes; thus they would have to be of short[er] duration and fall on unaccented beats. But the free style is not bound to this rule, so that these sevenths can last a full measure. [See example 5.10.]

It is to be noted here in general that, in the free style, passing notes need not always be passed over quickly and lightly as in the strict style. Thus when a harmony is sustained in the upper voices while prolonged passing notes are sounded in the bass, numerous unresolved dissonances often appear above these bass notes, as is made clear enough in example 5.11.

[87] In four-part compositions the fifth should not be used with this seventh chord; however, in a fuller texture it can be used to strengthen the harmony. In the latter case one has to watch out for forbidden fifth-

---

[d] Here and in the following paragraphs Kirnberger indicates that certain chords are not to be considered or treated as fundamental harmonies, but rather as passing chords that connect fundamental harmonies. (In *Die wahren Grundsätze zum Gebrauch der Harmonie* [Berlin and Königsberg, 1773], J. A. P. Schulz coins the term "Zwischenaccorde" to describe such chords.) Kirnberger's recognition of the fact that certain chords are subservient to others is important to the development of harmonic theory and may be considered as a precursor of Heinrich Schenker's distinction between chord and scale step [*Stufe*]. According to Schenker, several chords, each of which could be considered as an independent triad or seventh chord, can be subsumed under a single harmony or scale step; that is, the individual chords serve to prolong a single harmony, which thus exists at a higher or more abstract level than any of its individual parts. See paragraph 78 in his *Harmonielehre* (Stuttgart and Berlin, 1906), p. 181; English translation by Elisabeth Mann Borgese, edited and annotated by Oswald Jonas (Chicago, 1954), pp. 138–39.

EXAMPLE 5.10

EXAMPLE 5.11

progressions, particularly when the bass returns by step to the triad.

5. This free treatment also occurs with the first inversion of this seventh chord, as in example 5.12.[44]

[88] 6. Similarly, harmonies in the upper voices that are dissonant in

44. The half cadence common in the works of some French composers has its origin in this treatment of the six-five chord, to which they have given the name *accord de la sixte ajoutée* or chord of the added sixth. More will be said about this below in the chapter on cadences [chapter 6].

EXAMPLE 5.12

relation to a stationary bass are treated like nonresolving passing notes, regardless of their duration. [See examples 5.13 and 5.14.] In example 5.14, both sevenths at (a) are consonant, and the notes d and f are dissonant; at (b) both fourths are consonant, and again the notes d and f are passing dissonances.

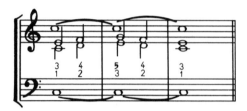

EXAMPLE 5.13

EXAMPLE 5.14

EXAMPLE 5.15

This free treatment of the seventh also occurs when the seventh is formed over a passing note in the bass that falls between the dominant seventh chord and its first inversion. [See example 5.15.]

III.   In the free style there are various cases where the seventh occurs without the preparation customary in strict composition.[e] See example 5.16.

[89] The first case is justified by the fact that the root progression is by fifth; in the second case the seventh, and in the third case the fifth, can be tolerated as passing notes in the free style.

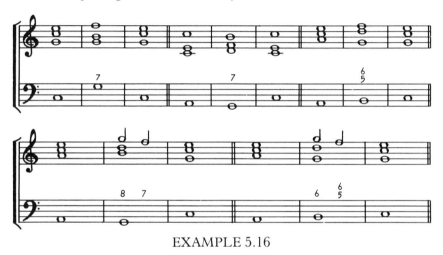

EXAMPLE 5.16

This gives rise to progressions involving two successive dissonant chords, which would seem to harsh in the strict style. Thus the progressions given at (A) in example 5.17, which are written according to the strict style, could occur as at (B) in the free style.

[90] The diminished seventh chord at (A) in example 5.18, which arises from the first inversion of the seventh chord with the suspended minor ninth (B), can be sounded freely at all times and in all its inversions. It is somewhat special because of its three superimposed minor thirds. This

---

[e]By Kirnberger's time it was generally accepted that the seventh did not require preparation. The fact that Kirnberger mentions it in this context is a reflection of his conservative attitude toward the treatment of dissonance. Although his discussion of the *galant* style is of historical importance, one gets the impression that he includes this information more out of duty than genuine interest. His sympathies seem to lie more with the strict style, which may be one reason that this chapter is so brief.

chord, which is the basis of all enharmonic progressions, will be considered in greater detail in the eighth chapter.

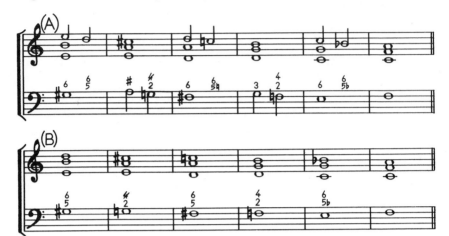

EXAMPLE 5.17

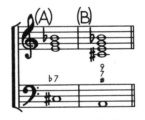

EXAMPLE 5.18

CHAPTER 6

Harmonic Periods and Cadences

[91] Chords are in music what words are in language. Just as a sentence in speech consists of several words that belong together and express a complete idea, a harmonic sentence or period consists of several chords that are connected and end with a close. And just as a succession of many sentences constitutes an entire speech, a composition consists of a succession of many periods.[a]

Before it can be shown how a complete composition is to be constructed, it is necessary to learn how individual harmonic periods are to be built. That is the purpose of this chapter.

Since a period consists of a succession of chords that are naturally related and end with a close, two matters are to be discussed here: (1) how a greater or lesser number of chords should be connected, and (2) how this succession of chords can be brought to a close with so-called cadences.

Chords can have two types of association, a general or broader one and a specific or narrower one. The general association lies in the fact that they are taken from one key and that the ear can sense this. This requires that the first chord in the succession must immediately suggest to the ear a specific diatonic scale of a major or minor mode, and that the remaining chords (their roots as well as their other intervals) must be taken from this scale.[45]

---

45. Periods whose chords are taken from several keys, i.e., chromatic and enharmonic progressions, will be discussed in the eighth chapter. However, the situation where perhaps one interval is not taken from the tonic scale will be given special attention below.

---

[a]The analogy between music and speech was common in the eighteenth century. An earlier discussion of this relationship can be found in Johann Mattheson's *Der vollkommene*

The key and mode is suggested most strongly to the ear when the initial chord of the period is the tonic triad, since this triad contains all the essential steps of the scale.[46] For that reason the period must begin with this triad.

[92] However, when this period is preceded by another that has concluded with the tonic triad of the new key, this rule is not necessary, since the ear has by then already become sufficiently familiar with the new scale. In this case the period can begin with an inversion of the tonic triad or some other chord taken from the new key.

This initial chord can be followed by any other chord belonging to the key, since they all have a general association with one another. However, neither the diminished triad on the seventh scale degree nor the triad on the third scale degree in a major mode should be sounded directly after the tonic triad, since these chords seem to suggest another key.

It is also necessary to consider the more specific association of chords. They can be brought into close association in three ways. First of all, two successive chords can have a close association by the relationship of their roots. We know that every note carries with it the feeling of its fifth, and that in general the transition from one note to another is easier the better these notes harmonize with one another. Thus the progression from one root to another is easiest through consonant leaps, i.e., fifths, fourths, and thirds. For this reason the chords shown at (A) in example 6.1 would be more closely related than those at (B).

Chords built on the fifth, fourth, third, and sixth degrees of the scale are related to the tonic not only by consonant leaps but also by the fact that each has one or two notes in common with the tonic triad. However, such

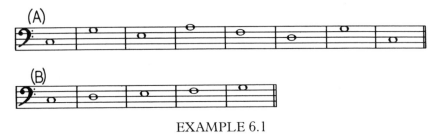

EXAMPLE 6.1

46. See the remarks concerning the triad on p. 54, above.

(Footnote a continued)
Capellmeister (Hamburg, 1739); see part II, chapter 9 ("Von den Ab- und Einschnitten der Klang-Rede"). See also Johann Walther's _Musikalisches Lexicon_ (Leipzig, 1732), which contains definitions of several terms common to both disciplines.

progressions, particularly those involving perfect consonances, have the drawback that each can be a point of rest, since the ear is so satisfied that it has no reason to expect anything further.

[93] For this reason it is also necessary to employ the second means of bringing chords into close association—using the inversions of chords instead of their root positions. Since the former do not harmonize as perfectly as the latter, they create the expectation of chords that are even more consonant. The most beautiful harmonic connection occurs when the ear is kept in a state of constant expectation of a more perfect harmony, which comes only at the end of the entire period, as in example 6.2.

EXAMPLE 6.2

However, there is even a better means of weaving chords together, so to speak, so that each leads the ear almost inevitably to the next. This method involves tying a few notes over, that is, allowing them to continue from one chord to another. Particularly when these tied notes are dissonant in relation to the second chord an additional harmony is made necessary by the expectation of their resolution. Therefore the chords in example 6.3 would be inseparably bound together.

EXAMPLE 6.3

These remarks are sufficient to show how the chords of a period can be joined together. Before discussing other characteristics of periods we must show how the close or end of periods could be articulated by means of cadences.

The feeling of rest or of complete conclusion of a succession of sounds can be obtained only by way of the perfect harmony and the perfect consonance. As long as the ear still perceives something imperfect, it expects the development or resolution of this imperfection. From this it follows that the last chord of the period, the chord which establishes the complete conclusion, must be consonant, and that the most perfect harmony, the triad in its most perfect form, produces the most perfect conclusion.

[94] If the phrase should be entirely in one key, the last chord must be the tonic triad. But just as one anticipates the final word in a period of speech before it is spoken and knows in advance that it is about to enter in order to conclude the meaning, the feeling of the final chord is awakened in advance at a perfect cadence of the harmonic period. Thus the most perfect conclusions will occur when the penultimate chord is a fifth above the tonic, as in example 6.4. This cadence will have the highest degree of perfection when the penultimate chord includes the seventh, since this makes the final tonic absolutely necessary. (See above, pp. 44 and 45.)

EXAMPLE 6.4

In this case one should consider not only the succession of roots, which fall a fifth at the most perfect cadence, but also the upper voices, whose final notes can also be determined by the penultimate chord.

The major third of the penultimate chord is the leading tone of the key in which the close occurs and goes to its octave. The seventh of the penultimate chord is the fourth above the tonic and thus resolves to its third. Therefore the most perfect type of cadence is that shown in example 6.5. This kind of cadence is suitable only at the end of a whole piece; for this reason it is called the *final cadence* or *principal close*.

EXAMPLE 6.5

This final cadence is somewhat less perfect when one leaps up to the tonic from the subdominant instead of falling from the dominant, as in example 6.6. [95] But in the minor mode, the minor third must be abandoned in favor of the major third just before the cadence and in the final chord itself, as is indicated here.

EXAMPLE 6.6

Sometimes this cadence is combined with the preceding one to establish complete repose through a double cadence. This can be done in various ways, as is evident from example 6.7.

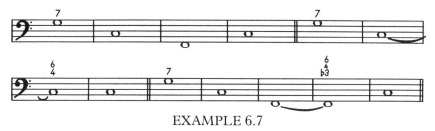

EXAMPLE 6.7

In the minor mode this double cadence provides the advantage of allowing one to conclude with the major third without harshness, as in example 6.8.

EXAMPLE 6.8

The cadence can occur in just this form at the end of a principal section in the middle of a composition; however, in this case, the final chord falls on some note other than the tonic, as in example 6.9.

EXAMPLE 6.9

Here the conclusion results from a digression (which will be discussed extensively in the following chapter) to the dominant. As before, the bass falls a fifth or ascends a fourth so that the penultimate bass note is the dominant of the final one, for this is an essential characteristic of the *full close* or *perfect cadence*.

[96] A principal section of a composition always ends with such a perfect cadence. Therefore it may be likened to [the end of] a paragraph in speech which concludes a succession of sentences that are individual yet related by a central topic, after which the speech pauses for a moment.

Just as a paragraph in speech consists of segments, phrases, and sentences that are marked by various punctuation symbols such as the comma (,), semicolon (;), colon (:), and period (.), the harmonic [equivalent of the] paragraph can also consist of several segments, phrases, and periods.[b]

In a long section the chord progression can be divided into individual periods and smaller rest points, where the ear is not completely satisfied and permanently put to rest, yet is allowed to rest momentarily.

Actually the ear finds rest on every triad because its harmony is so perfect that the ear is totally satisfied and not led on to anything else. Thus every perfect triad can, even without additional devices, establish a small rest point in the harmonic progression. [See example 6.10.] But this repose becomes more noticeable when the triad—for example, the dominant—is related to the tonic by a perfect consonance, particularly when it is approached by a consonant leap. In this case the repose becomes so noticeable that it is called a *half close* or a *half cadence*. [See example 6.11.] In a harmonic progression this cadence concludes an entire period, which in speech would perhaps be designated with a period sign.

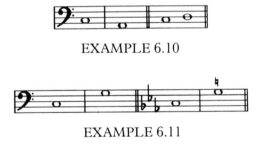

EXAMPLE 6.10

EXAMPLE 6.11

---

[b]Here Kirnberger uses the terms *Periode*, *Abschnitt*, and *Einschnitt* to describe successively smaller formal divisions in music as well as in speech. In this chapter they have been translated as "period," "phrase," and "segment," respectively. A more detailed discussion of this topic is found in Volume II, part 1, chapter 4 (third section) of this work, where these same terms have somewhat different meanings.

[97] French composers form this cadence in a special way—by adding the sixth to the penultimate triad, as in example 6.12. They call this sixth the *added sixth* and consider it, as we do with the seventh, an essential dissonance, which resolves upward here to the third of the following chord.[c] However, neither the German nor the Italian composers use this kind of cadence.

EXAMPLE 6.12

They do use this sixth as well as other dissonances at the half cadence, but only in passing, as can be seen in example 6.13. This does not occur in a more ponderous or slower tempo. However, these passing notes, like every other passing note, are not indicated in the figured bass.

EXAMPLE 6.13

There is still a third category of cadence, one that is reached by an unexpected progression. For this reason the Italians call it "inganno," which means something like *deception*. [98] This cadence occurs when the

[c] Here Kirnberger is referring specifically to Rameau's chord of the large or added sixth, as defined in Book II, chapter 7 (pp. 64–67; Gossett translation [New York, 1971], pp. 73–81) and Book III, chapter 16 (pp. 221–25; Gossett, pp. 240–45) of his *Traité de l'harmonie* (Paris, 1772).

dominant does not proceed to the tonic after everything has been prepared for a cadence, as in example 6.14.

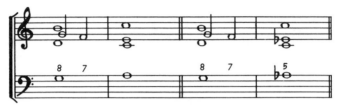

EXAMPLE 6.14

The French theorists call this close *cadence rompue*, or the *interrupted cadence*.

These are the three main types of cadences, the first of which produces complete repose and thus can be used to conclude main sections of a composition. The other two types do not produce complete repose, yet can also be used to conclude main sections; they are also suitable for dividing such sections into periods.

Each of these three main types can be varied or modified in many ways, whereby the feeling of rest which they provide is more or less weakened. The result is a great variety of smaller rest points that are achieved only by the harmonic progression.

The full cadence is most perfect when the seventh is added to the root of the penultimate triad, namely the dominant, and also when the octave of the final root appears in the top voice, as in example 6.15.

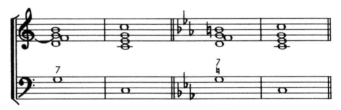

EXAMPLE 6.15

The modifications of this full cadence, which can be made in order to weaken it to a greater or lesser extent, can be recognized clearly enough from example 6.16. [99] However, cadences such as these—that are modified by chord inversion—produce rest points suitable only for certain periods and are no longer full cadences.

EXAMPLE 6.16

Where one has the freedom of resolving the dissonance in another voice, even the final chord of this cadence can be inverted, thereby preventing complete repose, as in example 6.17.

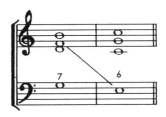

EXAMPLE 6.17

However, if one wants to keep the full cadence and yet prevent its effect of repose, the seventh need only be added to the tonic triad, whereby it becomes the dominant of a new key. [See example 6.18]

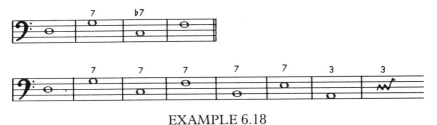

EXAMPLE 6.18

[100] It is also possible to weaken the half cadence by way of inversion; its various forms can be seen in example 6.19.

The modifications of the interrupted cadence are shown in example 6.20.

These are the many types of rest points that can be established by harmony. In the course of this work it will be shown how these rest points can also be made more or less perceptible in melody.

EXAMPLE 6.19

EXAMPLE 6.20

After having shown how entire main sections as well as periods, larger or smaller phrases, and segments are to be differentiated by various rest points, we still need to consider the length of periods.

In vocal compositions the text determines every phrase and period, since the harmony must make a resting point evident where the text demands it. However, in compositions written for instruments alone, the composer is completely in charge. Only in ballets and dances, which already have a predetermined rhythm, is the composer strictly bound to the character of the piece. Since everything pertaining to rhythm will be discussed in the second part of this treatise, we shall content ourselves here simply with a few general remarks concerning the length of periods.

Some time ago the so-called "stile coupé"—a [literary] style characterized by a succession of short periods—was in vogue in France; this style has also crept into music on occasion. [101] There are composers who seek beauty in making a cadence every other measure or even every measure. Where this is required by the expression of the text, there is nothing wrong with it. However, where one is not restricted in this way, this style soon becomes dull and boring. In music, as in speech, it is always better to write longer rather than shorter periods and to divide them, depending upon their length, into phrases and segments by way of weaker half and interrupted cadences. This results in the true periodic style in music as well as in speech.

In pieces that are written for voices or wind instruments such as the flute and oboe, the length of periods is limited, since most singers and players must stop to catch their breath. However, he who writes for the clavier, organs, or violins is not restricted in this way. Anyone who knows how to deal with harmony to a certain degree will not find it difficult to create rather long periods with only two or three chords. Instead of giving all kinds of rules it will be sufficient to demonstrate this with examples. [See examples 6.21–6.23.] One need only remember that long periods must be divided into phrases and smaller segments.

EXAMPLE 6.21

EXAMPLE 6.22

EXAMPLE 6.23

[102] The harmony of the last example is based on just two chords,[d] as can be seen from the fundamental bass, thus proving how easy it is to write long periods without becoming too monotonous.

It also deserves to be mentioned here that to make the harmony of a period somewhat more charming one can occasionally substitute major thirds for the natural minor thirds, as if the intention were to modulate, but only if these substitutions are forsaken immediately thereafter. Thus the period shown in example 6.24 is entirely in C major despite the accidental sharps.[e]

EXAMPLE 6.24

[d] Here Kirnberger means just two harmonies, the tonic and dominant, in each key.
[e] This example indicates Kirnberger's awareness of the important distinction between actual modulation and the practice of stressing harmonies within a single key by their dominants. This concept is developed in the next chapter.

CHAPTER 7

Modulation

[103] One sings or plays in a certain key as long as no notes other than those contained in the diatonic scale of that key are sounded in the melody and harmony. These notes for each tonic and each mode have been displayed above in table 2.2. As soon as a composition is somewhat long, it is not good to remain in the same key throughout; melody and harmony must gradually be led to different keys but at the end must be returned again to the original key.

In the preceding chapter it was assumed that a harmonic period would continue and conclude in the same key in which it begins. However, as stated above, longer compositions, which consist of several periods, require a diversity of keys. All follow the same pattern: first they continue for a while in the original key, then go to various other keys, but finally return to the main key, in which the piece ends.

Each key has its characteristic degrees and intervals which give it its own character and personality both in harmony and in melody and which distinguish it from all other keys. This will be recognized by anyone who carefully examines the table of keys in the second chapter; however, this distinction is even more striking to the ear.

It is impossible to explain exactly which features differentiate one key from another; but a trained ear perceives it, and, though it is impossible to establish definite rules, a composer sufficiently equipped with reason and sensitivity will always know which key to choose according to the character of what he wants to express. On the other hand, various definite rules can be given on how the harmony should gradually be led from the main key to other keys and how it should eventually be made to return to the main key.

These are the rules of modulation that are to be developed in this chapter.

In modern music we not only have twenty-four different scales, each having its own character, but we can also retain the ancient modes. This leads to an extraordinary diversity of harmony and modulation. It is possible to lead the harmony through various keys in such a way that the succeeding key always differs only a little from the preceding one; however, it is also possible that successive keys have little in common. [104] In the first case, the ear feels a pleasant change in which there is nothing harsh, abrupt, or incoherent. This kind of modulation is suited to pleasant and mild sentiments. However, in the other case, one is quickly swept away from one kind of sentiment to another; this is suited to violent and quickly changing affections. In either case the transitions must be composed in such a way that nothing is forced.

Here it is particularly important to note, as was already done above, that each key has its essential degrees which define it and its mode. These essential degrees are contained in the tonic triad. Thus, when such a triad occurs at the beginning of a composition or a period, the ear is directed to that key [center] and mode.

Only in cases where the ear is already used to a key to which all notes of the new triad belong is one uncertain whether or not the root of this triad should be considered as a tonic. For example, if an ear that is accustomed to C major hears a G major triad, this triad has nothing that points to a new key, because all its notes also belong to the C major scale. Thus, for the ear to lean toward G major, it would be necessary to introduce a note foreign to the key of C major shortly before or immediately thereafter.

For this reason the tonic triad is sufficient to announce the key only at the beginning of a piece, before the ear is accustomed to any scale. However, if one goes from one key to another, the triad in the new key must be preceded or immediately followed by a note foreign to the former key. This note, which is essential to the new key, erases, so to speak, the feeling of the old key. How this can be accomplished will be clearly demonstrated in the course of this chapter.

It is necessary to know three main points with respect to modulation: (1) to what keys one can modulate from each given key; (2) how long one can stay in the new key; and (3) how the modulation is to be introduced and accomplished. These three points are to be discussed here in this order. [105] It should be noted, however, that this chapter will deal only with the simplest and most standard modulations, where one goes from each key to those most closely related to it. Sudden digressions to remote keys will be considered separately in the following chapter.

I. When one has played for a while in the original key, the ear is so accustomed to this key that it feels the entire diatonic scale to some extent on each chord. If the harmony moves to a different key, the ear attunes itself to the scale of this new key in the same way as it did with the preceding one. It is easy to imagine and even easier to hear how difficult and unpleasant it is for the ear to attune itself suddenly to a scale that differs greatly from the one it has felt shortly before. If one is accustomed to C major and is supposed to perceive E major immediately thereafter, it would be necessary to change the scale C, D, E, F, G, A, B rapidly into C-sharp, D-sharp, E, F-sharp, G-sharp, A, B. This would be just as unpleasant as if one were to move from warmth to cold, or from darkness to bright light. Such rapid changes are contrary to our sensibilities. Generally all changes must happen gradually so as not to be offensive, and the present sentiment must never contrast greatly with the preceding one if we are not to be affected unpleasantly. By the same token the harmony must be treated in such a manner that the key to which one wants to modulate does not contrast too much with the preceding one, unless the expression of the piece requires such harshness. The latter situation will be discussed in the next chapter.

Thus, in modulation it is necessary above all to consider the relationship of keys. It is self-evident that those keys whose scales have most notes in common are most closely related. So it can be said that the key of C major is closely related to G major, since they differ only by one note; although C major has an F while G has an F-sharp, all other pitches are the same. On the other hand the keys of C major and F-sharp major are almost diametrically opposed, since they have only a single pitch in common.

However, two keys can differ by only one note and still be only slightly related. This happens when the note is entirely contrary to the nature of the other key. For example, C major and F major differ by just one note, which is B in C major and B-flat in F major. [106] However, this B is indispensable to C major, since it is the leading tone of the key. By changing this pitch, the C major scale suffers more than if any other note were to be changed. Therefore the key of F major is farther removed from C major than one in which a less essential note is changed.

It is not necessary to explore extensively the degrees of key relationship, since they can be perceived so easily that teachers of composition are almost always in agreement on this subject. Table 7.1 shows the degrees of relationship in major and minor keys.[a]

TABLE 7.1.

Major	V	vi	iii	IV	ii			major	G	a	e	F	d
						For example:							
Minor	v	III	iv	VI	VII			A minor	e	C	d	F	G

Each major key is most closely related to the major scale of its fifth, then to the minor scale of the third below, etc., as is shown in the table. The minor keys differ from the major keys from the third to the sixth degrees of relationship.[b] Thus, when the main key of a composition is in the major mode, one can modulate without harshness to the major keys on its dominant and subdominant, and to the minor keys on its submediant, mediant, and second scale degree.

When the main key is in the minor mode, one can modulate to the minor keys on its dominant and subdominant, and to the major keys on its mediant, submediant, and seventh scale degree. However, the major mode does not permit modulation to its seventh scale degree, nor does the minor mode to its second degree. The reason for this exception is obvious: the seventh of major keys and the second of minor keys do not support perfect triads, but diminished triads. In C major the triad on the seventh, B, is

[a] Although theorists of the eighteenth century were in general agreement as to which keys are most closely related, they did not always agree in their ranking of these key relationships. Heinichen, for example, ranked the closely related keys as follows: Major keys usually modulate to those on scale degrees 5, 3, and 6, but less commonly to those on 2 and 4; minor keys usually modulate to those on scale degrees 3, 5, and 7, and less commonly to those on 4 and 6. (See his Table of Modulations on p. 761 of *Der Generalbass in der Composition.*)

A later theorist who discussed modulation at some length was Heinrich Christoph Koch. In his *Versuch einer Anleitung zur Composition* (Leipzig, 1782–93), Koch, like Heinichen, divided the closely related keys into two levels. (See vol. 2, part 1, chapter 2.) His ranking was as follows: From major keys, the most common modulations are to those on scale degrees 5, 6, and 4, and less commonly to those on 3 and 2; from minor keys, the most common modulations are to those on scale degrees 3, 5, and 4, and less commonly to those on 7 and 3. It is interesting that some years later, in the article "Ausweichung" in his *Musikalisches Lexikon* (Frankfurt, 1802), Koch gave another and quite different ranking of these relationships. It differs from Kirnberger's only slightly—the first and second degrees of relationship for minor keys is reversed.

[b] According to this statement, Kirnberger apparently considered the first level of relationship to be that between a key and itself.

diminished, and since the scale of A minor is the same as the one in C major, the triad on the second of this key is also diminished.

These are the keys to which one can modulate directly from the main key, be it in the major or minor mode. In long compositions it is possible to go to the related keys of a secondary key to wich one has modulated directly from the main key. [107] However, it should be noted that these keys to which one cannot go directly can easily erase the feeling of the main key in which one has begun and will also end; also, one cannot return from them to the main key without extensive detours.

Let us suppose that in a piece in C major one had detoured to F-sharp minor and had to return to the original key. One will find that this return is very harsh and abrasive unless lengthy detours are taken. That is, from F-sharp minor one would have to go to B minor or directly to E minor, then to G major, and finally back to C major.

From this it follows that in common modulation one should not venture into distant keys and that it is safest to be satisfied with the five closest levels of relationship stated above.

In this type of modulation it is a general rule to proceed in such a way that the main key, in which the piece begins and ends, is never completely erased. Therefore one should modulate to another key only after the ear is almost satiated with the main key, and these secondary keys should not mask the main key to the extent that it is completely forgotten. Thus one must always stay in its neighborhood, so to speak, and renew its feeling from time to time. Wherever this is neglected, it is difficult to preserve harmonic unity. Since this point is very important for good modulation, let us dwell on it a little longer.

Let us suppose that the main key of a piece is C major and that a modulation from there to its dominant, G major, has occurred. If one then wanted to make this key the main key in the same manner as C major in order to modulate again from there to its related keys, little would remain of the tonal unity. For that reason one should not go from G major to its dominant, D major, as if the piece were composed in G major, but must modulate to D minor, a key that is related to the main key of C major. This would also be the case with other modulations. If a piece has begun in C major and then modulated to F major, it cannot progress from there to B-flat major or to G minor without destroying the feeling of the main key; but it can go to G major.

It can generally be seen from this remark that the keys to which one modulates directly from the main key cannot lead in turn to all of their closely related keys, but must forfeit those that are alien to the main key. [108] If the main key is C major, one cannot go from G major to its dominant (D major) or to its mediant (B minor). Similarly, F major forfeits its otherwise natural modulations to B-flat major and G minor; E minor forfeits those to B minor and D major; and D minor forfeits those to B-flat major and G minor.

Therefore it can be considered a rule (unless the piece is very long) that the main key should be sustained in such a way that one modulates only to those keys which can be reached without difficulties, namely, only to those indicated in the tables given above. However, none of the secondary keys should be considered as a main key from which one modulates again to its related keys. This is the simplest and most natural way of modulating. To present this clearly, we add the following model [example 7.1] where the modulation is led from the main key of C major through all its related keys and is finally returned to the main key.

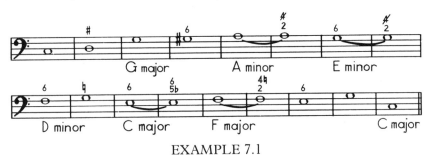

EXAMPLE 7.1

In very long compositions, for example where an entire psalm is to be set, variety of modulation can be achieved by considering the dominant and the subdominant, as well as the mediant and submediant, as main keys from which one also modulates to their related keys. This more extravagant type of modulation will be discussed in more detail in the following chapter.

II.   These remarks also serve in part to answer the second question concerning modulation—how long to remain in the new keys to which one has gone. This depends mainly on the length of the piece. Only in very long pieces is it acceptable to establish more remote keys in such a way that they come to be considered as replacements for the main key. [109] But in shorter pieces no secondary key should be treated as if it were a main key from which one modulates freely. Hence it is also clear that one should not stay in a secondary key for a long time, but would do well to return from it to a key that is not remote from the main key. Although we do not intend to define exactly how long one should stay in secondary keys, the following diagram [example 7.2] can serve as a guide. (A) is the model for major keys, and (B) for minor keys. Each note represents the key to which one has modulated, and its durational value expresses the relative amount of time one can remain in it.[c] If, for example, one has remained in the main key for two measures from the beginning, one can stay in its fifth for one measure and in its sixth for a half measure, etc. However, it is not absolutely necessary to follow this.

EXAMPLE 7.2

III.   It still remains to be investigated how in each case the modulation is to be organized and accomplished. The very term modulation [*Ausweichung*], which has been given to the transition from one key to another, already implies that this must happen gradually. If one wanted to go directly from one key to another without any preparation, the harmonic progression would be incoherent and very harsh. Therefore one must already sense at the end of a period the key in which the following period will continue, and the keys through which the harmony is led in an entire composition must be related or connected in this way.

        This is best accomplished when each period closes in the key of the following period. In this way the periods are closely connected. If one has begun in C major, for example, and wants to go from there to G major, one need only conclude the phrase or period leading from C major with a cadence in G major and continue this key in the following period.

----

[c] In the article "Ausweichung" in Sulzer's *Allgemeine Theorie der schönen Künste* (Leipzig, 1771–74), Kirnberger acknowledges Rousseau as his source for this model of durations. (See Rousseau's *Dictionnaire de musique* [Paris, 1768], p. 299 and plate B, figures 6 and 7.)

[110] In order to see clearly how this is accomplished, let us assume one is playing in C major and wants to continue the next phrase in G major. According to the preceding remark, the phrase in C major would have to close in G major. It would not be sufficient if the last harmony were the major triad of the key of G, since this triad also belongs to C major. Thus the ear would not receive the slightest inclination of a new key from the half cadence shown in example 7.3. The cadence must be preceded by something that arouses this feeling of the new key.

EXAMPLE 7.3

This can best be accomplished by stating the dominant chord of the new tonic, either with the major third or the minor seventh or both together, and then closing from there with a cadence to the new tonic. Instead of the half cadence mentioned previously, the one shown in example 7.4 would have to be used to make the complete modulation to G major perceptible.

EXAMPLE 7.4

The major third in the chord on D is foreign to the key of C major and therefore indicates a new key. At the same time it is the leading tone of the key of G and thus leads naturally to it. When one proceeds from this chord to the G chord through a full cadence, this new key is completely instilled in the ear. If one wants to make the feeling of the new tonic even more certain, the minor seventh need only be added to the major triad on D, whereby the cadence in G becomes necessary.[47] In this way modulation can be announced and completed.[48]

---

47. See what was said about the effect of these essential sevenths on p. 45, above.

48. Although thirds taken from outside the scale of a given key (which are indicated by accidental sharps or flats) usually indicate a modulation, this is not always the case. Often no modulation takes place, as was mentioned above (p. 120). For if one does not actually go to the announced key, or if one abandons it im-

[111] The major third on the dominant of the new key is not always sufficient to announce a modulation. It has this effect only if it is foreign to the key in which one is playing. This is the case in the cited examples, because the scale of C major does not have an F-sharp. But if one wanted to modulate from this key to F major, this major third on the dominant of the new key would have no power to announce the new key, since it also belongs to the key of C major. Thus, in the progression in example 7.5, the major third above C in the penultimate chord would not announce the new key even though it is the leading tone of F major, since it also belongs to C major. Consequently, despite the cadence, one would not have modulated to F by this means. In this case, the minor seventh serves to announce the new key, because it is foreign to C major. Therefore the modulation would be accomplished as shown in example 7.6.

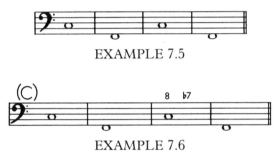

EXAMPLE 7.5

EXAMPLE 7.6

By replacing the octave in the penultimate chord with the minor seventh, which is foreign to the key of C major, one indicates in advance that this key is to be abandoned and necessitates the cadence in the new tonic, F.

[112] These are the means of announcing a new key and of actually entering it by means of a cadence. But instead of closing in the new tonic, one can also approach it by a half cadence on its dominant. For example, if in C major one were to arrive at a half cadence on D, this could also be a cadence leading to G major. This could also apply to other similar cases, as can be seen in example 7.7.

At (a) a modulation to G major would be accomplished by the half

---

(*Footnote 48 continued*)

mediately, no modulation has occurred. Thus the following period is entirely in C major.

EXAMPLE 7.7

cadence on D; at (b), to A minor; at (c), to D minor; and at (d), to E minor. However, if one actually wanted to close in the new tonic itself and yet avoid making a full cadence, one need only use an inversion of the penultimate chord. Thus the three modulations designated above with the letters (A), (B), and (C) [examples 7.4 and 7.6] could also be achieved by using the first inversion of the penultimate chord. [see example 7.8.]

EXAMPLE 7.8

Other inversions of the penultimate chord could also be used. Thus one could close in G major from C major in all the ways shown in example 7.9.

EXAMPLE 7.9

The first and third type of close is called the *bass cadence*, the second and fourth the *descant* [soprano] *cadence*, and the fifth and sixth the *tenor cadence*.

The modulation is thus prepared by progressing to the dominant of the new key. [113] If the minor seventh and major third are both present in this harmony, the cadence in the new key becomes necessary. One can arrive at this dominant of the new key as quickly as desired. It is possible to proceed from any chord taken from the scale of the main key, either directly by a single step or at most by two steps, to the dominant of every other key closely related to the main key, and then to complete the cadence. To make this point perfectly clear, we would like to present all these modulations from the key of C major in a table.

Let us assume that one has continued for a while in the main key and now wants to modulate to a different key. The fastest way of modulating from each key to every other key can be seen in table 7.2.

TABLE 7.2.

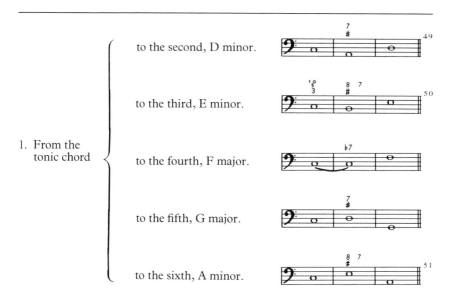

1. From the tonic chord

to the second, D minor.

to the third, E minor.

to the fourth, F major.

to the fifth, G major.

to the sixth, A minor.

49. Instead of this cadence, the following one would be preferable, because it is better that the note raised by a sharp be in the same voice from which it originates.

50. This transition from the C chord to the cadence in E minor is harsh. Usually the chord on A or G, or the sixth chord on E, precedes the dominant, as here:

51. It was mentioned above that the progression from the tonic to the chord of its major third would be harsh. Thus it would be better to approach the chord on E from the fifth or sixth [degrees] of the main key. This close would be the most direct:

TABLE 7.2. *(continued)*

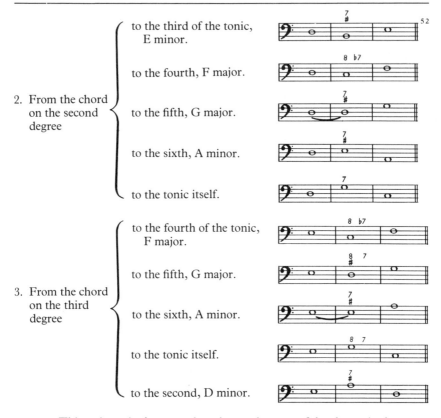

	to the third of the tonic, E minor.
2. From the chord on the second degree	to the fourth, F major.
	to the fifth, G major.
	to the sixth, A minor.
	to the tonic itself.
3. From the chord on the third degree	to the fourth of the tonic, F major.
	to the fifth, G major.
	to the sixth, A minor.
	to the tonic itself.
	to the second, D minor.

52. This cadence is clumsy and unpleasant because of the change in the upper voices from f to f-sharp, which then leads to e, as can be seen from this realization:

To avoid this harshness it is better to place the A chord or the sixth chord on C between D and B.

TABLE 7.2. (*continued*)

53. See note 49, above.
54. See note 49, above.
55. Note 51 must also be applied to this cadence.

It is easy to apply these different modulations to other keys simply by paying attention to the relationship between the chord from which the modulation is initiated and the key to which the modulation is aimed. That is, just as one modulates from the main key of C major in all the ways shown here, one can also modulate from every other main key in a similar way. These modulations can also be used as formulas to digress quickly into distant keys, as will be demonstrated in the following chapter.

Although all the modulations shown are certainly feasible, those in which the dominant of the new key is preceded by the chord on its subdominant, submediant, or seventh are really the best.

It often happens that a modulation is fully prepared but does not actually occur. The ear is deceived, since a new key is only suggested and then abandoned without actually being reached, as in example 7.10.

EXAMPLE 7.10

[118] In both cases the key of G major is suggested by the second chord, and yet there was no close in that key.

Even if the close in the new key had actually occurred through a cadence, the feeling of that key can immediately be erased by adding the seventh to the triad, which suggests modulation to yet another key, as in example 7.11.

EXAMPLE 7.11

Here one expects a cadence in A minor after the second chord. Although this chord does indeed leap to A, the added minor seventh and the major instead of the minor third already indicate that the harmony is not going to continue in A minor. The same also occurs in the following chords.

One can even go directly to a new dominant of another key by omitting the chord that naturally follows the seventh chord. For instance, instead of the progression at (A) in example 7.12, the one at (B) can be used.

Wherever the expression requires it, it is possible in this way to lead the ear from one expectation ot another and to keep it in a constant state of unrest for as long as desired.

EXAMPLE 7.12

Chromatic bass progressions also belong here, since the key to which one has modulated is quickly abandoned; from there one modulates to the next key by using the first inversion rather than the root position of its dominant chord, as in example 7.13.

EXAMPLE 7.13

To conclude this chapter we would like to present the general rules of modulation as briefly as possible.

1. First of all, in every composition the main key that has been chosen must be completely established, which is accomplished by using no chords for several measures other than those that are contained in the diatonic scale of that key. [119] Depending upon the length of the entire composition, one can establish the main key by such chords for six, eight, and up to twelve or even more measures.

2. Then one modulates to another key closely related to it, most naturally to its dominant. This is done either directly and in the shortest way, or indirectly by passing through other keys in which one remains, however, for only one or two measures.

3. After modulating to the dominant of the main key, one also remains there for six, eight, or more measures, depending upon the length of the composition. From there one proceeds again either directly or indirectly—dwelling briefly in passing keys—to the mediant or submediant of the main key. One also remains there for a while, as before in the dominant.

4. From this mediant or submediant one proceeds again in the manner described above to other keys related to the main key but not previously visited, and also remains there for a while.

5. Finally, one modulates to one of the keys most distantly related to the main key, likewise remains there for a few measures, and from there returns to the main key through two or three other keys, in which one remains only very briefly. However, before closing completely in the main key, one must direct the modulation again to its dominant, remain there for a while, and then end the entire piece with a cadence in the main key.

6. If the composition is very long and the memory of the main key has been lost to some extent by dwelling on other keys, one can use a so-called *point d'orgue* on the dominant before the final cadence, whereby the desire for the main key is notably increased.

7. In this case one can also use a *point d'orgue* after the cadence in the main key and then repeat the final cadence.

These rules are clarified by the following illustrations which can serve as examples. The square notes indicate keys in which one remains for six, eight, or more measures; the white notes indicate those which one touches on only in passing, without remaining there longer than one or at most two measures; the black notes indicate notes by which the cadence is prepared or where the actual shift to the new key occurs.

[120] What was said above in the second rule—that one modulates from the main key to its dominant either directly or by touching on other keys—is clarified by table 7.3.[d]

TABLE 7.3.

Direct Modulation.

Indirection Modulation.

1. Through one passing key (A minor or D minor).

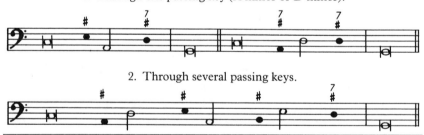

2. Through several passing keys.

[d]An important and highly perceptive aspect of Kirnberger's discussion of modulation is the distinction he draws between keys that are the goal of modulation and those that are momentarily emphasized in the process of changing from one stable area to another. This distinction is an extension of his earlier observation about the difference between change of key and the practice of emphasizing secondary triads within a key. (See chapter 6, example 6.24 and note e.)

Just as one modulates from the main key to the dominant in a great variety of ways, either directly or through one or more passing keys, one proceeds in much the same manner from the dominant to other keys, and from there again to other keys, until one returns at last to the main key. Example 7.14 represents a modulation scheme for a long composition; it is a model that can be modified in many ways.[e]

EXAMPLE 7.14

[e]This model, which summarizes the main points in this chapter, demonstrates Kirnberger's conception of the relationship between modulation and form. The barlines delineate the primary modulations and thus the major formal divisions of this hypothetical piece.

CHAPTER 8

Modulation to Remote Keys and Sudden Digressions

[121] In the preceding chapter, consideration was given only to those modulations [involving keys] to which one can go directly from the main key. Furthermore it was assumed that the harmony would remain in the closest degrees of relationship with the main key throughout the entire piece. Considerable diversity of modulation can be achieved even in longer compositions by this means alone.

Experienced harmonists, however, are not always satisfied with such a timid way of modulating. They digress into more remote keys where the ear sometimes loses the main key entirely, yet know how to direct the modulation back to it at just the right moment. Sometimes a digression to a somewhat more remote key is also necessary for expressive reasons. This free and more daring type of modulation is to be discussed here.

Generally this type of modulation is based on the principle that one of the keys to which one has modulated is treated as the main key, from which one in turn modulates again to its related keys according to the rules given in the preceding chapter.

Thus the first step to a further extension of modulation consists in treating the dominant or subdominant of the main key like the main key itself. In both cases one arrives at two new keys that are not directly related to the original key. If, for example, the main key is C major, the standard modulations—according to the preceding chapter—are limited to the keys of G major, F major, A minor, E minor, and D minor, because only these are directly related to C major. If G major is then treated as the main key, it is possible to modulate to D major, C major, E minor, B minor, and A minor. Thus one obtains the keys of D major and B minor, which are not available in the first type of modulation.

138

If one modulates from the main key to its dominant or subdominant, these keys are in the same mode as the main key, be it major or minor, as was shown in the preceding chapter. Now if this dominant is in turn made the main key, its dominant also has the same mode; but it would not have the same mode as if one were to modulate to it directly from the original key. [122] [For example,] one can modulate directly from C major to D minor. But if the dominant of C major, namely G major, is treated as the main key after modulating to it, one modulates again from there to its dominant D, that is D major, and thus obtains a key foreign to the original one. When G major replaces C major [as the main key], a second foreign key, B minor, is also obtained. It is well known that every [major] key has the same pitches as the key of the opposite mode a third below it. Thus [the pairs] C major and A minor, D major and B minor, F major and D minor, and G major and E minor share the same pitches. Therefore, by treating the dominant of the original key as a main key, two new keys are always obtained—the dominant of this dominant and the [minor] key a third below it.

Likewise, if the subdominant (F) in C major is treated like a main key, two new keys, B-flat major and G minor, are made available for modulation.

If more keys are desired, one goes a step further and treats one of these new keys as a main key, thereby obtaining two additional keys. That is, from the previously mentioned D major one obtains A major and F-sharp minor; and the previously mentioned B-flat major provides the new keys of E-flat major and C minor.

However, one should be content with this, since an even greater removal from the main key would lead too far. Those pieces which modulate in a circle through all keys are only a curiosity and are of no use otherwise.

Table 8.1 shows the most distant modulations from the main key of C major.

TABLE 8.1.

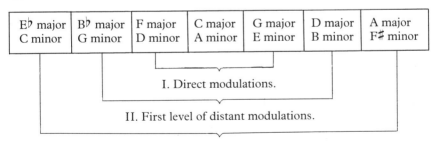

E♭ major / C minor	B♭ major / G minor	F major / D minor	C major / A minor	G major / E minor	D major / B minor	A major / F♯ minor

I. Direct modulations.

II. First level of distant modulations.

III. Second level of distant modulations.

TABLE 8.2.

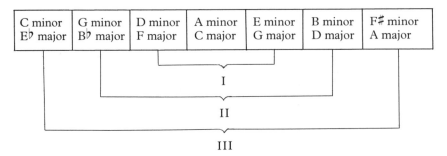

C minor E♭ major	G minor B♭ major	D minor F major	A minor C major	E minor G major	B minor D major	F♯ minor A major

I

II

III

[123] Those keys related to a main key in the minor mode by the first and second levels of distant modulation are found in a similar way. They are presented in table 8.2.

To avoid harshness in these remote modulations, a key in the second and third levels of relationship should always be approached from a key in the first and second levels, respectively. Thus, if the piece has begun in C major, one cannot modulate, for example, to either D major or A major unless those keys are preceded by D minor and A minor. The same rule applies to the remaining keys.

Furthermore, there are special procedures by which one can suggest that a key to which one has modulated is now to be treated as the main key. This can happen either by remaining in the new key for a long time and preparing the cadence over several measures, whereby the ear becomes accustomed to the new key; or, after cadencing in the new key, by repeating the main idea in that key in the same manner as it was stated in the original key at the beginning of the piece. Both procedures can be seen clearly in example 8.1.

[124] Before the cadence on G, the f-sharp that announces the cadence is heard several times here, and in this way one is kept in expectation of the new key for so long that the ear finally accepts it as the main key. Then the main idea is repeated in the new key exactly as it appeared in the original key.

This may suffice regarding gradual modulations to remote keys.

Occasionally it may be necessary to modulate quickly to keys that are remotely related to the main key. Therefore the shortest ways to accomplish this must also be discussed here.

This generally happens in the following way. One takes the dominant of

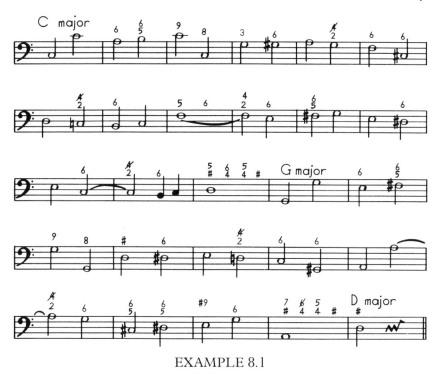

EXAMPLE 8.1

one of the keys to which one can go directly from the main key and, without closing from there to its tonic, reinterprets it as a tonic triad, from which it is now possible to progress by one step to any triad contained in its scale.

If the intention were to get very quickly to the remote chords of F-sharp major or D-sharp minor from the main key of C major, one imagines a modulation from C major to E minor, which can occur directly. The major triad on B, as the dominant of E, is needed for this. If one now conceives of this B major chord as a principal tonic, it is possible to go directly from there to the chord of its dominant (F-sharp major) or its mediant (D-sharp minor).

Table 8.3 is inserted here to show at a glance the many possible ways of modulating quickly from a major or minor key to remote keys. [125] C major and its submediant A minor—both of which, as is known, have the same scale—are presented here as the main keys from which the modulation is to occur.

TABLE 8.3.

	I C major	II D minor	III E minor	IV F major	V G major	VI A minor
I G major			B minor		D major	
II A major	A major	B minor	C♯ minor	D major	E major	F♯ minor
III B major	B major	C♯ minor	D♯ minor	E major	F♯ major	G♯ minor
IV C major						
V D major	D major		F♯ minor		A major	B minor
VI E major	E major	F♯ minor	G♯ minor	A major	B major	C♯ minor

The top row represents the keys to which one can modulate directly from C major and A minor according to the remarks contained in the preceding chapter. The left-most column shows the dominant chords that are necessary to close in the keys contained in the top row. If one now imagines while playing one of these chords that it is a tonic triad of a main key, it is possible to see the keys to which one can now go from this main key [by examining] the row next to it. However, the table shows only those keys not directly related to C major or A minor.

Suppose, for example, that the E major chord were sounded as if the intention were to close in A minor. If this chord is then considered as a tonic chord, one can go from there immediately to F-sharp minor, or G-sharp minor, or B major, etc.—all chords that are quite remote from C major.

If the intention is to stray suddenly even further [from the original key], one treats one of the foreign chords obtained in the manner described above as a main key and then proceeds as before. [126] To modulate quickly from C major to C-sharp major, one first goes to D-sharp minor in the manner indicated in table 8.3. Since D-sharp minor relates to C-sharp major exactly as D minor relates to C major, one goes from D-sharp minor to C-sharp major in the same manner shown in table 7.2.

Such modulations should be used, however, only where the expression demands it, that is, where the feelings are to be led rapidly from one sentiment to another. This must be left to the discretion of the composer. Such modulations cannot occur in compositions that are governed by a single affection throughout. If one wants to make a formal cadence in one of these remote keys, a formula for accomplishing this can always be found in table 7.2. This will be made clear enough by a single example.

Let us assume that we are in the main key of C major and have sounded the chord on E with the major third, as if we intended to proceed from there to a cadence in A minor. If this chord is now considered as the tonic triad in a new main key, it is possible to cadence in each key contained in the bottom row of table 8.3 by taking one or two steps. The shortest way to do this from the E major chord is by means of the formulas listed on p. 131, above. That is, one need only replace C major with E major as the tonic. Thus, in this case, the cadence to D minor listed in the table provides the formula for the cadence to F-sharp minor, and the cadence to E minor listed in the table provides the formula for the cadence to G-sharp minor, and so on.

However, suppose one does not want to close directly from the E major chord but first wants to go to some other chord belonging to the E major scale, for example F-sharp minor. Then the cadence patterns listed on p. 132 will serve as formulas for leading from, say, this F-sharp minor chord, as the chord on the second degree of the scale, to cadences on any of the remaining degrees.

It still remains to be noted that although in the given tables the note at which the shift to the new key occurs has a triad or seventh chord as its harmony, the first inversions of these chords are often preferable.

If one wants to make the cadences in remote keys less noticeable and to keep the ear in uncertainty about the modulation, this is best done by using ties. [127] If, for example, the intention is to go quickly but somewhat unnoticed from C major to B minor, and this is to be accomplished through the major triad on A, one would progress as at (B) in example 8.2 instead of making a formal close, as at (A).

Still another means of arriving very quickly at remote keys is the following. Instead of considering the bass note of any given chord as the second, third, fourth, etc., from its tonic, one need only make it an interval

EXAMPLE 8.2

from some other tonic. Then one gives it a harmony befitting its purpose according to the most natural figuration of the scale and goes from there to its tonic.[56] One example will clarify this.

[128] If, in the key of C major, one had arrived at the major triad on B, which is the seventh of this tonic, and then wanted to go quickly to A major, one would consider the bass note B as the second of the new tonic, assign it the appropriate harmony, and go directly from there to A in the same manner as from D to C in C major. [See example 8.3.]

Those who have a certain amount of training in harmony will always see with ease how the bass note at which the shift occurs would have to be harmonized so that the ear is directed toward the scale of the new tonic, and

EXAMPLE 8.3

56. This natural figuration of the scale consists of assigning figures to all notes of the diatonic scale in such a way that the chords are simple triads or seventh chords, or their inversions, built on the tonic and its dominant and subdominant. Thus the C major scale would be figured in the following way.

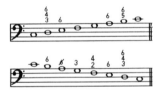

Here every chord is either the triad or the seventh chord, or an inversion of these chords, on the tonic and both its dominants. The scale of a minor key, for example A minor, would be figured in this way:

When the minor or natural sixth is used in the ascending scale, it cannot be continued beyond that point because one would have to progress by an augmented second (F–G-sharp) in order to arrive at the leading tone. Thus in the ascending scale, one must either go directly to F-sharp or sound it immediately after the F.

in addition how everything can be prepared in advance by the penultimate chord. Thus it was easy to see here that the major third above B had to be changed to the minor third (as the seventh of the dominant in the new tonic), and that not the minor but the major sixth had to be used, since it is the leading tone of the new tonic.

Those who think the free sounding of the minor third is too harsh in such a case can introduce it freely in the preceding chord, as in example 8.4.

EXAMPLE 8.4

Just as the bass note at which the shift occurs was considered as the second of the new tonic in both these examples and therefore was figured with $\frac{6}{4}$, it can also be made some other interval [in relation to the new tonic], $\frac{3}{3}$ as can be seen clearly enough in example 8.5. [129] At (a) the bass note B-sharp functions in the same way as the seventh [degree] in A minor and is figured in such a way that it could lead directly to its octave in C-sharp minor.[a] At (b) the C becomes the seventh [degree] of the following key of D-flat major; at (c) the $\frac{4+}{2}$ chord on B functions in the same way as the $\frac{4}{2}$ chord of F in the C major scale, so that one could close directly to the sixth chord of the new tonic in F[-sharp] major; and at (d) the B major chord

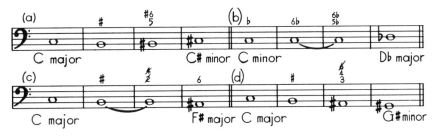

EXAMPLE 8.5

[a] It should be kept in mind that Kirnberger uses C major and A minor as the models for all the keys. Thus progressions in other keys are often described in relation to the one or the other of these two.

functions in the same way as the C major chord in the descending B [*sic*, A] minor scale in order to close in G-sharp minor through the chord of the major sixth.

Finally, there still remains to be discussed a quick and somewhat violent way of modulating to very remote keys, a way that is based on the enharmonic treatment of harmony. This is accomplished by means of the chord with the minor seventh and minor ninth, which can have four different roots without changing its nature, since it has the special quality of being constructed of three superimposed thirds. To grasp this clearly, consider the nine-seven chord in example 8.6. As it stands here it is the chord on D as the dominant of G major or minor, to which it would have to close. However, without changing a note, it can also be the nine-seven chord with the major third of three other roots. If the e-flat is changed to d-sharp, which is the same on the keyboard, it is the nine-seven chord with the major third on B, as at (a) in example 8.7; if c is changed to b-sharp, it is the same chord on the root G-sharp, as at (b); and, finally, the root is F if f-sharp is changed to g-flat, as at (c).

EXAMPLE 8.6   EXAMPLE 8.7

[130] Each of these four roots is the dominant of a particular tonic to which the chord resolves at the cadence. Thus it is possible to close directly from this chord in four keys: (1) in G when D is the root; (2) in E when B is the root; (3) in C-sharp when G-sharp is the root; and (4) in B-flat major when F is the root.

If the first inversion of such a nine-seven chord is used instead of [having] one of its roots in the bass, the ninth becomes the seventh.[b] Thus,

[b]To understand what is said here and in the following paragraphs about the inversions of the diminished seventh chord, the reader must remember that Kirnberger considers this chord to be an unauthentic seventh chord, whose root is a major third below the bass note. The seventh, then, is a nonessential dissonance, whose resolution is delayed until the following harmony. Thus the root of the chord f-sharp–a–c–e-flat is D, since e-flat, as the ninth from D,

instead of closing to the tonic of the actual root, it is possible to arrive at a completely foreign tonic by means of an enharmonic shift, as can be seen clearly in example 8.8.

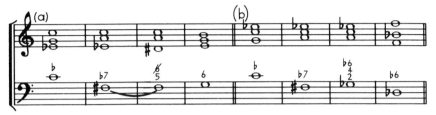

EXAMPLE 8.8

In the first progression, the second chord is really the nine-seven chord on D, but in its first inversion, where the ninth has now become the seventh. Instead of resolving downward immediately like a suspension, the ninth is held over to the next chord. In the third chord, this ninth is enharmonically changed from e-flat to d-sharp, whereby the chord becomes a nine-seven chord on B, which is used here in its second inversion. From here it must lead to a close on E, while the same chord without the enharmonic shift (if it had remained as in the second measure) would have caused a close on G.

[131] In the second progression, another enharmonic shift occurs in the third measure. Here the bass note is really the ninth of F, the dominant of B-flat, to which the close occurs.[c]

The enharmonic shift always occurs when one of the intervals of the diminished seventh chord appears first as an augmented second and later, when the chord is repeated, as a minor third, or vice versa. In this way the chord assumes a different nature and requires a different progression. From this it is thus evident how chords in very remote keys may be reached quickly by means of enharmonic change.

This advantage is increased in the following way. If a given diminished

---

is a displacement of d, the octave. And since the diminished seventh chord is a displacement of the essential seventh chord in the six-five position, it is considered by Kirnberger to be in first inversion. Similarly, the chord a–c–e-flat–f-sharp would be considered to be in second inversion, since it is a displacement of a–c–d–f-sharp, the essential seventh chord in the four-three position. The same principle applies to the other positions of the diminished seventh chord and to all other unauthentic seventh chords. (See note g in chapter 4, above.)

[c]Note the unusual resolution of the dissonant bass note g-flat, which would normally resolve down by step to f in the next measure. Another unusual resolution, in this case of the leading tone A-sharp, occurs at the end of example 8.2.

seventh chord does not lead to the desired remote chord, another chord of this type can immediately be obtained by moving the first chord up or down by a half step, from which one can go to four new keys. Example 8.9 may clarify this.

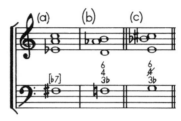

EXAMPLE 8.9

According to the previously discussed technique, one could go either directly or by one of the three enharmonic shifts from the chord at (a) to G, B-flat, C-sharp, or E. However, if none of these keys, but instead E-flat or F-sharp, is needed, this chord can be immediately followed by the one at (b), which is the third inversion of the nine-seven chord a fifth below the previous root, D. From this chord one can reach C, E-flat, F-sharp, and A in the manner described above.

[132] Similarly one can get from the first nine-seven chord to the nine-seven chord of its dominant by moving the bass up by a half step, as at (c); this leads to the following modulations: D, F, G-sharp, and B. This repetition of the chord of the minor [diminished] seventh by moving it up or down by a half step can be continued through many chords in succession. Two examples of this from J. S. Bach's *Clavierübungen* are added here. [See example 8.10.]

EXAMPLE 8.10

It can easily be seen from the above that one could progress by a few steps from any given chord in a particular key to any needed chord in the entire range of all twenty-four keys.

These progressions can be made smoother by repeating or inverting the diminished seventh chord until the ear no longer perceives which of the notes form a minor third or an augmented second, or they can be made smoother by tying some of the notes, as in example 8.11.

EXAMPLE 8.11

It can be stated in general that enharmonic progressions are not absolutely necessary for modulating quickly. They were very much in use at the time of Marcello and sometimes may have been used in such abundance only for the purpose of making it difficult for even connoisseurs of harmony to guess their proper treatment and to reduce certain chords to their true fundamental harmony.[57] [133] If one wants to create a sudden surprise and puzzle the listener to a certain extent, this can be achieved without these enharmonic progressions simply by going from the seventh chord or its inversions to entirely remote keys. Example 8.12 can serve as an illustration of this.

The most powerful way to achieve a sudden surprise is to use simple triads to go to very remote chords. Older composers knew very well how to

EXAMPLE 8.12

57. On this occasion we can note in general that today's composers are beginning to refrain from various affectations of this sort. Many inversions of dissonant chords in succession, the omission of resolution and the free introduction of new dissonances that should have been prepared by the omitted chord, the replacement of major intervals by minor ones and vice versa—all of these were used much more frequently before than now. Herr Capellmeister Bach, in the second part of his *Versuch über die wahre Art das Clavier zu spielen* [Berlin, 1762], chapter 38, also praises contemporary taste, which sanctions such harmonic peculiarities only occasionally and never without necessity.

do this before chromatic intervals were introduced. Those who know Froberger's works will be able to see what a splendid effect he managed to
achieve by a successful choice of chords that sound foreign yet are not too
remote from the main key. In example 8.13 rather remote keys are reached
by simple triads and their inversions.

EXAMPLE 8.13

CHAPTER 9

Harmonic and Nonharmonic Melodic Progressions

[134] So far we have considered harmony only in terms of chords or in the situation where consonant or dissonant notes are heard simultaneously. Before the theory of harmony that has been discussed thus far can be applied to the composition of a piece of music, it is also necessary to consider harmony in terms of the succession of individual notes.

To be sure, the concept of harmony, of consonance and dissonance, seems to be suited only to notes that are heard simultaneously. However, since the ear retains the preceding note at the entrance of each subsequent note, it compares the two; for this reason some progressions are light and agreeable, others heavy and even unpleasant. In certain cases, one also perceives something analogous to the resolution of dissonances in the progression of individual notes. For example, when the entire diatonic scale of a key is sung up to its major seventh, one immediately feels that this last note must lead to the octave, which is felt almost simultaneously with the major seventh. If the ear is to be satisfied, the octave must follow.

Thus there are two reasons why certain melodic progressions are to be rejected. Either they are contrary to the expectation of the ear, which definitely expects certain notes to lead to others, such as the ascent of the major seventh to the octave and the descent of the second to the unison in the Phrygian mode; or they are very difficult to sing because of their strong dissonance, like the tritone F–B. From this it follows that the melodic progression of a voice is subject to certain harmonic rules, even when it is considered without reference to other voices. These rules are to be discussed in this chapter.[a]

[a]Further discussion of the harmonic implications in melody are contained in subsequent chapters, particularly in chapter 3 of Volume II, part 1.

We must keep in mind from the beginning that the treatment of harmony is subject to the rules of either the free or the strict style, as was discussed above.[58] What is forbidden in the strict style is not only permissible in the freer style but often sounds very good because the expression is often assisted by such deviations from the rules. [135] This is particularly true in situations where disagreeable passions are to be expressed. Therefore most of the rules of progression stated here tolerate an exception on occasion for expressive reasons.

Generally the rules of progression are based on the premise that the melody should be gentle and pleasant. Since there are instances where it must be less gentle and pleasing for expressive reasons, these rules need not be followed throughout, as long as one avoids the totally ugly or even the impossible.

The simplest and most pleasing melody is without doubt one that proceeds only through the pure diatonic steps of the chosen key. This occurs for the same reason that we get complete satisfaction from the consonant harmony; that is, the ratios of intervals in this diatonic progression are always the simplest and most comprehensible.[59]

However, it happens that a few intervals must be raised or lowered when modulating to other keys or otherwise using notes foreign to the present key. In doing so, progressions can arise that must be avoided.

The principal rule that has to be observed in this case is the following. Never progress by augmented intervals unless the [second note of the] interval can be led directly to the note above it, as from a leading tone to a new tonic. Thus the following progressions [example 9.1], both ascending and descending, would not be allowed. [136] Even the major seventh [ex-

EXAMPLE 9.1[60]

58. In the beginning of chapter 5, on p. 99.
59. See what was said about this in chapter 2, on pp. 37–38.
60. A few overzealous theorists also mention an augmented third, which, however, is basically imaginary. One will never find intervals such as the following imagined thirds in the works of classical composers.

ample 9.2] must be reckoned among these. Such progressions occur in an ascending form only if the raised note is resolved upward like a leading tone, as in example 9.3.

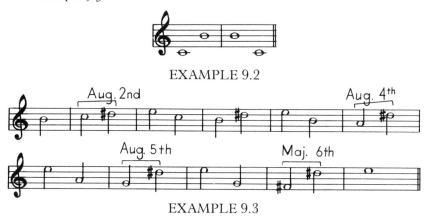

EXAMPLE 9.2

EXAMPLE 9.3

The above-mentioned forbidden progressions by augmented intervals are not improved by filling them in with passing notes. Thus the progressions at (A) in example 9.4 would still be bad if they were to occur as at (B). [137] This ascending and descending augmented fourth can be used in this way only if it is led a half step further up or down, as in example 9.5.[61] The

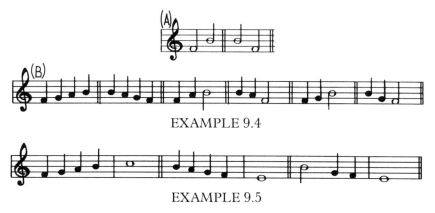

EXAMPLE 9.4

EXAMPLE 9.5

61. However, this does not occur in the minor mode, where the augmented fourth must fall a whole step, since it is very difficult to sing. Thus the following progression would not be good.

augmented prime or the augmented octave that results from its inversion [*sic*, transposition] can occur only in passing, as in example 9.6. The same is true when it appears as the augmented fifth from the bass, as in example 9.7. Here the situation is the same as with passing notes that are not considered part of the harmony and not figured in the thorough bass. Only in the more serious style and in slower tempi does this not occur.

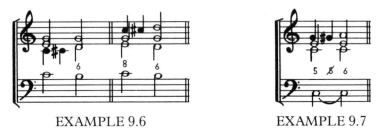

EXAMPLE 9.6   EXAMPLE 9.7

In earlier times, neither the ascending nor descending leap of a major sixth was allowed; but now it is used without hesitation. But it must be kept in mind that this sixth would be almost impossible to sing in certain harmonic progressions, as in example 9.8.

EXAMPLE 9.8

[138] However, this can also happen with intervals that are otherwise permitted. Forbidden progressions can become permissible by inverting them, as can be seen in example 9.9.

Diminished intervals, for the most part, create bad progressions. It is not permissible to ascend from f-sharp to a-flat, or, in reverse, to descend from a-flat to f-sharp, unless, in the first case, one passes through g, or, in the second case, this g is heard after the f-sharp, for this f-sharp, as the leading tone of g, creates the expectation of the g. Therefore the forbidden progression at (A) in example 9.10 would be acceptable as at (B). [139] Similarly, the ascending and descending leap of a diminished fourth, such as g-sharp–c, is made more acceptable when the note a, which should follow g-sharp, is sounded in the bass, as in example 9.11 at (A); it could also occur as at (B).

EXAMPLE 9.9⁶²

EXAMPLE 9.10

EXAMPLE 9.11

62. The older composers forbid both these progressions, while the younger ones allow them. However, the first c–g-sharp, the descending diminished fourth, is easier to sing than the second one, which ascends. Even the leaps of a small fifth shown in the preceding two examples were not allowed formerly, but are used today without hesitation.

When a single-line melody is composed in such a way that its harmony is implied and sounds like a two- or three-part piece, the forbidden progressions no longer sound bad. Thus the phrases at (A) in example 9.12 would be feasible, because they sound almost as if they were written as at (B) below.

EXAMPLE 9.12

There are cases where each voice has a good progression and where even the harmony of all voices seems faultless, but where the progression between two voices is disagreeable; this is generally called the unharmonic *cross relation*. The unharmonic cross relation that results from two successive major thirds in parallel motion is disagreeable; but in contrary motion they are acceptable, as can be seen in example 9.13. [140] In the first example the tritone c–f-sharp is felt too strongly, but less so in the second; in the third nothing adverse is noticeable. This remark also applies to example 9.14, where the augmented fifth results from a cross relation.

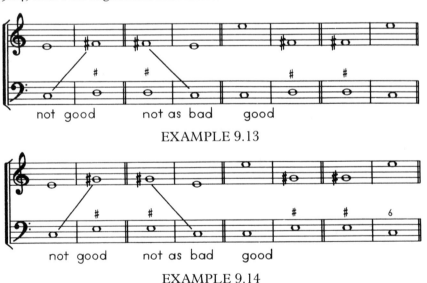

EXAMPLE 9.13

EXAMPLE 9.14

It remains to be noted regarding successive thirds that two major thirds can follow one another when the two voices in which they occur move up or down by a half step, as at (a) in example 9.15, or when an additional third voice is tied over, as at (b). However, thirds sound best when the major third alternates with the minor, or vice versa, as in example 9.16.

EXAMPLE 9.15

EXAMPLE 9.16

It is generally very difficult to use a series of successive thirds in a four-part texture in such a way that forbidden fifths and octaves are avoided. [141] This will be discovered by all who try to realize the phrase in example 9.17 in four parts.

EXAMPLE 9.17

CHAPTER 10

Simple Counterpoint in Two and More Parts

Long ago, before the present system of notation came into use, pitches were designated by simple points that were placed on parallel lines. As many lines were used as the system had pitches, and each note was indicated by a point on the appropriate line. Later, when compositions for two and more voices were written, the points indicating the pitches of the other voices had to be placed against the points of the existing voice. This resulted in the expression "to set point against point" [*contrapunktiren*], which means to add one or more voices to a given voice. Thus we have retained the word *counterpoint*, which refers to the art of composing one or more voices to a given monophonic melody according to the rules of good harmony.

If one is concerned only with pure harmony and the good progression of voices as they are written, this is called *simple counterpoint*. But if the voices are composed in such a way that one or more of them can be taken higher or lower—so that all of its notes can be transposed up or down by a second, third, fourth, etc.—without violating the purity of harmony, this type of writing is called *double counterpoint*, which, as is easy to see, is much more difficult than the simple.

[142] This chapter deals only with simple counterpoint; the requirements of double counterpoint will be explained in the second volume. Simple counterpoint is called *plain* or *equal* when each note of the given melody, which is called the *cantus firmus*, is accompanied by only one note of the same duration in another voice—a whole note against a whole note, a half against a half, etc. It is called *unequal* or *florid* when several notes are set against one note of the *cantus firmus*. If strict or equal counterpoint is well understood, the florid causes little difficulty. Therefore diligent practice in

158

strict counterpoint is particularly important to the art of strict composition; this is to be our principal concern here. We advise prospective composers not to concern themselves with composing figured or so-called "galant" pieces until they have acquired such dexterity in this counterpoint that its composition is thoroughly strict.

Simple plain counterpoint can be for two, three, four, or more voices. It is best to begin with four voices, because it is not possible to write for two or three voices perfectly until one can do so for four voices. Since complete harmony is in four parts, the harmony in two- and three-part compositions must always be incomplete. Therefore it is impossible to judge with certainty what must be omitted from the harmony in the various situations that arise until one has a thorough knowledge of four-part composition.

Consequently, this counterpoint should be considered as a succession of complete chords. If the writing is to be correct and strict: (1) the chords must follow one another coherently according to the rules of harmony; (2) each voice must have a flowing melody and a strict progression; and (3) several of the voices together must sound strict and have nothing disagreeable in their progression. Errors against strictness of composition result mainly from four causes: (1) from the lack of coherence; (2) from the immediate repetition of perfect consonances, the octave and fifth, between two voices, which renders the melodic line somewhat empty, indefinite, and therefore disagreeable; (3) from difficult and unharmonic progressions in one voice; and (4) from unharmonic cross relations between two voices.

The most important considerations regarding the avoidance of these errors are scattered throughout the preceding chapters. Thus all that remains for us to demonstrate here is the more precise application of the rules previously stated here and there. [143] Most teachers of strict composition have directed their efforts above all to the establishment of precise rules whereby the second error, namely, progression by octaves and fifths, can be avoided, since this error is committed most easily and makes the melodic line extremely barren and disagreeable.

These rules have to do with the progression or motion of voices insofar as they move away from or towards each other. These rules are found everywhere; yet we intend to repeat them here for the sake of completeness.

Two voices progress in *similar motion* when they ascend or fall together; they progress in *contrary motion* when one ascends while the other falls, or when one voice is stationary while the other ascends or descends. The latter situation is called *oblique motion* by some, but it also belongs under contrary motion.

Forbidden octave- and fifth-progressions will be avoided in most cases by observing the following three rules about these motions.

1. One must progress from one perfect consonance, that is, an octave or fifth, to another by contrary or oblique motion.

2. The same is to be observed when going from an imperfect to a perfect consonance.

3. One can progress by all types of motion from a perfect to an imperfect consonance, or from an imperfect to another imperfect consonance.

Composing becomes free of offensive errors by the observance of these rules—those stated about the preparation and resolution of disonance, and those mentioned about the avoidance of unharmonic progression and cross relations. However, the observance of these very rules is often so difficult that one can scarcely see how errors are to be avoided. For that reason it is necessary for us to cite various rules that are special to and practical for such situations. In addition, though the writing may be strict, it may still be imperfect; that is, it can still be very flat and empty, or be harsh in various ways. And for this reason it is necessary to make to few special rules, which are to be stated here.

We mention in advance that everything stated here concerns only strictness and euphony, and that nothing is to be said yet about the power of expression. [144] Melody can be better or worse with one and the same succession of chords, depending upon whether one increases the distance between the chord tones or brings them close together. If one acts without deliberation in this matter, either the melody can become a confused rattling, or the voices relate to each other so little that the harmony is no longer clear.

Rules for the proper treatment of close or open harmony have been given to us by nature itself. By now it is a well-known observation that the sound of a completely pure string that is not tuned too high is a mixture of many pitches that fuse into one single main pitch. If, for example, one bows the string that produces the pitch of great C, whose length we shall express by the number 1, the pitches that would have to be expressed by 1/2, 1/3, 1/4, 1/5, 1/6, etc., are mixed together with this note. Consider the following succession of numbers, each of which expresses the length of a string and its appropriate pitch. All these pitches, most of which correspond quite closely with those in our tempered system, sound in the pitch C, and this very mixture without doubt produces the amenity of the sound.

1, 1/2, 1/3, 1/4, 1/5, 1/6, 1/7,ᵃ 1/8, 1/9, 1/10, 1/11, 1/12, 1/13,
C, c,   g,   c¹, e¹, g¹, i¹,   c², d², e²,   ★,   g²,   ★,

1/14, 1/15, 1/16, 1/17, 1/18, 1/19, 1/20, 1/21, 1/22, 1/23, 1/24, 1/25,
i²,   b²,   c³,   c♯³, d³,   d♯³, e³,   ★,   ★,   ★,   g³,   g♯³,

1/26, 1/27, 1/28, 1/29, 1/30, 1/31, 1/32.
★,   ★,   i³,   ★,   b³,   ★,   c⁴.

It can be deduced from this that, to sound pleasing, lower pitches must be separated by a greater distance, but higher ones must be brought closer together. Nature allows nothing to be heard between C and c; only one note, g, the fifth of c, between c and c¹; three others between c¹ and c²; a number of others that are only a semitone apart between c² and c³; and those situated between c³ and c⁴ lie even closer together.

The composer must follow nature's suggestion by separating lower notes and bringing the higher ones close together. No other note must stand between the lowest bass note and its octave; and this octave must come no closer than a fifth to the next note, and the third octave no closer than a third. [145] In the higher register the harmony can be closer. In the second-line octave, passing [major] seconds can be used; and in the third-line, passing semitones.

In the high registers it is not always possible, of course, to place notes as close as intimated by the preceding representation of harmonic tones. From that, one learns in general only that closeness of harmony has to be sought above all in the upper voices. It would be most inferior if the lowest inner voice were to be close to the bass and the two upper voices far from the third inner voice. If the uppermost voices have to go very high, the bass as well as the lowest inner voice must also be moved up. In general the bass cannot be separated from the outermost voice by more than two octaves, unless in works for many voices the space between the lowest and highest parts is filled by many inner voices.

This may suffice regarding close and open harmony.

Besides this, the following main points must be given consideration in four-part writing: (1) that the harmony have appropriate variety and diversity along with good continuity; (2) that the progression in all voices, together as well as separate, be strict; (3) that each voice have a simple and

---

ᵃThe reader is reminded that Kirnberger uses the letter i to designate the natural seventh. See note 24 and note c in chapter 2, above.

flowing line, yet all voices combine together well. Each of these three points deserves to be considered in somewhat greater detail.

1. How harmony in a period could be made totally cohesive was stated in detail above in the sixth chapter.[63] Concerning variety and diversity, it was also noted that fairly long periods could be formed with a few fundamental chords and their inversions.[64] We recommend that the prospective composer consider this seriously, so that he may avoid the disgusting monotony into which so many new composers tend to fall by remaining on one harmony for many measures, by retaining one triad or at best exchanging it with the sixth chord, and sometimes by not being able to make progress with the harmony over a long span of measures.

To please beginners, we want to clarify what has been said about continuity and diversity of harmony by just a couple of examples. [146] See illustrations (a), (b), and (c) in example 10.1. In the first, the harmony lacks

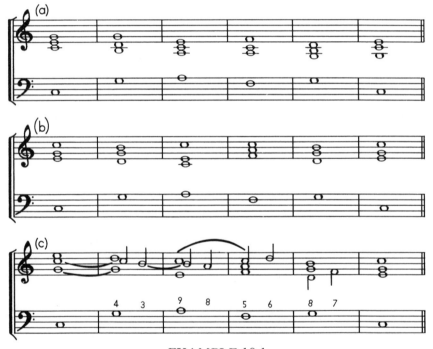

EXAMPLE 10.1

63. See above, pp. 109–11.
64. See above, pp. 119–20.

continuity because one can stop on each chord. Because perfect consonances are always situated in the top voice, the ear is satisfied at each
harmony, as at a close; consequently, there is no reason to expect anything
further. In the second example the harmony has greater continuity because
the top voice usually has the thirds of the roots; since these are not sufficiently restful, further progression is expected. However, in the third example the connection is still closer as a result of the ties or suspensions.

What has been said about lack of variety will become clear from example
10.2. [147] A bass figured as it is here allows only a repetition of the same
harmony to be heard, even though it appears to the eye to have diversity.
Basically it does not sound much different than if it were played as written
below in the fundamental bass.

EXAMPLE 10.2

It must be kept in mind that even when a melody repeats the same note
several times in succession, the harmony may be varied sufficiently, since
the same note can now be the third, now the sixth, fifth, or octave of the same
or another root, and thus new harmonies always occur. He who has mastered harmony can always use other harmonies or inversions of the original
ones with repetitions of the same melodic passages.[65] One can even take the

65. Knowledge of double counterpoint greatly facilitates this variety of harmony. Regarding this we shall cite only a single example. The following passage by
Capellmeister Graun is very agreeable.

If the bass of the first measure were to be repeated in the second measure, this
passage would lose all its beauty. It is notable that each bass note is taken a third
lower with the repetition of the same notes in the upper voices. This transposition is
based on counterpoint at the tenth.

harmony of the remaining voices from different keys [as accompaniment] to the same melody. Since there is sufficient means to maintain diversity, monotony of harmony is even less excusable.

On occasion there are melodies to which the same bass note can be retained for several measures without becoming tedious. In this case one has to be on guard against the bad habit of inferior composers of changing the bass notes—which should consist of half, quarter, or eighth notes in keeping with the character of the works—into quarter, eighth, and sixteenth notes, whereby the bass accompaniment turns into a type of drum beat.

[148] A few great composers sometimes allow the same bass to continue for many measures. However, by examining only the upper voices it will be found that a delightful variety and diversity of harmony is formed above the same bass note. Thus one must not presume that the harmony lacks variety wherever the same notes are repeated several times in one or two voices. Great composers also know how to stir the ear by diversity where the eye believes it perceives monotony. But those who do not understand this search in vain to make their tedious monotony tolerable by endless alterations between *piano* and *forte*. However, one must guard against holding or repeating one note too long in the highest voice. It is not tolerable for more than two or at most four measures.

For the sake of good diversity of harmony one can never recommend enough to young composers that they study the four-part works of Handel, Bach, and Graun with persistent diligence. But before they are able to do this with desirable success, they must be familiar with double counterpoint.

2. Strictness of progression for each individual voice as well as for all four voices simultaneously depends in large part on the precise observance of the general rules concerning progression (see above, p. 159), and the special rules stated above in some of the preceding chapters. If dissonances are properly prepared and resolved, if one carefully observes the warnings given in the ninth chapter about harmonic and unharmonic progression, and finally if one has become sufficiently familar with what was fully prescribed in the fourth chapter about every four-part chord, about omission of some and doubling of other intervals, and about the avoidance of forbidden fifths and octaves, then one has no need of knowing much more about this point. We want to mention here only a few observations not contained in the preceding chapters.

The third can never be omitted from the harmony. From this it follows that in four-part writing the octave from the bass of a sixth chord should not be doubled twice in succession, because either the sixth, which is essential to this chord, or the third would then have to be omitted. Therefore the first inversion of the C triad cannot occur as at (A) in example 10.3, but as at (B).

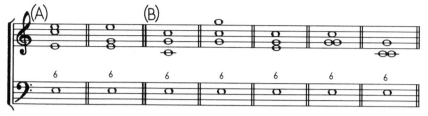

EXAMPLE 10.3

[149] Several fourths in succession must not be used when the lowest inner voice is separated from the two highest ones and is close to the bass. In such a situation they are just as offensive as successive fifths. But when all the upper voices are close together and less far removed from the bass, one can write as many fourths in succession as desired.

Sometimes it happens that one imagines hearing forbidden fifths and octaves even though they cannot be discovered in the notes. This can happen when the two highest voices are played by the same kind of instrument, since the ear sometimes confuses the first and second violin with one another. Here we shall provide only one example as warning to composers: The phrase at (A) in example 10.4 sounds as if it were written as at (B).

[150] Even though one has to watch out for forbidden fifths and octaves

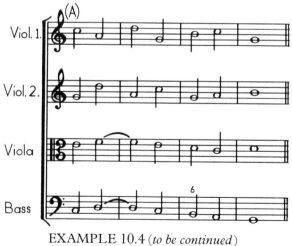

EXAMPLE 10.4 (*to be continued*)

EXAMPLE 10.4 (*continued*)

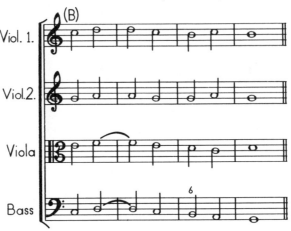

in four-part writing, there are situations where they can be written because their bad effect can be lessened.

Thus several fifths can be written in succession when one ascends four tones from the fifths, particularly when these fifths occur between the tenor and bass, as in example 10.5

EXAMPLE 10.5

Here fifths appear at (a), (b), (c), and (d). Since the fifth from the bass at (a) ascends four steps, this makes the following fifth at (b) permissible; and since this one also ascends by four steps, the following one at (c) is permitted. At (d) there is an additional one that can be justified by the passing notes in the bass. But here the fifth of the bass at the five-four chord has been doubled, thereby avoiding the two fifths that would have resulted in the soprano and tenor if the octave of the bass had been used.

[151] Thus such fifths are used even by good harmonists, though only in an emergency. We mention this so that young composers, should they come

across such places in the works of great masters, do not presume that they need not be quite so careful about being strict. Those great composers know how to disguise the errors that necessity extorts from them, so to speak. Wherever such places are found, one must consider carefully how they were treated by them. Thus it would be futile to justify the fifths at (A) in example 10.6 on the basis that one had found the passage at (B) in the work of a great master. Nevertheless, even though forbidden fifths and octaves become tolerable in four-part writing as a result of such leaps of a fourth, it is better to take care and instead to omit something from the harmony. Thus the passage at (A) in example 10.7 would be preferable to the one at (B).

[152] In three-part writing the disagreeable effect of fifths and octaves is no longer obscured by the above-mentioned leaps of a fourth. Thus they are permissible in this manner perhaps only in pseudocounterpoint.[b] On the

EXAMPLE 10.6

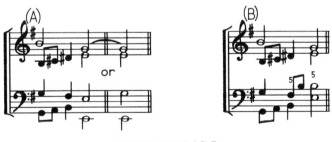

EXAMPLE 10.7

[b]Kirnberger does not explain what he means by *künstlichen contrapunkten*.

contrary, they can be used without hesitation in writing for more than four parts; yet they are always best in contrary motion.

Two fifths, where one is perfect, the other small, can be used in succession without hesitation, especially in descending motion, as in example 10.8. Yet J. S. Bach had such a sensitive ear that even this was sometimes offensive to him. Thus we find that he avoided the perfect fifth following the small one, as at (a) in example 10.9, by doubling the fifth of the triad, as at (b) or (c).

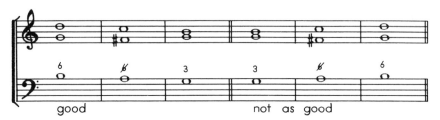

EXAMPLE 10.8

EXAMPLE 10.9

[153] Capellmeister Graun preferred the second type to the first, especially when the minor third from the bass was not in the signature but had to be formed by raising the diminished third with a sharp. He preferred to double the small fifth, as at (b) or (c) in example 10.10, rather than the large one, as at (a).

EXAMPLE 10.10

In certain situations some try to avoid forbidden fifths by having two voices proceed together to the third. But when this third is major, especially when it is accidental and indicated by a sharp, as in the last measure of [the first progression in] example 10.11, this method is not good. Moreover, the voice directly above the bass could not be sung as written here at (a).[c]

EXAMPLE 10.11

A special but permissible case of writing fifths and octaves in contrary motion in order to avoid direct fifths is shown in example 10.12.

EXAMPLE 10.12

[154] Forbidden fifths can also be avoided by the crossing of two voices, as is shown in example 10.13, where without this crossing a forbidden progression by augmented second (a) or fourth (b) would occur. Indeed, at (c) there are two perfect fifths that exist only as a result of the stepwise progression but are not at all displeasing owing to the dissonant four-two chord.

The crossing of two voices is permitted to avoid octaves and fifths. [See example 10.14.] [155] It is also permissible when a triad or its first inversion, the sixth chord, results from crossing of the bass, as at (a) in example 10.15. It is prohibited only when the six-four chord results from the crossing of the tenor below the bass at the end of a period, as at (b).

[c]Kirnberger does not explain why the tenor voice at (a) in example 10.11 would be difficult to sing. Possibly he objects to the direct progression of the chromatically altered d to e-sharp, which would normally lead to e-natural.

EXAMPLE 10.13

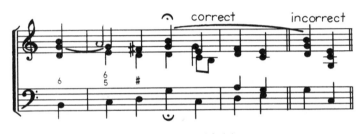

EXAMPLE 10.14

EXAMPLE 10.15

In the situation where the consonant six-four chord can be used in the middle of a period, it makes no difference whether the bass or tenor has the lowest note.

This restriction refers only to such cases where, for example, a vocal composition in four parts is sung without organ with a sixteen-foot stop or a string bass.

However, the tenor can go below the bass in a similar way without error only if a string bass or a lower bass on the organ supports the higher one. Thus the progression at (A) in example 10.16 would be incorrect without a string bass and good with one. [156] With the support of a lower bass this passage would sound as at (B).

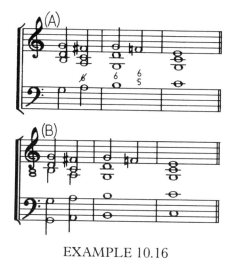

EXAMPLE 10.16

How even more liberties may be taken in so-called florid counterpoint will be shown in the next chapter.

Those fifths and octaves that are avoided by the crossing of parts in instrumental ensembles or vocal music cannot occur in this manner on the organ, piano, or harpsichord, because the crossing of voices is not noticeable there.

3. But the greatest strictness of writing does not insure that the four-part piece will be perfect; each voice must also have its own proper and flowing line, and all voices together must combine favorably.

Above all, each voice must have its individual and flowing line. One must not fancy having written four parts when several voices are doubled at the octave.[66] [157] In the entire science of composition there is perhaps

66. One occasionally comes across compositions that appear as if they consist of very many voices, but which in fact have only three or four. The alto goes with the bass and the tenor with the soprano in octaves. In this way one could easily make a composition that in fact has only three voices appear as if it consisted of 10, 12, and more voices. Consider, for example, the following arrangement:

nothing more difficult than for each of the four voices to have its own flowing line as well as for a single character to be retained in them all, so that a single perfect totality results from their union. In this respect the late Capellmeister Bach of Leipzig has perhaps surpassed all composers in the world. For that reason his chorales as well as his larger works are to be recommended most highly to all composers as the best models for diligent study.[67] Even skilled composers will be able to convince themselves of this more easily if they attempt to add an alto and tenor to the bass and soprano of one of his chorales, and to make these voices just as singable and as expressive as are the other two.

The good line of each voice depends mainly on simple progressions of small intervals. Wherever there are many large leaps in one voice, the line loses its gracefulness, and the voices cross one another, causing the ear to become totally confused. Since it is impossible to establish in rules what is required for this, the best advice that can be given to prospective composers

------

(*Footnote 66 continued*)

Together with the first soprano would go:

the first oboe	} in unison
the first violin	
the first flute an octave higher	
the first tenor	} an octave lower
the first horn	

Together with the second soprano or alto:

the second oboe	} in unison
the second violin	
the second flute an octave higher	
the second tenor	} an octave lower
the second horn	

The vocal bass would normally go with the second tenor in unison with the bass [violoncello].

| the viola | an octave higher |
| the string bass | an octave lower |

This would give the appearance of sixteen voices, which are basically only three.

67. Because of the great profit that young composers can derive from the works of this great man, I have resolved to publish a collection of a hundred of his chorales in the near future. [Through Kirnberger's diligent efforts a collection of Bach's four-part chorales (*BWV* 253–438) was eventually published by C. P. E. Bach in four volumes (Leipzig, 1784–87).]

is that they study the works of our greatest classical composers with persistent diligence and use them as models.

We shall show by just a single example how bad and unsingable certain
forbidden progressions are. [158] By examining the tenor voice in example
10.17, which is taken from the chorale *Von Gott will ich nicht lassen*, one will
discover that it would be almost impossible to sing in this way. From c[1] of
the second measure to d-sharp[1] in the third, there is an augmented second;
and in the same voice from the third to the fourth measure, from d-sharp[1]
down to g, there is an augmented fifth. At the same time there is an
augmented fourth in the alto from f-sharp[1] down to c[[1]].

EXAMPLE 10.17

At (a) in example 10.18, the progression from c-sharp[1] to its diminished
third e-flat[[1]] is particularly bad and impossible to sing, despite the intervening g, which likewise is a forbidden leap of a fourth. This c-sharp, since it is
the leading tone, must first be followed by the harmony d before one can go
from there to e-flat, as at (b), not to mention the octaves, which occur from e-
flat to d with the bass in the first example.

EXAMPLE 10.18

Although we are dealing here only with plain counterpoint—where
note is set against note—it can still be noted in advance that it is very bad in
four- or even in three-part works for a voice to be so composed that it stands
out greatly from the others, whereby these voices serve only to accompany

it, as it were. [159] This goes totally against the nature of four-part writing.[68] Wherever possible, the voices must have equal beauty.

Nevertheless, particular care must be taken that the highest voice have the greatest strictness and attractive harmony in relation to the bass, since the ear is most sensitive to the highest notes. Thirds and sixths, which can be alternated, are best suited to the highest voice. Here and there a fifth, even less frequently an octave, can be used. The greatest harmonists assert that harmony, even in works for very many voices, always suffers a bit when the octave of the bass is situated in the outermost voice. However, this cannot always be avoided without damaging the smoothness of one of the voices.

Direct passing octaves and fifths between the highest voice and bass must also be assiduously avoided. It is not necessary to consider the outer voices in relation to middle voices with such care, although even there passing fifths are noticeable to a fine ear. One even finds that the late Bach has sometimes avoided hidden fifths in the inner voices by doubling the fifth instead of the octave of an ordinary chord, as at (a) in example 10.19.

EXAMPLE 10.19

[160] Although it is better at the end to double the octave after the major third of the dominant of a key, one is sometimes obliged to disregard good voice leading and to use the fifth instead of the octave in order to avoid octaves in relation to the bass. [See example 10.20.] Since one has to be particularly careful about having a good melody in each voice, and, as is well known, the major third of the dominant leads best and most pleasingly to the octave of the following bass, one should try to arrange the harmony in

68. One sometimes encounters a trio in which the first voice completely obscures the others to the extent that they lack melodic coherence. This error is made most often by composers who particularly want to display in a most brilliant light the part and instrument they play themselves. But they do not consider that those who have the other parts cannot possibly play with the proper feeling in such a situation. How is one to play well if nothing of the affection and of the true expression of the piece is contained in his entire part, but is concentrated solely in a single voice?

EXAMPLE 10.20

advance so that difficulties do not arise. If chorales are heard with trombones and cornets or trumpets playing the soprano, and the alto trombone has the above-mentioned third, one will realize how awful it sounds if the third does not ascend to the octave of the bass.

Since the alto trombone, next to the cornet, stands out most clearly, nothing is more unbearable than if such a third, instead of going up by a half step, progresses down by a major third, in which case it becomes difficult and unpleasant to sing.

Such chorales, in which the alto progresses like this down by a major third from the third of the dominant, occur only when choirs are very full or accompanied by instruments. But it has a bad effect when there are only four singers because the alto voice stands out just as much as does the alto trombone in relation to the cornet. In the next voice, namely, the tenor, the third is allowed more freedom. [See example 10.21.]

EXAMPLE 10.21

[161] The following chorales [examples 10.22–25] are inserted here as models of strict and good four-part writing.[69]

69. In these chorales almost all dissonant chords have been avoided, and only the triad and its first inversion, the sixth chord, used, since in this style the greatest caution is necessary with regard to fifths and octaves.

Furthermore one cannot aspire here to have a particularly good melody in all parts. It is sufficient simply to avoid fifths and octaves as well as all forbidden

EXAMPLE 10.22 (*to be continued*)

progressions, and likewise not to exceed the ranges of the vocal parts, which can be managed either with open or close harmony.

On this occasion it is important to know that the soprano part in the chorus does not go above g² or below d¹. The tenor has the same range but an octave lower, from d up to g¹.

The alto has the same range as the soprano, but a fifth lower, namely, from g to c¹ [c²].

The bass is an octave lower than the alto, namely, from A to c¹. It can go up to d¹ without hesitation.

EXAMPLE 10.22 (*continued*)

EXAMPLE 10.23

EXAMPLE 10.23 (*continued*)

EXAMPLE 10.24 (*to be continued*)

EXAMPLE 10.24 (*continued*)

EXAMPLE 10.25 (*to be continued*)

EXAMPLE 10.25 (*continued*)

EXAMPLE 10.25 (*continued*)

[170] In three-voice writing careful consideration must be given to the following special rules in addition to the general rules of strict harmony.

[171] When the upper parts are widely separated from the bass, for example by more than ten tones, they may not progress in fourths. But this is tolerable when the bass is closer to the middle voice. Example 10.26 would sound very bad. On the other hand the upper voices could remain as they are here if the bass were to be placed an octave higher. Yet this would still not help at all if the upper voices were sung and the bass played by an instrument. One knows from experience that in such a case, even with the best orchestra, almost nothing at all is heard besides the voices of the singers.

EXAMPLE 10.26

From this it follows that in three-part writing both the upper voices must always be written in such a way that the bass could be taken away. For that reason one has to watch out here for many sixths in succession that form progressions of fourths in the upper voices. If the two concertizing [*concertirend*] voices always progress by thirds and sixths, the piece becomes rather paltry, although it sometimes sounds well in very short passages.[70]

To clarify this we recommend study of examples 10.27 and 10.28. [172] These examples are composed for two singers but are as if for three with the addition of the bass. In the first, the singers proceed in sixths and thirds; in the second, consecutive thirds as well as sixths are avoided. This type is preferable to the first. However, in general, such compositions for two singers must be written in consideration of the vocal parts, that is, in the manner of two-part works, which will be discussed later.

When the upper two voices are concertizing, one has to take care in this type of composition that these voices are not too far apart, as they would be,

EXAMPLE 10.27

70. In general, duos for two concertizing voices and a bass or more accompanying parts must be written in such a way that the two voices alone sound as beautiful as a strict two-part piece. This can be achieved only by composers who are sufficiently versed in the science of fugue and its required techniques, such as strict and free imitation, and canon. The most perfect models of this style are the works of Handel, Bach, and Graun. The last I hope to publish soon for young composers and amateurs. [See *Duetti, terzetti, quintetti, sestetti ed alcuni chori della opere del signore Carlo Enrico Graun*, I–IV (Berlin and Königsberg, 1773–74).]

EXAMPLE 10.28

for example, if the highest part were composed for flute or violin and the second for bassoon or violoncello, or, in vocal writing if there were only a soprano and a bass.

[173] Here, too, one usually would not want to let one voice cross over or under the other, because this damages the melodic line of the highest part. This occurs only with trios and duets of two concertizing voices. Nevertheless it is sometimes necessary to do this when fifths and octaves cannot be avoided in any other way.

In a three-part composition where two equal instruments are concertizing, there is no advantage in having one imitate the other, since it always sounds like a repetition of the preceding. Two unlike instruments can do this, but with like ones transpositions in counterpoint at the octave help. The two upper parts for violin at (A) in example 10.29 would sound exactly as at (B). It would sound better if some notes were transposed in counterpoint at the octave, as at (C).

[174] Whenever possible the octave or fifth of the bass is to be avoided in the highest voice, except at the beginning and end or to articulate phrases better. Since they sound too complete, they set the ear at rest to some degree. Preferably the third above the bass should occur in the highest voice, so that the ear can never rest except at real phrase divisions. In this way the melody acquires complete coherence.

Care should also be taken not to let the bass cross over one of the upper voices, since the nature of the chord is thereby altered. This is especially true

EXAMPLE 10.29

EXAMPLE 10.30

with a triad that sounds like a six-four chord, as can be seen in example 10.30, where the last chord sounds exactly like the six-four chord at *.

This should suffice regarding three-part composition.

Writing in two parts is the most difficult of all and cannot be done perfectly well until complete knowledge of four-part writing has been achieved. There are two types. Either there is only one solo voice accompanied by a thorough bass, or there are two concertizing voices without other accompaniment. Writing is most difficult in the latter situation, because one is much too restricted. Neither the octave nor fifth can ever be placed in the highest part, except where required at cadences. Since the third is indispensable to the harmony, a close would always be formed whenever the octave or fifth occurs in the highest voice. Therefore only thirds and sixths, with the fourth and seventh as their displacements, can be used in the highest voice. The ninth can also be used; however, the bass or lower voice must not remain stationary for the resolution but must either move up by a third so that the ninth is resolved to a sixth, or down by a third so that the ninth is resolved to a tenth, as is shown in example 10.31.

EXAMPLE 10.31

[175] In writing for two voices, one must be careful at cadences not to let the second voice close from the dominant to the tonic, as the bass normally does. If the upper voice closes through the fifth of the dominant, as at (a) in example 10.32, the third of this dominant, or the leading tone of the tonic, is used in the lower voice. But if the upper voice closes from the leading tone, the lower voice goes from the second scale degree to the tonic, as at (b); in this situation the bass cadence could also be used in the lower voice, as at (c). However, it is necessary that the lower voice have the dominant of the tonic as its penultimate note when the close is not to the principal tonic, as in the preceding examples, but goes instead to its lower third, as at (d), where the cadence leads to A minor instead of C major, even though the upper voice progresses as it did at (b) and (c). In place of g in the lower voice one could not use its dominant d here, as happened in example (b). If a half cadence is made on the dominant of the key, and the fifth of this dominant is in the highest voice, the second voice must then have the third of this dominant; but if the third is in the highest voice, the second voice can have this dominant itself. Most *bicinia* for trumpets as well as horns close with the tonic in the upper voice and the third in the lower voice. But it is better when

EXAMPLE 10.32

both close to the octave, or possibly even to the unison, which is particularly necessary with low instruments.

Because of the danger that a third part may be felt as missing, this writing for two parts—two flutes, or other instruments or voices that sound alike—is so difficult that I know only of the flute duets of W. Friedemann Bach, eldest son of J. S. Bach, that can serve as perfect models of this type of composition. [176] Many duets are subject to the danger that more than one voice could be added to them.

It is even more difficult to write a simple melody without any accompaniment so harmonically that it would not be possible to add a voice without error, even disregarding the fact that the added voice would be most unsingable and awkward. Of this type we have the six unaccompanied sonatas for violin and six for violoncello by J. S. Bach. But here we are simply talking about compositions written for one voice.

These, then, are the most important rules that, when observed, make writing in four, three, or two parts strict and also pleasing to the ear.

Writing for many voices—five, six, and more—is less difficult because the greatest strictness no longer matters in the middle voices. Frequent hidden octaves and fifths, even direct ones in contrary motion, can occur in the inner voices, so that the bad sound that they produce in works for fewer voices is obscured and rendered imperceptible by the other parts.

In writing for many voices, the same chords are used as would be used in writing for four voices, except that one or more intervals in these chords are doubled without omitting others, so that the correct number of voices results.

In writing for five parts, the fifth voice usually doubles the octave of the triad, next its fifth, and rarely the third, because the latter often results in forbidden octaves. Therefore the three forms of the triad arranged as a five-part chord are those shown in example 10.33.

With the sixth chord, the sixth, third, and octave of the bass can be doubled; but the latter must be used with greater caution because the octave

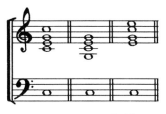

EXAMPLE 10.33

is the third of the actual root. [177] Therefore there are also three forms of the four-part [*sic*, five-part] sixth chord, as shown in example 10.34.

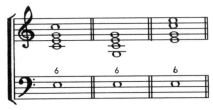

EXAMPLE 10.34

At full cadences it is necessary to double the octave of the bass, and it would be wrong not to do so, as can be seen from example 10.35.

EXAMPLE 10.35

If the octave of the root is retained, no doubling is necessary with the seventh chord, since it has four parts already. But if the octave is omitted, the fifth or third can be doubled. As is the case with the triad, the major third can rarely be doubled, but doubling of the minor third presents no difficulty. However, the seventh itself can never be doubled.

With the inversions of the seventh chord it is easy to determine which interval should be doubled as long as one is careful that the seventh of the root is never doubled. Thus the fifth in the six-five chord and the third in the six-four-three chord must not be doubled; and in the four-two chord the octave of the bass must not occur in the upper voices.

With the nonessential dissonances, the ninth and the fourth, either the fifth or the octave of the root is doubled. But with the ninth, the fifth is preferable to the octave.

[178] These very remarks about doubling also apply to writing for six and more parts, where two intervals rather than one are doubled; namely, both the octave and the fifth.

In writing for six voices, particular care has to be taken with the seven-

EXAMPLE 10.36

six-four-two chord not to confuse it with the nine-seven-six-four chord. In the first, the consonances from the fifth of the bass, as the proper root, are doubled; but with the other, the consonances from the bass itself, as can be seen in example 10.36.[71] These progressions occur only with so-called organ point,[72a] where the bass is stationary. In the second measure, the first harmony of the upper voices is the seventh chord on E, which is the actual root here and the dominant of the key to which it closes. [179] From this it is clearly evident that the note b, which is the second in measure two, becomes the ninth in measure three. As the second, it is the fifth of the real root and is consonant, because the note a is the nonessential dissonance. Therefore this second can progress freely, since the note a resolves to the third of the actual root. But since the b of the second measure is stationary and becomes the displacement of the octave in the last measure, it must resolve downward. According to what has been stated above, it can also be seen that the figures

$$\begin{matrix} 9 \\ 7 \\ 6 \\ 2 \end{matrix} \; or \; \begin{matrix} 9 \\ 4 \end{matrix}$$

71. The feature that clearly distinguishes the seven-six-four-two chord from the nine-seven-six-four chord is that the major seventh in the seven-six-four-two chord can be delayed by the nonessential dissonance, the octave, as at (a). But this cannot occur with the nine-seven-six-four chord, as at (b).

72a. An organ point is actually a full close prolonged by melodic or harmonic elaborations; it normally is found at the end of a composition, but sometimes even in the middle. The bass sustains the dominant of the key to which it is closing, above which many types of harmonies, connected as a rule with one another by ties and suspensions, are heard in the upper voices, until the full cadence finally follows. This lingering on a sustained bass note sometimes occurs on the tonic itself, where, after the final cadence has already been introduced, the cadence is repeated again from the tonic triad through many harmonies.

could only be used on the downbeat. It is unnecessary to discuss in detail the doubling of intervals of dissonant chords in seven, eight, or more parts, since one can be guided by what has already been said.

Since it is a general rule that only the consonances from the true root must be doubled, the main thing with all doublings is that the true root be kept in view, and, in conformity to the remark just made, that the second be properly distinguished from the ninth. To clarify the matter more fully, let us imagine the five-part progressions in example 10.37, which we want to make sound even fuller. Everyone can easily see how the doubling of the voices must happen here from what has already been stated, since it is obvious which note is the root in each measure. But if these progressions should appear as in example 10.38, the actual root at (a) would be b with the seventh; consequently the consonances of this note b would be doubled here, especially those—as was already demonstrated—that sound the best

EXAMPLE 10.37

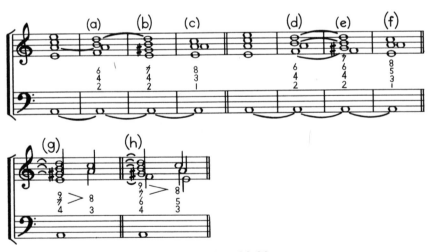

EXAMPLE 10.38

in four parts.[72b] [180] At (b) the true root is e with the seventh. At (d) the chord is the same as at (a), but at (e) the ninth (here the 6 of the bass) is added to the seventh of the root E. At (g) the harmony of the upper voices at the downbeat is the same as at (b), but since the bass has the actual root here and the dissonances are suspensions, the consonances from the bass must be doubled, since at (a) the consonances of the root E were to be doubled. The chord at (h) is related to the one at (g) in a similar way.

Examples 10.39 and 10.40 can be considered as illustrations of a very fine five-part and a six-part vocal composition.

EXAMPLE 10.39 (*to be continued*)

72b. Since with such stationary basses the consonances of the actual root become dissonances in relation to the bass note, the doubled notes are dissonances of the bass. For this reason some believe that the dissonances may also be doubled. However, these doubled dissonances are really consonances of the root.

EXAMPLE 10.39 (*continued*)

EXAMPLE 10.39 (*continued*)

EXAMPLE 10.40 (*to be continued*)

EXAMPLE 10.40 (*continued*)

EXAMPLE 10.40 (*continued*)

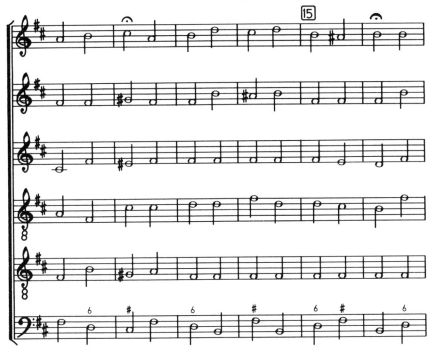

EXAMPLE 10.40 (*continued*)

[185] In the first chord of the second part of the chorale on page 196, above, the B minor chord could have been used instead of the E chord, as shown at (a) on page 198. But then the bass is four tones above the tenor, and thus the triad is actually changed into the six-four chord, which cannot be used at the beginning. Since a string bass or organ stop of sixteen feet is always assumed in the accompaniment of such a chorale, the fundamental is still below the tenor, which thus remains an inner voice.

In the chorale itself, as it stands on p. 196, this B has not been placed in the bass because from there to E-sharp would have formed a forbidden leap of an augmented fourth. This is improved by inverting the B–E-sharp, thus making it easier to sing.

The main melodic line or *cantus firmus* can be placed in any voice when writing for more voices; however, when it is placed in the bass, one must be careful that it conclude with cadences that belong to the main key.

EXAMPLE 10.41 (*to be continued*)

EXAMPLE 10.41 (*continued*)

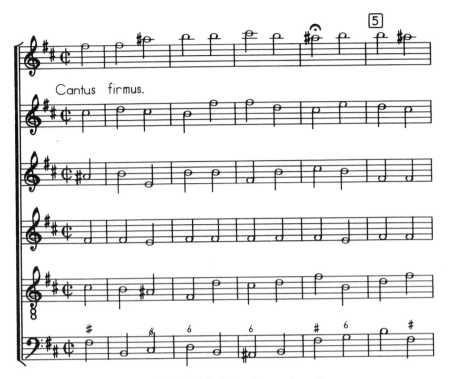

EXAMPLE 10.42 (*to be continued*)

EXAMPLE 10.42 (*continued*)

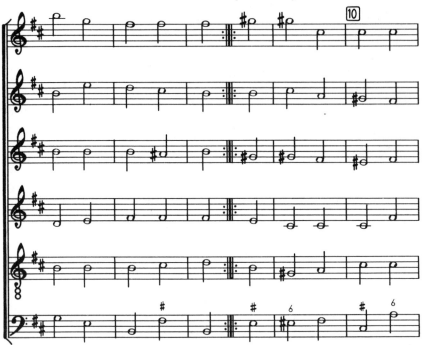

EXAMPLE 10.42 (*continued*)

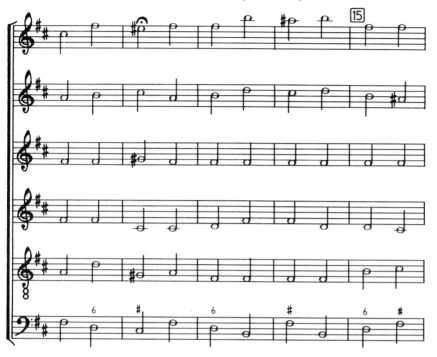

EXAMPLE 10.42 (*continued*)

CHAPTER 11

Embellished or Florid Simple Counterpoint

[189] Melody is similar to walking in several respects. Simple plain melody, which is called chorale, resembles the common walk, which progresses by equal steps; embellished melody, on the other hand, is analogous to the decorative motions that occur in dances, where each step is embellished. It is very important in music that one grasp this similarity, since the most essential qualities of embellished melody are best understood through this comparison.

Consider the melody in example 11.1. [190] Note that the manner in which the voice progresses is identical to the common ordinary walk. Here each note and each syllable of the text represents a step to further progress. All these steps are identical with regard to stress as well as rate of occurrence. One can proceed quicker or slower with these steps without the motion losing its simple unaffected nature or its even character; this can also happen with melody. The preceding melody can also be sung twice as fast, as in example 11.2. Likewise with example 11.3.

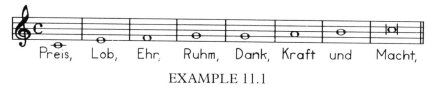

Preis, Lob, Ehr, Ruhm, Dank, Kraft und Macht,

EXAMPLE 11.1

Preis, Lob, Ehr, Ruhm, Dank, Kraft, und Macht,

EXAMPLE 11.2

Trau auf Gott in al - len Sa - chen

EXAMPLE 11.3

Only the last step is held longer, since one cannot stop suddenly, as is also the case with walking. Here two tones occupy the same time as only one did previously. The same number of steps are taken as before, but in half the time. these same steps could also be made twice as fast again, as at (A) and (B) in example 11.4.

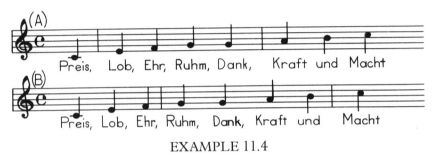

(A)

Preis, Lob, Ehr, Ruhm, Dank, Kraft und Macht

(B)

Preis, Lob, Ehr, Ruhm, Dank, Kraft und Macht

EXAMPLE 11.4

The time taken for one step in the first melody [example 11.1] is just the same as that taken by four steps in the last one [at (B) in example 11.4]; this time is called a measure. Therefore a time or measure can encompass one or more steps, depending on whether the melody is fast or slow. However, all measures must have the same number of steps as long as they progress at the same rate of speed. [191] Thus the number of notes that are sung in a specific portion of time, or in a measure, determines the fast or slow motion of a melody. Occasionally the term measure is applied to this motion. Thus one says, for instance, that the melody is in 2/4 or 4/4 time, etc., in order to indicate that two or four steps occur in one measure.[73]

It must be carefully noted that the nature of the plain or unembellished simple melody lies in the fact that each note occupies one step, that is, one of the principal time divisions of the measure—a whole measure when it is not

73. One should note that it is not the purpose here to explain the various kinds of measures and to account for their impact on expression. This material will be discussed in the second volume. Here only the different note values in relation to one another will be considered.

partitioned into several time divisions throughout the entire piece, as in example 11.1; a half measure when it is partitioned into two time divisions throughout, as in example 11.2; a quarter measure when each is partitioned into four time divisions, as in example 11.4. Hence these are the types of simple melody.

On the other hand, the embellished or florid melody is distinguished by having notes that do not correspond to a step, or do not occupy a full time division of the measure, as in example 11.5. Here the two notes before the first barline amount to only one step; the following eight notes between the first and second barlines occupy four steps. However, the steps are embellished, just as one might make a little side motion with the lifted foot instead of moving straight forward.

EXAMPLE 11.5

Just as each step in walking can be embellished by various little motions before the foot comes down again, melodic steps can also be decorated by several notes. After the note that actually represents the downstep or the beginning of the step has been given, many types of notes—involving conjunct or disjunct motion—can be used as decoration during the time that the downstep would have been held in a simple melody; however, all these notes together with the downstep must occupy no more than one principal time division of the measure. [192] Whenever there are several voices, one of them can have just plain or simple steps while another is decorated, as in example 11.6.

Here the bass has the simple melody, in which each note constitutes one step; each step in the upper voice encompasses four notes, the first of which

EXAMPLE 11.6

always represents the downstep of the foot, while the following three are little motions that decorate the step. However, these four notes must occupy no more time than is required of one step in this 4/4 measure. In technical language this way of embellishing the melody is called *counterpoint per diminutionem*, since the notes have to be diminished in their duration or type. Accordingly this can be called *florid counterpoint* or florid writing.

In addition to florid writing, there is yet another type that arises when the notes enter other than would seem to be required by the time divisions of the measure. Theorists call this *anticipation* or *retardation* of the melody.[74] Both will be clarified by the following examples. [193] First consider the two-part unembellished passage in example 11.7, and then the same notes altered as in example 11.8.

EXAMPLE 11.7

EXAMPLE 11.8

In the progressions designated by (a), one observes that the bass begins on the first step before the upper voice enters. This has the effect on all following steps that the two voices never enter at the same time, but at different points of time. These staggered attacks cause the passage to have an entirely different motion and character than the first type [example 11.7], even though the same notes occur in both. These attacks that are staggered between two parts are called *contretems* by the French. Furthermore the harmony is completely changed, since every note in the upper voice remains

74. *Anticipatio* and *retardatio*.

for an eighth of a measure after the entrance of the new bass note, against which the note in the upper voice is dissonant. Consequently, consonances and dissonances are always heard in alternation here, while everything was consonant in example 11.7.

In the progressions designated by (b), the two voices enter together on the first beat. However, since the upper voice does not occupy the entire step, but moves to another note halfway through it and then continues this way, this has the same two-fold effect as the situation at (a).

We will call this type of writing *syncopation*,[a] and this manner of composition *syncopated counterpoint*.

[194] These are the two types of florid counterpoint. In the first type there are auxiliary notes that are not necessary to the progression of the melody but merely decorate it. In the other type the melody deviates from its direct course, although no notes other than those necessary for each step occur. Both types can serve to give the melody the true character of expression that it is supposed to have, and sometimes also to embellish it pleasantly. In each type a certain caution is necessary—otherwise the melody could easily lose its euphonious quality and become disagreeable. What is to be observed in this matter is to be discussed in this chapter. But before these rules can be stated, a few explanations must first be given.

Here we are considering every main part of the measure as a full step or as the downstep of the foot, so that if one wished to indicate the motion of the melody by beating time, one beat would have to occur on each time division of the measure. However, the first beat would always be the most emphatic. There are motions or types of progressions where the situation is different, and where, for example, only the first time division of the measure corresponds to the downstep of the foot, while the others represent only hasty downsteps, even though they pose as real steps. Such measures represent a step as it occurs in dances under the name "pas," which are often composed of several hasty steps, like the "pas" of a minuet. These types of measures will not be discussed here, but only those in which each main time division of the measure is regarded as a downbeat, that is, as a complete step or "pas." Here the intention is merely to show how one simple step that is a principal note could be embellished.

---

[a]The term used here by Kirnberger is *ungleicher Gesang*, which might literally be translated as "uneven" or "staggered" motion; throughout this chapter it has been translated as *syncopation*. The reader is cautioned that the term syncopation, as used here, has a limited meaning; it refers specifically to the staggered motion that results from anticipation or retardation of one part.

For this reasons we will always introduce two voices here: one has only ponderous notes falling on the downbeat or downstep, which represent the really heavy steps of the gait or syllables of words; the other voice, however, will take just as many steps, but embellish them.

Thus we first have to consider *florid*, then *syncopated* writing here. The florid melody can be of two types: either the notes serving as embellishment are taken from the harmony of the principal note, as in example 11.9, which we will call *arpeggiation*; or they are not all taken from the harmony of the principal note, but some are sounded only as pleasant or suitable transitions to the next notes. [195] Such notes are called *passing tones*.

EXAMPLE 11.9

The transition through notes that do not belong to the harmony can be achieved in two ways. Either the passing note comes after the main note, as at (a) in example 11.10; this is called the *regular passing note*. Or the passing note falls directly at the beginning of the step or time division of the measure, and the main note follows directly after it, as at (b); this is called the *irregular passing note*. Sometimes both types alternate with one another, as at (c).[75] [196] Thus we will call this *passing motion*. This may be sufficient to clarify the technical terms.

Therefore we have three situations to be considered here: (1) *arpeggiation*; (2) *passing motion*; (3) *syncopation*. Each will be examined here individually, although all three are often used in a single composition, even in

75. In technical language the first type is called *transitus regularis*, the second *transitus irregularis*, and the third *transitus mixtus*.

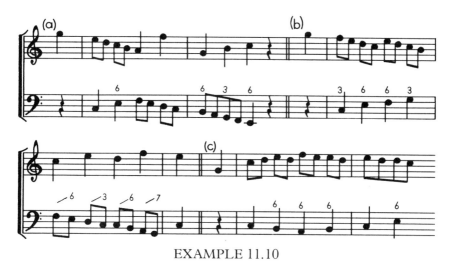

EXAMPLE 11.10

a single measure. However, before we examine each type, we must first present a few general rules about florid or embellished writing.

It is an essential quality of every composition of this type that its motion sound entirely unambiguous and its pace be properly measured by the meter, and not obscured or made uncertain by the embellishments. One must be able to perceive throughout with the greatest ease whether a measure contains two, four, or eight beats[b] in duple time, or three or six in triple time.

Thus, if the embellishments in one voice are such that the motion becomes uncertain, another voice must make it clear. For example, if half or whole notes appear in one voice in 4/4 time, another voice must have quarter notes. The same is true of similar cases.

Example 11.11 can serve as an example of this. [197] Since the motion is not indicated by the bass in the first two measures, it is determined by the upper part. But in the fourth measure it becomes clear from the bass, and in the third from the two parts together. The motion is expressed most easily and clearly by the bass notes. And this point must be carefully observed by the composer, since otherwise his writing will be confused. Particularly where the beats are obscured by ties in one voice must the motion be made clear in another part, as at the asterisks.

---

[b] For the remainder of the chapter the word *Schritt*, literally "step," has been translated as *beat* (of the measure). Kirnberger continues to use this word, rather than *Taktschlag*, because of the analogy drawn earlier between melody and walking.

EXAMPLE 11.11

To be sure, there are situations where great masters neglect this precise designation of the motion in single measures; but this happens for good reasons, either because the expression demands it, or because the intention is to stir the listener with something strange or unusual. An instance of this, from the opera *Cleopatra* by Graun, is given in example 11.12.[c]

EXAMPLE 11.12

[198] In the third and fourth measures both voices have a quarter note after the first eighth, even though the bass should have two eighths according to the rule given above. But, of course, one realizes that the composer wished to intensify the expression by stopping or remaining on this note.

Example 11.13 is from the opera *Tamerlano* by Handel.[d] At two places

[c]Carl Heinrich Graun's *Cleopatra e Cesare* was first performed at the inauguration of the Royal Opera in Berlin, 7 December 1742.

[d]George Frederic Handel's *Tamerlano* was premiered at the King's Theatre in London, 31 October 1724. This excerpt is the opening eight measures of an aria sung by Irene near the end of act 2. The double measures shown by Kirnberger are notated as two single measures in the following modern edition: Händel, *Werke*, vol. 69, ed. F. Chrysander (Leipzig, 1876); reprinted, 1966, by the Gregg Press (Ridgewood, N. J.), p. 84.

No che sei tan-to co-stan-te   nel-la   fe-de a me pro·mes·sa

EXAMPLE 11.13

in this example, two measures are joined so that they become one,[76] which produces a desirable emphasis here. All great masters make such exceptions, but they do it with deliberation.[77]

[199] On this occasion it must also be noted that the resolution of all nonessential dissonances should never occur on the same beat as the disso-

76. Although the second and third measures are joined together, they are still treated in the phrase in such a way that they are counted as two real measures. If one were to count from one barline to the next as one measure, the result would be a phrase of three measures. This style sometimes occurs in ballets, for instance in a *passepied*, *lourée*, and the like. However, the number of measures in a segment [of a phrase] must always be standard.

77. There are examples by very fine masters in which the parts move in different meters throughout. In this case the meter could be indicated for each particular part, as great composers have done with two parts by designating one with 12/8 and another with C, the symbol for common time. We note on this occasion that it is not right for the performer to divide half or even whole notes that sometimes occur in even 4/4 time into quarter notes by bow pressure or, on wind instruments, by blowing more strongly. This should not even be done when two notes are connected by a tie—the composer has already taken care that the motion is indicated in the other parts. On the other hand, the composer must not put the player in a difficult situation by having him pause where it is impossible to do so. This would happen if he wanted to write a pause where there must be a note. It is impossible to pause: (1) after a passage with very fast notes, because it is not possible to stop short with a sixteenth or thirty-second note but necessary that a longer note follow as a resting point; (2) after a dissonance, which must be followed by a consonance in the same part. The following examples will clarify both. Example A cannot be played as it is written, because it is impossible to stop with the notes marked by an asterisk. Therefore this passage would have to be written as at B.

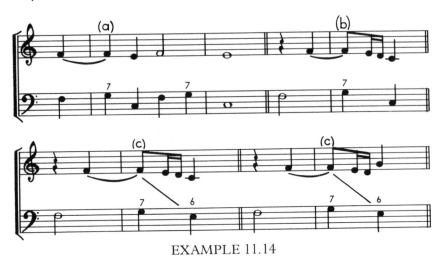

EXAMPLE 11.14

nance, but always on the following one, as at (a) in example 11.14; thus the resolution of the seventh at (b) would be incorrect. If one wanted to retain this same motion, the resolution would have to occur in the bass, as at (c).

[200] If a rest occurs in the bass at a place where a note defining the beat should occur, the notes in the upper voices must harmonize either with the preceding or following bass note; a new harmony cannot be used at the rest, since it would have no foundation. Therefore, example 11.15 would be totally wrong.

EXAMPLE 11.15

However, a dissonance can occur in the upper parts over a rest in the bass when it resolves above the following bass note, after the rest; but this dissonance must have its foundation in the preceding bass note. Example 11.16 is allowed, just as if a foundation were there.

[201] But where new harmonies appear above rests in the bass, the basis upon which the singer is to sense his notes is taken away to some extent. And

EXAMPLE 11.16

when harmonies appear frequently without foundation, the singer finally assumes that the parts are wrong, and this causes confusion. To understand how a singer is troubled by such errors, consider example 11.17. At (a), after the six-five chord on f-sharp, it is almost impossible for a sensitive singer to sing the G chord, since he still has the preceding unresolved six-five chord in his ear; he necessarily longs to hear the resolution of the fifth from the bass, as the seventh from the root.

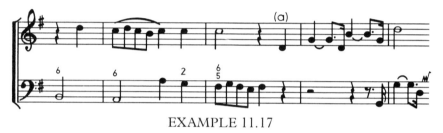

EXAMPLE 11.17

Wherever several notes occur on one beat, only one of them is the main note, and the others serve as decoration, whether this happens in one or several parts, with the same or a different harmony. [See example 11.18.]

EXAMPLE 11.18

The following is to be noted here in general. (1) Regarding the value or length of these notes that serve merely as decoration, one must pay attention to the type of motion that prevails in a piece. It is obvious that a slow tempo tolerates smaller decorations than a fast one. (2) The character of a piece or the prevailing expression requires or allows more or fewer embellishments. [202] A piece of a tender nature tolerates more little ornaments than a heroic piece. But it is not possible to give definite rules about this. A composer of genius and taste senses without rules the extent and limit that is to be observed.

However, since the different types of principal characters occur in the common dance melodies, aspiring composers can consider the works of the greatest masters in this genere as models which they must always follow. Here are a few observations that will make this study somewhat easier for a beginner.

Fast compositions in 4/4 time, as it appears in the *bourrée* or also in the *gavotte*, do not easily tolerate notes smaller than eighth notes. The same meter, but in a slow tempo, as it usually appears in *overtures* and *entrées*, tolerates sixteenth and even thirty-second notes.

In 3/4 meter of moderate tempo, as it appears in *minuets*, notes smaller than eighth notes are not to be used. However, the *sarabande*, which is also in 3/4 meter but has a slower tempo, tolerates sixteenth notes. The *polonaise*, which is faster than a sarabande and one-third slower than a minuet—so that a time span of eight measures in a polonaise is equal to twelve measures of a minuet—also tolerates only sixteenths as the fastest notes. But in polonaises that are designed for dancing, one should scrupulously avoid the manner common in Germany of placing two sixteenths after an eighth.

Passepieds in 3/8 meter also can tolerate only sixteenth notes. Those ballets that have changes of melodic motion almost every eight measures, like the *chaconne*, for example, tend now and then to have even thirty-second notes instead of the customary sixteenth notes. The tempo of each type can easily be determined from the fastest notes of a piece. The organization of each type will be discussed in more detail in the second volume.[78]

[203] Regarding embellishments in general, it is finally to be noted that they are not arbitrary but must be chosen with taste and feeling according to the character of a piece. Everyone senses that a fast spirited piece requires different embellishments than a tender or sad piece.[79] This will be discussed

---

78. Every beginner who wants to become well grounded in composition is advised to become familiar with the disposition of all types of ballets, because all types of characters and rhythm occur and can be observed most accurately in them. If one has no skill in these character pieces, it is impossible to give a definite character to a piece, which even every fugue must have. Those who study the fugues of J. S. Bach will find that each one always has its precisely defined character. This will not be attained by those who are incapable of giving a character to nonfugal compositions.

79. One occasionally hears singers use certain embellishments and mannerisms that were written down by the master for an adagio in other pieces as well, whereby the character of a piece is frequently damaged. The same is also to be observed in so-called cadenzas for the singer. These must always be in keeping with the character of a piece. A soloist must not presume that he can make do with a few rehearsed cadenzas everywhere.

in more detail in its proper place. Here it is appropriate to remark that similar embellishments and generally similar progressions must be chosen for places of similar character in a piece. Melodies as they sometimes appear by untrained composers—where all embellishments are arbitrary, where no measure in a piece has any similarity whatsoever with another—give the ear a confusing succession of notes that never say anything intelligible.

Observation of the similarity of embellishments is called *imitation* in the theory of composition; it is generally expressed by the Latin word *imitatio*.

However, one distinguishes between *free* and *strict* imitations. The latter appear mainly in fugues and fugal pieces, about which more will be said in the second part. Free imitations, however, must also be used in compositions that have nothing in common with fugues. As was stated, they are based on a similarity of progression and ornamentation. Instances of similar progressions are shown in example 11.19.

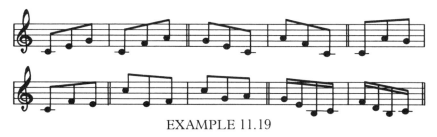

EXAMPLE 11.19

[204] A piece acquires its definite character from such imitations. But, as a result, the process of composing also becomes more difficult; it becomes all the more difficult the more precise is the similarity.

To give the beginner a clear concept of such imitations, we want to clarify the matter by an example [example 11.20]. Here one first sees a two-part chorale, after which the soprano is written in florid counterpoint in such a way that the ornamentation written above the first bass note is repeated above each following one at different intervals—that is, at the fourth on the first part of the second measure, at the third above the

EXAMPLE 11.20

following bass note, then at the fifth, and last at the octave. Such imitations become much easier if one chooses to stick less strictly to the degrees of ascent and descent as they appear in the first figure, and also if one inverts the figure completely.

In pieces with several main melodies, such free imitations in the different parts must be made audible. In this way the whole receives its unity of character.

[205] Now it is time for us to consider each type of florid counterpoint separately.

I. The first is *arpeggiation,* which, as was already explained, results when two, three, four, or more notes from the consonant harmony are written in succession against one note of the bass or fundamental part.[e]

Here it is to be noted in general that one main voice is, to a certain degree, transformed into several voices by arpeggiation. When, for example, two eighths in arpeggiation are written in place of each quarter that constitutes a beat, the composition could be heard as having three parts. For that reason arpeggiation must be structured in such a way that a strict three-part composition would result if successive notes were heard simultaneously.

Thus, if two notes from the arpeggiated harmony are soundes simultaneously, one must add to the bass note those notes that are required in three-part writing according to what has been said about this in the preceding chapter. Thus, for example, one cannot use the fifth and octave above the bass with the triad; the third must be present except at the beginning of a piece, where the octave can be sounded after the fifth.

We shall clarify this by a few examples. The two-part passage at (A) in example 11.21 would, because of the arpeggiations, sound like the three-part passage at (B).

[206] This three-part piece is strict throughout, and the two successive fifths in contrary motion at (a) in example 11.21 are not an error, since they sound as at (b) in the three-part piece. For just this reason the three successive fifths at (a) in example 11.22 would be permitted, since the phrase sounds as if it were written as at (b).

Although one must always be careful in two- and three-part writing to

---

[e]Kirnberger's views on arpeggiation (*Brechung*) were probably influenced directly by Heinichen's discussion of the "Harpeggio" in *Der Generalbass in der Composition,* pp. 556 ff.

EXAMPLE 11.21

EXAMPLE 11.22

place the thirds and sixths of the bass in the top voice, the octave is nevertheless permissible when the arpeggiated two-part composition sounds like a four-part piece, as in example 11.23, where the octave occurs at (a).

[207] On the other hand, the octave is incorrectly written above the sixth chord on B at (a) in example 11.24, since the sixth of this sixth chord must be doubled as at (a) in example 11.25, or the third as at (b).

EXAMPLE 11.23

EXAMPLE 11.24

EXAMPLE 11.25

Arpeggiation involving two notes against one permits two variants, since one can write, for example, c^1–e^1 or the reverse e^1–c^1, or, by octave displacement of a note, c^1–e or e–c^1. One should try to vary these when the situation occurs repeatedly but should always choose the type that provides the strictest writing. However, in general, one can obtain different melodies to the same harmony by means of these variants. Example 11.26 can serve to illustrate this.

EXAMPLE 11.26

[208] The most pronounced variants are obtained by inversion of intervals, as in example 11.27. In the first case (a), the progression in the first measure is the same as in the second case (b); here, however, the leap of a seventh in the second measure has been transformed [in (b)] into a descending second by inversion. Such variants have two advantages. First, the melody is changed unexpectedly over the same harmony, and second, one can help the singer, who perhaps could not reach so high.

EXAMPLE 11.27

This variety increases considerably when three or even four notes occur against one, as we shall see later on.

Sometimes the best composers allow themselves liberties from the rules stated here; however, the beginner must not think that they have done this out of ignorance of these rules or that the rules themselves were not valid. Only he who has advanced so far that he can trust his ear can digress from the rules in special situations that tolerate it. Example 11.28 can serve as an illustration of such liberties; the passage at (a) would sound as at (b) if the notes were aligned vertically.

EXAMPLE 11.28

[209] Even octaves sounding after the beat are permitted when they occur as at (a) in example 11.29, but not as at (b). Even worse would be the octaves and fifths of the type shown in example 11.30.

There are also cases where great composers deliberately write direct

EXAMPLE 11.29

EXAMPLE 11.30

fifths in succession when the bass ascends while the upper part descends.[f] But this happens only in fast pieces, in order to obtain a good line in the bass or to avoid bass notes that had already occurred shortly before. [See example 11.31.]

EXAMPLE 11.31

[210] In all examples of arpeggiation given thus far, the bass progresses steadily in undivided notes and the arpeggiated ones are in the upper part. This can also be inverted, and the arpeggiated notes placed in the bass. Or the arpeggiation can be alternated between the upper and lower parts; also, one voice can be sustained while the other makes a step. However, the given

[f]Example 11.31 contains direct octaves, not fifths as indicated by Kirnberger.

rules of good harmony must always be observed. Example 11.32 will suffice to illustrate this. [211] Here the six-four chord in the second measure is the second inversion of the triad, and not the dissonant six-four chord.

EXAMPLE 11.32

If three arpeggiated notes are written against one, the composition is also treated as if it were written in four parts. Particular care has to be taken that each dissonance in the arpeggiation is resolved in the same voice, just as it would have to occur if the arpeggiated notes were sounded simultaneously. [See example 11.33.]

EXAMPLE 11.33

The ninth variation of the well-known Tartini Minuet in A major, edited by me in the *Vermischte Musicalien* [1769], can be cited as a model of a strict four-part composition resulting from arpeggiated chords. All the arpeggiated notes except the third quarter of the eighth measure can be written simultaneously, and the writing remains entirely strict. Only in the middle of the above-mentioned measure does an octave appear, which could easily be corrected if b¹ were replaced by e¹. The octaves c-sharp³ and f-sharp² in the inner parts of the seventh measures are unnoticeable. In fact, only the octaves, which the ear notices easily, are forbidden, since one writes not for the eye, but for the ear.

Where three arpeggiated notes occur against one, six immediate variants appear, as can be seen in example 11.34. [212] But if one wants to increase the number of variants by putting the octave or third instead of the fifth on top, as it always is here, a total of eighteen variants results.

EXAMPLE 11.34

Variety can be increased even further if the harmony is used in more open or closed position. Thus, for instance, each of the open-position harmonies in example 11.35 admits six additional variants.

EXAMPLE 11.35

From this it can sufficiently be seen what diversity of melodic progressions can occur over the same harmony. Certainly not all permutations are always good, just as is the case with so-called *anagrams*, or the permutations of the letters of a word, not all of which produce intelligible words. Meanwhile it is good for a beginner to practice such permutations diligently, since this gives him skill in finding melodic variants without effort. One must leave it to the ear and taste of each composer to decide which of these variants are useful or not. We want to cite just a single example of this. If one chose to transform the passage at (a) in example 11.36 into that at (b) or (c), these permutations would not be approved by good composers, since they sound like octaves.

[213] If the upper part has four notes to one in the bass, one must proceed according to the rules of writing in five parts; great difficulties arise from making the writing so strict that no error would result if the notes were sounded simultaneously. Nevertheless there are works by J. S. Bach in which strict composition has been observed in connection with four-part arpeggiation. This may suffice regarding arpeggiations.

EXAMPLE 11.36

II. Next to be considered in greater detail is *passing motion*, which always involves a few dissonant notes. The simplest case is that of two notes on one beat, the first of which is consonant and the other dissonant, as at (A) in example 11.37. Here the dissonance always falls on the second half of a beat, and one has to take care that it does not fall on the second beat itself; one could fall into this error by not paying precise attention to the type of motion. Thus, for instance, the passage at (B) would be incorrect in common 4/4 time because the passing dissonances fall on the following beat; however, in *alla breve* time, it would be correct.

EXAMPLE 11.37

[214] A passing note is most natural and pleasing when it leads from a note to its third, be it ascending or descending, as at (a) in example 11.38; they can also be written as leaps, as at (b).

Irregular passing notes must never be used at the beginning of a piece.

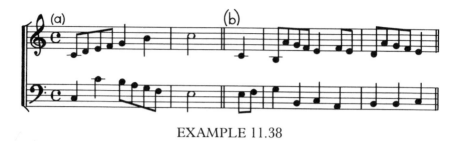

EXAMPLE 11.38

The beginning at (A) in example 11.39 would be wrong. It must be preceded by at least one consonance of the main key, even if it were only in one voice, as at (B).

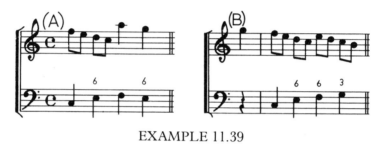

EXAMPLE 11.39

[215] Although the regular passing note is more agreeable, the alternation of both types makes a composition more charming. At first it is certainly not as comprehensible as one having only regular passing notes, but for just that reason it becomes pleasing after repeated hearings.

A very thorough knowledge of harmony is necessary to distinguish both types of passing notes when they constantly alternate in a piece, or always to recognize the main note in the constant alternation. Without this, one cannot figure the bass as a thorough bass. For that reason a piece is printed at the end of this volume, which beginners can use for practice in this very necessary knowledge of regular and irregular passing notes.

If four notes occur in a part on one beat, various regular and irregular passing motions, consonant as well as dissonant notes, result. The most pleasant and easiest occurs when a consonance always follows a dissonance, as in example 11.40.

Two dissonant notes can also follow one another; however, by leap this is seldom good. Of the five progressions in example 11.41, the first two are the best, the third is still permissible, but the fourth and fifth are not good.

One usually does not write three dissonant notes in succession when there are four notes on one beat.

EXAMPLE 11.40

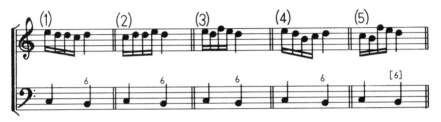

EXAMPLE 11.41

[216] When passing notes occur simultaneously in more than one voice, thirds and sixths sound best, as at (a) in example 11.42. But when three successive notes in two voices do not sound as at (b), the piece can easily become confusing. Sometimes even four successive notes are dissonant here. Because of the speed and the light comprehensible melody, it is still tolerable; but in a slower tempo this would be intolerable. However, even at a fast tempo, one must not do this too often, particularly if several voices were to rush along in the same manner; this makes the piece most confusing. Here it is better to take Capellmeister Graun, the most euphonious and thoughtful composer of beautiful melody, rather than Händel or J. S. Bach, as a model. The latter was most venturesome in this respect, and therefore his works require a very special execution that is exactly suited to his style; without this, many of his works would hardly be bearable. [217] Those who do not understand harmony completely must not dare to play his difficult pieces; but if one comes upon the correct execution, even his most learned fugues sound beautiful.

EXAMPLE 11.42

What has been said in the remarks on *arpeggiation* regarding the variety that results from permutations can also be applied here. but because of the dissonances, more consideration and deliberation is necessary here than there. Example 11.43 provides samples of this type of variation.

EXAMPLE 11.43

III. Finally *syncopation* is to be considered. *Retardation* or *anticipation* is determined according to the voice that has the syncopation. In example 11.44, one sees at (a) a two-voice passage in which both voices progress

EXAMPLE 11.44 (*to be continued*)

EXAMPLE 11.44 (*continued*)

together.[80] At (b) this passage is changed so that the soprano falls behind; but at (c) it comes first. What is to be remembered about this can be stated most clearly by the remarks that are to be made about the various situations occurring here.

[219] It must be noted in general that syncopation occurs only in situations where both parts would be consonant throughout if they were to progress simultaneously, as in all the examples here.

At (d) the basic notes are the same as at (a), except that instead of triads their first inversions have been used. At (e) the preceding passage has been changed so that the soprano comes first. However, it should not be written as here, since a seventh appears each time the soprano ascends; the seventh is so noticeable that one expects its resolution, which does not follow. However, descending, the passage sounds somewhat like fifths. At (f) everything is correct, ascending as well as descending. [220] At (g) the voices progress

80. When each of the two voices progresses in seconds but the two are separated by a third, as here, syncopation can very easily be employed by the singer, even when it is not indicated by the composer. However, the voice part must not be accompanied by flutes or violins playing with it in unison. These would progress simultaneously with the bass, and the singer would then be blamed for hurrying or falling behind. A singer who wants to make such alterations must look carefully at the score so as not to make the changes at the wrong time or contrary to the nature of the accompaniment.

by leaps, and immediately thereafter the same passage is syncopated. This is possible when consonant notes are involved. However, one has to take care that it does not sound like octaves or fifths, as it does in the following passage at *, where the phrase sounds as if it were written as at †, or, when the tempo is fast, as at ‡. At (h) the upper part forms thirds or sixths in relation to the bass. Syncopation is also very appropriate here, as in the following examples. However, the passage would not be good if written as at (i), where the fourth from the bass is sounded freely on the fourth quarter of the first measure.

This may suffice regarding syncopation.

To provide beginners with strict and good examples of florid counterpoint in addition to the rules stated here, a few chorales are inserted at the end of this chapter, about which several things need to be said.

The first is not really in florid counterpoint, yet written with far more harmonic variety than those at the end of the preceding chapter. This type can be considered as midway between simple and florid counterpoint. The models given in the preceding chapter have an entirely consonant harmony, as is generally appropriate for use in churches where the entire congregation sings and where the bass must be just as easily singable as one of the other voices. But here the harmony is already more varied, and interwoven with many types of dissonances. If only the bass is correct in such pieces, the upper voices can be added to it more easily than in the type that is totally simple, where everything is consonant, for in this latter situation great care must be taken not to write forbidden fifth and octave progressions.

By the way, this first chorale was written by HER ROYAL HIGH-NESS, PRINCESS AMALIA OF PRUSSIA.[81] [221] One might note something else special about its *cantus firmus*—that it has been set in three ways by the famous J. S. Bach as well as by the late Capellmeister Graun, as at (A), (B), and (C) in example 11.45.[g]

---

81. The others are by two young composers who have been instructed by me according to the rules presented in this work.

---

gAll these harmonizations appear to be by Bach. See chorales 74, 80, 89, 98, and 345 in the *371 Chorales and 69 Chorale Melodies by Johann Sebastian Bach*, edited by Albert Riemenschneider (New York: G. Schirmer), 1941.

EXAMPLE 11.45

[222] The first setting without doubt follows exactly the spirit intended by the originator of this melody, that is, in the Phrygian mode. The second begins in the subdominant of the Phrygian mode, or, if one wants, in the Aeolian mode, and closes later in the dominant. The third is in the Ionian mode. The latter seems least appropriate to the spirit intended by the originator but probably has been set by both the mentioned composers in this way because the congregation sings the same bass in most churches. In this situation, it is best that the organ retain this bass. When the entire congregation sings, a detestable cacophony would result if the organ were to sustain E major at the end of the first verse, while the entire church sang in C major.[82]

It can be seen from these three examples how different basses can be written to one melody, thereby giving it different characters, and how this melody can then be used equally well in different songs of very dissimilar content. [223] In the second part of this work it will be shown in greater detail how several basses can be composed to one melody, no matter in which voice it lies. Meanwhile it will be sufficient to add only one more example [example 11.46], which is taken from Handel's opera *Tamerlano*.[h]

For the benefit of the beginner of composition we cannot let it go unmentioned here that a most diligent training in chorales is a highly useful and even indispensable matter, and that those who consider such exercises as superfluous or even pedantic are caught in a very detrimental bias. Such exercises are the true foundation not only of strict composition but also for good and proper expression in vocal compositions.

Every aria is basically nothing more than a chorale composed according to the most correct declamation, in which each syllable of the text has only one note, which is more or less embellished according to the demands of expression. The true basis of beauty in an aria always depends on the simple

82. Much time and considerable skill is needed on the part of an organist to train a whole congregation in a good manner of singing. The function of the organ in chorales that are sung by an entire congregation is simply to keep the people on pitch. That is what the organist must aim for, and not for unnecessary excesses and decorations of the melody on each syllable, which often makes it difficult to perceive what sort of song is being played or in what key it is sung.

hThe first part of this example is taken from the introduction (mm.13–19) of Asteria's aria, "Se potessi un di placare," which closes act 2 of *Tamerlano*. The last two measures do not appear in the edition (pp. 86–88) cited in note d of this chapter. Kirnberger's indications "at the 3rd, 5th, 7th" apparently refer to the intervals above d, the first pitch of the ascending bass line.

EXAMPLE 11.46

melody that is left when all its decorative notes are eliminated. If this simple melody is incorrect in terms of declamation, progression, or harmony, mistakes cannot be completely hidden by embellishment.

[224] Whoever wants to take pains to strip the most beautiful arias of all embellishments will see that the remaining notes always have the shape of a well-composed and correctly declaimed chorale.[83] Examples 11.47 and 11.48 will show this sufficiently.[i]

[226] It is also useful to the future composer of arias that he frequently exchange the principal melody in his diligent practice of chorale writing and use it now in one voice, now in another, for skill in writing melodic parts depends on this. An aria in which the first violin has a melody that is above the soprano and is entirely different from the vocal part is written according to the same rules as a chorale in which the principal melody is in the alto.

83. That the principal harmony and simple melody must be made perceptible in all embellished arias, particularly in adagios, is most clearly evident from the fact that the best arias are those in which the accompanying parts have only the main notes of the harmony; most slow arias by the famous Hasse are composed in this way. This has the advantage of leaving the singer freedom to add his embellishment at will and to anticipate and retard as he pleases. This would not be possible if the first or second violin already had the embellishments of the vocal part, as was mentioned previously (see note 80, above).

---

[i]These two examples should be of particular interest to the student of reductive theory, particularly since such examples are quite rare in the eighteenth century. One earlier source that contains a number of interesting voice-leading reductions is J. D. Heinichen's *Der Generalbass in der Composition*, part 2, chapter 1 (pp. 585–724).

Aria from the opera *Tamerlano* by Graun[j]

EXAMPLE 11.47

Aria from the opera *Silla* by Graun[k]

EXAMPLE 11.48 (*to be continued*)

[j]This example is the opening vocal phrase of the aria sung by Andronico at the end of act I of *Tamerlano*. The bass line differs somewhat (though not significantly) from the one printed on p. 39 of the edition cited in note d of this chapter.

[k]The first performance of Graun's *Silla* was given at the Royal Opera in Berlin, 27 March 1753.

EXAMPLE 11.48 (*continued*)

EXAMPLE 11.49 (*to be continued*)

EXAMPLE 11.49 (*continued*)

EXAMPLE 11.49 (continued)

EXAMPLE 11.50 (*to be continued*)

EXAMPLE 11.50 (*continued*)

EXAMPLE 11.51 (*to be continued*)

EXAMPLE 11.51 (*continued*)

EXAMPLE 11.51 (*continued*)

EXAMPLE 11.51 (*continued*)

EXAMPLE 11.52 (*to be continued*)

EXAMPLE 11.52 (continued)

EXAMPLE 11.52 (*continued*)

EXAMPLE 11.52 (continued)

EXAMPLE 11.53 (*to be continued*)

EXAMPLE 11.53 (*continued*)

EXAMPLE 11.53 (*continued*)

EXAMPLE 11.53 (*continued*)

EXAMPLE 11.54 (*to be continued*)

EXAMPLE 11.54 (*continued*)

EXAMPLE 11.55 (*to be continued*)

EXAMPLE 11.55 *(continued)*

EXAMPLE 11.55 (*continued*)

EXAMPLE 11.55 (*continued*)

EXAMPLE 11.56 (*to be continued*)

EXAMPLE 11.56 (*continued*)

EXAMPLE 11.56 (*continued*)

EXAMPLE 11.57 (*to be continued*)

EXAMPLE 11.57 (*continued*)

EXAMPLE 11.57 (*continued*)

EXAMPLE 11.57 (*continued*)

EXAMPLE 11.57 (*continued*)

EXAMPLE 11.57 (*continued*)

EXAMPLE 11.57 (*continued*)

Appendix

[248] It was been mentioned with regard to regular and irregular passing notes that it is sometimes very difficult to find the principal notes and to detect the true harmony as conceived by the composer. So that beginners can practice the correct judgment in a few rather complex situations, the following keyboard piece has been inserted here, and, below the actual parts, three additional staves with bass clef have been added to clarify the harmony.

The lowest of these three staves is really what the French composers call the fundamental bass. It contains the true fundamental chords, that is, the triads and seventh chords on which the harmony is based throughout.

The next staff shows the nonessential dissonances, or suspensions, where they occur.

But the top staff [of the three added] presents the thorough bass and shows which inversion of the triad or seventh chord the composer has used at each harmony. Suspensions are also indicated there.

Once beginners have acquired skill in the accurate analysis of harmony in this piece,[a] we recommend to all of them that they also study the works of great masters in a similarly thorough way. In that way they will be in a position to solve the most difficult harmonic structures. Moreover, they will find that harmonies about which people sometimes form very strange notions and in which some people imagine finding quite odd composite or superimposed chords, are in fact nothing other than mere triads or seventh chords. These are the only true fundamental chords, from which all others

[a]A different interpretation of the opening measures of this fugue was given some years later by A. F. C. Kollmann in his treatise, *A New Theory of Musical Harmony* (London, 1806),

266

arise by inversion and suspension, as has been frequently shown throughout this work.

Many have been persuaded by French writers that we owe this simple theory of harmony to Rameau, whom the French would like to praise as the first profound teacher of harmony. However, nothing is more certain than the fact that this very theory of fundamental chords and the variety resulting from their inversions were known better and more thoroughly by the old German composers long before Rameau wrote. He has not yet grasped the theory of simplicity of harmony in its true purity, since sometimes he actually considers passing tones as fundamental notes. This is the basis, for example, of his chord *de sixte ajouteé*, which he considers as a fundamental chord. [249] For example, he views the $\frac{6}{5}$ harmony on the second quarter

plate xx, no. 4:

Kollmann's interpretation of the a-sharp in m. 5 as an appoggiatura follows naturally after the preceding suspensions in mm. 2 and 4. Kirnberger's rules for the treatment of dissonance, even in the lighter style, are too strict to accommodate this possibility.

of the following progression as a fundamental harmony, and the sixth in it as an essential dissonance, which is just passing.

EXAMPLE A-1

German and non-German composers form half cadences not only with the passing sixth, like Rameau, but also with the augmented fourth from the bass (as the leading tone of the following tonic), which makes the cadence more piquant, as here:

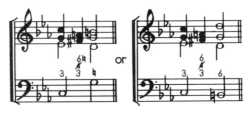

EXAMPLE A-2

From this it can clearly be seen that both these notes are simply passing, since there would be no other way to explain how the augmented fourth occurs here in the harmony.

Certainly no true connoisseur of harmony would justify a phrase like the following by Rameau.

EXAMPLE A-3

In the attached piece there is a place where the above-mentioned situation occurs, namely, on the third eighth of measure 58. A instead of B with $\frac{7}{\sharp}$ should be in the bass. Here this A is the main note, but B, which

precedes it from above as a sixteenth note, is an irregular passing note; the
4+ or d-sharp is the second dissonance.

But on the lowest staff, B has been indicated as the fundamental chord
so that the preparation of the following dissonant chord might be achieved.
[250] In the soprano the d-sharp is really a "Nachschlag" or passing note to
e, the fifth of the bass A, but instead has been written directly above the A.
But in the bass the irregular passing note, where B is dissonant before A, is
to be considered as here:

EXAMPLE A-4

Instead of a and c¹ being dissonant in relation to B, but d-sharp
consonant, here a, as the octave from the bass, and also c, as its third, are
consonant. But d-sharp in the soprano, as a regular passing note, and B in
the bass, as an irregular passing note, are dissonant.

[*Harmonic Analysis of Kirnberger's Fugue in E Minor*]

Die Kunst

des reinen

Satzes in der Musik

aus sicheren Grundsätzen hergeleitet und mit deutlichen

Beyspielen erläutert

von

Joh. Phil. Kirnberger

Ihrer Königl. Hoheit der Prinzeßin Amalia von Preußen Hof=Musicus.

Zweyter Theil.

Erste Abtheilung.

Berlin und Königsberg,

bey G. J. Decker und G. L. Hartung, 1776.

30

THE ART
OF
STRICT MUSICAL COMPOSITION,

derived from reliable principles and
illustrated with clear examples

by
JOH. PHIL. KIRNBERGER
Court Musician to Her Royal Highness,
Princess Amalia of Prussia

VOLUME II

Preface

I had hoped to present the second volume of this work to lovers of musical composition shortly after publication of the first volume. But I have been detained too long from realizing my intention, partly as a result of other necessary work and partly as a result of obstacles, the details of which would be of no importance to the reader. In order to avoid the suspicion that this volume would never come out, I had to make the decision to publish only the first part of the second volume for now.

What I will actually discuss in the second volume is stated in the brief introduction that precedes this part. In addition, I want only to mention that following the theory of double counterpoint I will describe the various specific genres and forms of compositions in contemporary music and communicate my ideas concerning the best organization of these compositions. I will aim above all at determining the true character of the various commonly accepted dance melodies, since a thorough knowledge of them greatly facilitates the invention of melodies that have a definite expression of some sentiment or passion.

I have reason to be pleased with the good reception of the first volume and the approval I have received from true connoisseurs of harmony, and I hope that they will not withhold approval of this volume. But it does not bother me at all that some things have displeased people who have not really explored very deeply the nature of harmony. I would have liked to remove their doubts about my theory, but it is not in my power to give them the experience and refined ear that they seem to lack. Therefore I must leave them to their differing opinion.

I believe I may promise to the sympathetic reader that the other part of this second volume, half of which has long been ready, will certainly be published by Easter of next year.

Introduction

[1] Every melody consists of a succession of smoothly connected notes that have a particular passionate expression. Nature has apparently given man the talent to sing in order that he may maintain and strengthen himself in the sentiments that melody is capable of expressing.

That this is the primary and most natural use of melody is evident from the fact that even the most barbaric and half-wild people begin to sing cheerful songs when they want to be happy; but when they want to excite themselves for battle and strife, they do it with war songs that are wild and awaken their courage.

The same can be seen daily among us. Even those who have learned nothing about music sing or whistle their own melodies when filled with tender sentiments in order to maintain and strengthen themselves in the sentiment that pleases them.

Thus melody is not an invention of art but a manifestation of nature in sensitive men. Certainly people were singing long before it occurred to some rational mind to establish what is known today as the scale or tone-system, to define intervals, and to pay attention to the meter and rhythm characteristic of natural melody.

Music considered as an art does nothing else than to enhance the characteristics of natural melody and to seek in the nature of the matter itself rules by whose observance melody becomes more perfect.

The first step that art had to take was to establish the scale or system from which all notes of melody are to be derived. It is likely that each nation originally had its own scale in conformity with the nature of its hearing and national character; this scale differed from those of other nations by the height of the voice as well as by specially defined intervals. We find traces of this still today in the designation of different scales of the ancient Greek nations, from which one may assume that each tribe—Ionian, Dorian, Aeolian, Phrygian, etc.—had its own scale.

It is not improbable that the different national melodies were also originally distinguished from one another by meter, motion, rhythm, and character, and that, for example, a Phrygian song differed from a Lydian or Ionian one with regard to the above-mentioned features, just as a minuet differs from a sarabande today.

[2] Only after music had become a systematic and deliberate art were the scales of different nations gathered together into a single universal tone system, were new intervals added, were motion, meter, and rhythm more closely examined, and their effect on the character and expression of melody more precisely observed. Thus the rules of the art evolved gradually. These rules enable those who have a natural talent for melody to compose single melodies as well as polyphonic works that infinitely exceed those natural melodies in perfection.

In the first volume of this work I have dealt precisely and thoroughly with scales and the intervals contained in each one, with harmonies of many parts, modulation, and the correct harmonic and melodic progression of tones that were invented and introduced by the greatest masters of the art.

Now I come to the special features of song or melody that give it its character and expression. It is not difficult to see that this character depends on the choice of key, the succession of harmonies, the type of modulation, on motion, rhythm, and meter. Thus these are the principal points that I have to discuss in this second volume.

Newer music, however, differs from that of the ancient Greeks mainly by virtue of the fact that we compose our most refined and important works with several melodies that progress simultaneously, and yet really amount to a single polyphonic piece. Therefore I had to take care in this volume to show the various means by which such a polyphonic piece receives its necessary variety in addition to its true unity. This then led me to the extensive treatment of so-called double counterpoint.

These, then, are the various main points that a composer has to observe with regard to the desirable qualities of a piece, be it monophonic or polyphonic. I will now discuss these points in the order that seems most natural to me.

CHAPTER 1

Different Types of Harmonic Accompaniment to a Given Melody: Concerning Their Correctness and Expression

[3] Simple counterpoint in two and more parts was sufficiently discussed with respect to purity or correctness of harmony in the tenth and following chapter of the first volume of this work. Since in this second volume we have to consider composition with regard to beauty and power of expression, it seems worthwhile to note here first of all that a composition of the highest degree of harmonic purity can still be very bad and of very little value. Despite this purity, it can be stiff and unsingable, or monotonous, boring and antiquated, or without any power, energy, and expression.

Thus, just as it is absolutely necessary that a composer be in command of the strict harmonic style of writing, it is also certain that this strictness alone is the least of his merits. Music has a certain relation to rhetoric. The primary attribute of a speaker is that he comprehend the grammar of his language, that is, that he know how to express himself distinctly and correctly. But this alone is of little help to him. The most correct expression of language is a futile art if one has nothing important or interesting to say.

[4] Before we enter into a detailed discussion of beauty and power in melody, we find it necessary to demonstrate here in a special introductory chapter how complete knowledge of harmony not only leads to purity but also to melodic beauty and expression. This appears to be all the more necessary because of the current prejudice that the so-called scholastic rules of harmony and particularly the art of double counterpoint are of use only to the strict style but are almost useless or of little value for beauty and desirable expression of song or melody. This prejudice, which is of considerable detriment to music, appears to be gaining ground at this time in particular.

In order to guard against this destructive prejudice as much as possible,

I have taken it upon myself to show in this chapter what is required in setting to a given melody a bass that is not only strict, perhaps even pedantic, but that, in addition to being pure, is also suitable to several inner voices, yet permits in all voices a pleasant and expressive line that is consistent with its special purpose.

I must repeat that I am not presenting here everything that pertains to beauty and practical expression of melody, but for now will consider complete knowledge of harmony simply as a means that will facilitate the attainment of beauty as well as of expression.

Therefore I am assuming that a young composer, once he has learned the rules of strict harmony, will want to gain further skill at writing a figured bass to a given *cantus firmus* as the highest voice; this bass must not only be completely strict but also be written in such a way that it forms a good and flowing composition with the given *cantus firmus* and so that two additional inner voices can be derived from it. It is my intention to show what is needed for the composition of such a bass.

First let us presuppose a melody that contains no notes other than those found in the common or original diatonic scale C, D, E, F, G, A, B, c. If this ascending scale is regarded as a melody, a strict bass can be added to it that consists only of triads on the tonic, dominant, and subdominant, as can be clearly seen in example 1.1.

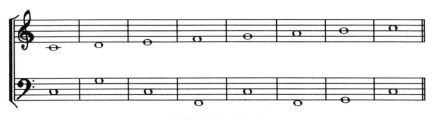

EXAMPLE 1.1

[5] From this it can be seen that to every purely diatonic melody it is possible to add a bass that consists of nothing but triads built on the tonic, dominant, and subdominant. Therefore this is the first and simplest type of harmonic bass.

However, the bass in the preceding example is not the only one suitable to the ascending scale that is regarded as a melody. It can easily be seen that triads on other degrees of the scale could also be used in addition to these three. We will consider this as the second type of bass.

Thirdly, the bass can be treated in such a way that in the middle of a composition one employs dominant chords of those keys to which it is possible to modulate from the main key.

Finally, even two, three, and up to four dominant chords can be used in succession, and enharmonic digressions to more remote keys can occur.

The following may now be noted regarding these four types or methods of composing a bass.[a]

It hardly needs to be mentioned that a bass consisting of only three chords would lapse very soon into an unpleasant monotony; consequently, this first manner of composing a bass would hardly be of any use if it were not aided by inversions of the triads. A bass that basically consists of just three triads can still attain variety and diversity by means of appropriate inversions.

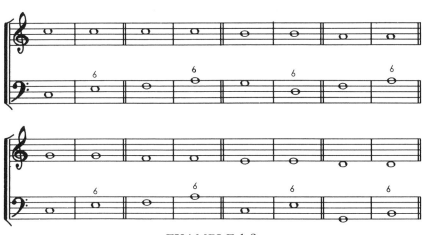

EXAMPLE 1.2

[6] From example 1.2, which is in the key of C major, one can see how the harmony of a bass could be changed for the same note in the top voice, and which bass notes can be used for each degree of the scale when no more than the three fundamental harmonies mentioned above are employed.

If, for example, c were to occur twice in succession in the melody, one of

[a] The following discussion, which constitutes a practical application and synthesis of many of the concepts presented in the first volume of this work, is without doubt one of the most thorough and systematic ever written about the subject of harmonizing a given melody. Kirnberger's approach to this subject—to begin with the simplest harmonizations and to progress from there through various steps to more complex solutions—is an excellent method of teaching this skill.

these can be harmonized by the triad on C or its first inversion, that is, by E with the sixth chord; but the second time this c in the soprano can be harmonized by the triad on F, either F itself in the bass or A with the sixth chord. The same applies to g in the melody, which can belong to the tonic as well as the dominant harmony. In this type of bass, d and b in the top voice belong only to the dominant harmony.

Since the dominant chord always implies the essential seventh above its root, this type of bass that is added to a given melody becomes much more varied if the essential seventh chord with its inversions is used.

Thus it is clear that, when necessary, a good bass consisting only of the tonic, dominant, and subdominant triads could be added to a melody that does not digress from the diatonic scale. One has to be careful only with the progression from G to F, or from the dominant chord to the subdominant, because it sounds harsh due to the omission of the tonic chord, and particularly because of the two major thirds and unharmonic cross relation caused by the tritone f–b. [7] This progression is good only when a caesura, or rest point, falls between the two chords. It is good to use in other circumstances, but only if both or at least one of the chords is inverted.

The same is also true of the progression from F to G, or from the subdominant to the dominant; only in inversion is it not harsh. Thus the bass in example 1.3, in which both progressions occur, is without fault.

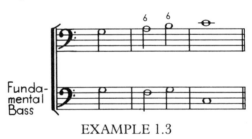

EXAMPLE 1.3

I must note in addition that this type of writing—where only the three basic chords mentioned are used without ever digressing to other keys—is the most elementary type of composition and is suitable only for the most common listener, whose ear is incapable of grasping anything more complex.

In this category belong all kinds of musettes, peasant dances, and street songs; marches of this type can also be found occasionally.

As soon as a melody digresses to secondary keys, this gives the listener something more to think about, even if only the same three chords are used in the new keys. Of this type there are even entire arias and choruses in operas written according to today's new Italian taste; their authors are not able to attempt anything more complex without revealing their incompetence at treating harmony.

Here I will include a chorale in which there is no deviation whatsoever from the tonic scale in either the melody or the harmony. [See examples 1.4 and 1.5.] [8] Further below, it is to be shown how such melodies can be made much more forceful by the harmony.

[9] Example 1.6 is another chorale; it modulates to the dominant of the main key but basically contains only the three mentioned chords, which are merely transposed to another key.

In this chorale, the three chords of the main key are transposed up a fifth in connection with the digression to the dominant, that is, to the chords on G, C and D with the major third.

The first chord is the tonic; from (a) to (b) the chords already belong.to G major. The G chord at (a) is already to be considered as the tonic of G

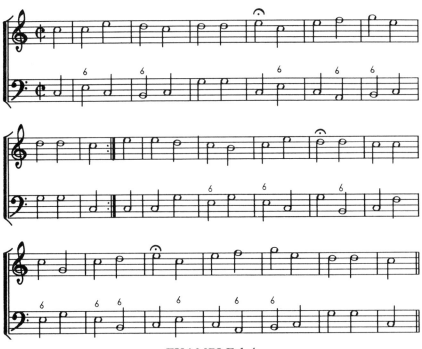

EXAMPLE 1.4

EXAMPLE 1.5

EXAMPLE 1.6

major, and the following D chord as the dominant of G. From (c) to (d) the chords belong again to C. From (e) to (f) they belong to the secondary key of G major; from there to the end, all chords belong once again to the main key of C major.

[10] If one wanted to establish the key more firmly in the first verse of this strophe and not modulate immediately to G major, one could make do with the three chords of C major, as in example 1.7.

The progressions at (b) are preferable to those at (a) for the reason given

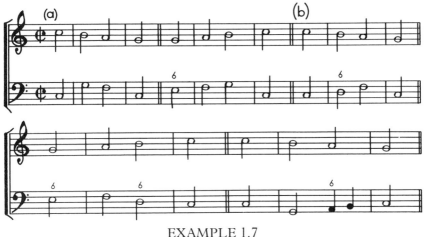

EXAMPLE 1.7

above regarding the progression of the fundamental bass by seconds.

Furthermore, it can easily be understood that with this restriction it is impossible to comply with all rules that must be observed with regard to the treatment of two outer voices. Neither contrary motion nor avoidance of perfect consonances in the middle of a period can be maintained throughout with this monotony of fundamental harmonies. Therefore, such a bass is only good at the lowest level and serves only to familiarize the beginner with the primary and most natural harmonies and progressions.

However, if such a bass is treated according to florid or embellished counterpoint, and passing notes, suspensions, and essential dissonances are used with these triads and sixth chords, contrary motion is obtained more easily, the chords are more closely connected, and the more frequent rest points, which result from the use of perfect consonances in the periods, can be removed more easily, as in example 1.8.

[11] Basically, however, the entire chorale has little charm and force because of the all-too-great monotony of its fundamental harmonies.[1]

1. The irregular passing note at (a) could easily have been avoided and the composition made more euphonious by going from the first bass note to c by means of the regular passing note d, as here:

However, as a result, the progression would have become unpleasant. Therefore the following important remark needs to be made here: One should never use a

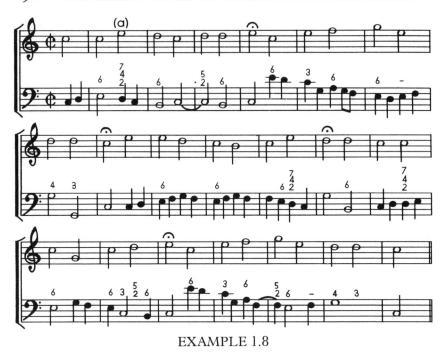

EXAMPLE 1.8

[12] To give the expression more life, the harmony must be rich in diverse chords; this is the origin of the second type mentioned above. Thus, the triads on the supertonic, mediant, and submediant are used here in addition to those on the tonic, dominant, and subdominant. In major keys, even the diminished triad on the step below the tonic is used, which in minor keys is the triad on the second degree.

Here we also wish to state what is necessary concerning the progression of these chords.

From the tonic chord one can go directly to the triad of its supertonic but can return from there only through the dominant triad, as shown in example 1.9.

(*Footnote 1 continued*)

long note after two short ones on an unaccented beat without reason (unless such motion were appropriate in another voice), since it violates the character of accented and unaccented beats.

This remark also applies to the treatment of the second [*sic*, third] quarter of the eleventh and thirteenth measures. In such situations the irregular passing note is most important.

EXAMPLE 1.9

The dominant chord can be omitted, but only if both or one of these chords is used in inversion, as in example 1.10.[b]

EXAMPLE 1.10

The omission is felt more strongly with the progression at (a), and thus must not be used without need. This omission is more tolerable in connection with the dominant, namely, when the A minor chord leads to the dominant triad in C major, as in example 1.11.

EXAMPLE 1.11

[13] The reason for this is that the D minor chord, which is omitted here, is not as crucial as the dominant chord in the situation above.

Therefore, one also cannot go directly from the tonic chord to the chord of its mediant but must go to it indirectly through the chord of the submediant or dominant, as in example 1.12.

EXAMPLE 1.12

The middle chord can be omitted if inversions of these chords are used. One can return from the mediant to the tonic in all sorts of ways, as at (a)

[b] The idea of omission is an important feature of Kirnberger's harmonic theories. In the discussion that follows, Kirnberger explains those progressions that appear to contradict his rules—for example, certain progressions by step or by ascending third—as resulting from omission of an intervening chord. This is consistent with his earlier discussion of omission in connection with the resolution of dissonance. See, for example, Volume I, chapter 5, section II, points (3) and (4).

EXAMPLE 1.13

in example 1.13; likewise from the tonic triad to the triad of its submediant, as at (b). But from the submediant it is better to go to the sixth chord of the tonic, as at (c), rather than return directly to its triad. One can also go directly from the submediant to the triad on the subdominant, as at (d); likewise to the supertonic, as at (e), or its inversion, as at (f).

Finally, in major keys, one cannot go directly from the tonic chord to the diminished triad but instead must go through the chords on the submediant, subdominant, or supertonic, as in example 1.14.

EXAMPLE 1.14

It is even less satisfactory to go directly from this diminished triad to the tonic; this is possible only through the mediant triad, as at (a) in example 1.15.

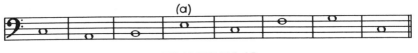

EXAMPLE 1.15

[14] The remaining progressions that can be used with these triads, as long as the notes themselves do not digress from the natural scale, are determined in major as well as minor keys by the following rules.

No progression by second occurs other than: (1) upward from a major to a minor chord, as from C to D, or from G to A; (2) from a minor chord to the diminished triad, as from A to B; and (3) in a minor key when the bass ascends by only a half step with two major triads, the first of which is the dominant, as in example 1.16, which is in A minor.

EXAMPLE 1.16

All remaining progressions by second require intervening chords, which at best can be omitted only when inversions are used. Yet, in a minor key, the progressions shown in example 1.17, where the diminished triad is omitted, are also useful.

EXAMPLE 1.17

Progression by ascending third can only occur with intervening chords. If direct, inversions must be used.

One can progress directly from each chord down by third, as in example 1.18.

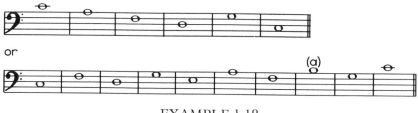

EXAMPLE 1.18

At (a) it appears doubtful whether this B should support the diminished triad or the six-five chord. [15] However, since the diminished triad progresses most naturally to the triad on the dominant, and since this E minor chord would be entirely inappropriate here after the B,[c] there can be no doubt that it is the six-five chord on B, that is, the first inversion of the following G chord with the essential seventh. For if one were to add only the third, fifth, and octave to this B, the sixth would be missed.

Likewise one can progress directly by fourth and fifth from each chord, except from the diminished triad to the chord of its fifth, as at (a) in example 1.19; the latter progression must occur in inversion, as at (b).

With this in mind, every attentive student would add a bass to the above chorale that would vaguely resemble example 1.20.

[16] This bass gives much more life to the chorale than the bass of the

[c]This E minor chord is hypothetical. It is mentioned here by Kirnberger in reference to the situation shown in example 1.15, where the E minor chord at (a) comes between the diminished chord on B and the triad on C. But, as stated, this possibility would be most inappropriate in this context.

EXAMPLE 1.19

EXAMPLE 1.20

first type merely by the greater variety of its fundamental harmonies, which generally provide the opportunity for giving the bass a more noble line.

In addition to these triads, dissonant chords can also be used when the dissonances are properly prepared by the preceding chord. However, it must be possible to delay the resolutions of these dissonances until the following harmony since we are dealing here only with simple counterpoint, where note is set against note. Or they must be derived from the essential seventh chord, whose resolution always occurs only at the following harmony. Thus the six-five chord could be used in place of the sixth chord in the third, seventh, and penultimate measures of the chorale above, since the fifth is prepared by the preceding chord.

From this it is clear that this second manner of treating the bass already permits great variety, particularly when all customary inversions of chords containing nonessential and essential dissonances, and similarly both types of regular and irregular passing motions are used, which give it even more variety. Such a bass can be useful and adequate for all types of musical compositions that are merely supposed to sound well.

The third manner of writing a bass results from taking every opportunity to use chords outside of the scale. However, these chords must be dominants of triads contained in the scale of the main key. For example, in the key of C major one has the dominant chord A major of D minor, B major of E minor, D major of G major, and E major of A minor. Such digressions from the scale of the main key give the bass a stranger flavor and stimulate attention by the quality of the dominant chords, which continually suggest a subsequent chord. [17] Thus the lower bass in example 1.21 is much more striking than the upper one.

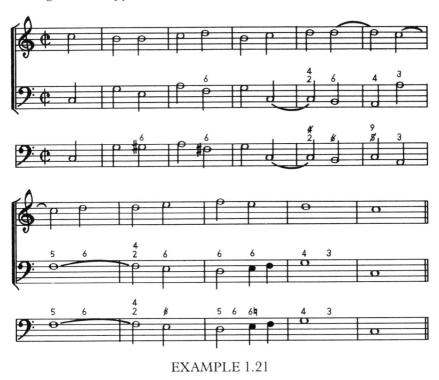

EXAMPLE 1.21

Of course, one can go even further with these dominant chords and use even those of the dominants of keys of which one can digress. Such remote keys have the greatest impact when they are used successfully. But great care is necessary here, because those who do not pay attention can easily digress so far that a return is difficult and the main key is no longer felt. Only the dominant chords of dominants whose tonic is a secondary key of the main key are appropriate for this use, and then it is necessary that the real dominant chord follow directly after it. [18] Example 1.22 presents the most natural ways of preparing these chords. The tonic is C with the major third.

EXAMPLE 1.22

However, F-sharp major before B major as the dominant of E minor would be a mistake in C major, since no digression occurs to B because of its remoteness from the main key. The phrase at (A) in example 1.23, in which even a further step is taken, would be much less acceptable in C major. But the phrase at (B), where even four dominant chords follow one another, is acceptable; all these chords belong to keys to which one can modulate from C major.

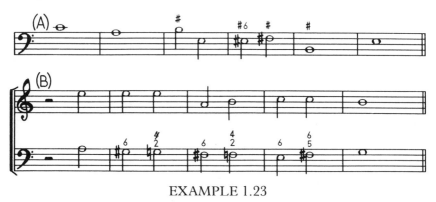

EXAMPLE 1.23

Such digressions, however, must be used only at a time and place where they are a means of expression or where they support it. Imagine the words *Herzlich lieb hab' ich dich, O Herr!* under the *cantus firmus* in example 1.23.

In this case, the bass at (a), which expresses something wild and violent by means of the sudden succession of dominant chords, would be totally inappropriate; a simple bass that remains more faithful to the scale of the main key, which for this phrase can be C major as well as A minor, would be preferable. [19] The matter would be entirely different if, instead, the words *O Ewigkeit, du Donnerwort!* were placed below the *cantus firmus*; here the bass at (a) is appropriate.

This can already serve as a tentative proof of the extent to which harmony is capable of expressions, and how nonsensical it is to ascribe all expression just to melody, which, when its harmonic accompaniment is altered, often changes just as much in expression. Of course, we are only speaking here of such melodies that permit changes in the harmonic accompaniment, of which, however, there are many. In the others, which are already expressive in themselves, harmony can still function as a support of the expression.

Besides, many phrases, which otherwise would be harsh and empty, can be made more correct and euphonious by means of these interpolated dominant chords. Consider the three basses in example 1.24 to the same melody.

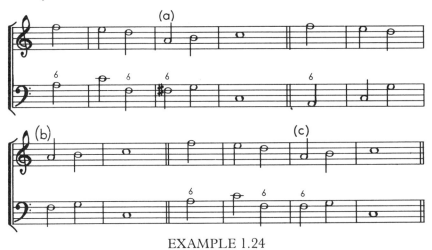

EXAMPLE 1.24

The F-sharp at (a) in the first bass, as the inversion of the dominant chord before the dominant of C, improves the two forbidden successive major thirds that occur at (b), where the stepwise progression of the fundamental bass, which is heard without inversion, sounds very harsh. [20] At (c) the two consecutive major thirds are more tolerable than in the preceding example, yet this bass is still very lifeless because of the repetition of the same sixth chord on F. However, all these irregularities are removed by the F-sharp of the first example, and thus the first is the best harmonic accompaninment to this melody.

Finally, if required by the expression, sudden digressions to remote keys, enharmonic progressions and transitions, sudden shifts, and similar harmonic devices that can produce great effects can be applied to a *cantus firmus*. This is the fourth manner of composing a bass to a given melody. It is self-evident that this fourth type is suited only to the expression of violent and most highly intense sentiments. But this demands a master of harmony who is already familiar with what has been said in the first volume, particularly in the eighth chapter. For that reason, instead of further lectures about this material, I will add here the beginning of a chorale with different basses that increase in affect. This will show how varied the harmony to a melody can be, depending on what purpose or expression it requires. But first I would like to present for consideration the following doctrines that must be observed by young composers who want to practice this way in strict composition as well as in expression.

1. Each bass line as well as the harmonies that accompany it must be homogeneous. That is, the progressions must not be simple or diatonic at one time and extravagant and enharmonic at another; nor should they remain on one harmony for a long time and then suddenly go from one harmony to the next; nor should they progress in simple counterpoint at one time but in florid or embellished counterpoint at another. None of these should occur unless the *cantus firmus* has words that suddenly change in affect, and yet moderation and purposefulness are to be observed here; otherwise the whole can easily become clumsy and comical. [21] The various types of accompaniment must be considered as materials for a character piece: Just as one building is constructed of ashlar, another of limestone, and yet another of wood instead of stone, depending upon the character of the building, and just as an inept mixture of building materials would be inappropriate for a building, the same is true with a musical composition if a certain harmonious mixture of chords and progressions is not observed.

2. The harmonies must be chosen according to the affect of the whole— consonant and simple for quiet expression, more elaborate for the affective style, and most extravagant for the most passionate expressions.

3. The bass must be written in such a way that each of the inner voices has a singable melody that is not contrary to the expression.

4. [The composer] must also pay attention to cadences so that he does not close where the meaning of the words does not tolerate a rest point, or, vice versa, that he does not cause something further to be expected where the phrase or period should have come to an end.

In the following harmonizations [example 1.25], different cadences are used, some of which produce more, some less or no repose at all. Since our intention here is not to show how the bass must be written to conform most perfectly to the words of the melody *Ach Gott und Herr, wie gross und schwer sind mein begangne Sünden!*, but only to demonstrate how varied the bass could be to this melody according to the nature of the expression, hopefully no one will object that the cadences in these examples are often contrary to the meaning of the preceding words. By the way, everything pertaining to the mechanics of cadences has already been discussed in the sixth chapter of the first volume.

[30] Here there are twenty-six basses to one melody, each of which is best suited to this or that expression.[d]

In the first harmonization only the most natural and most easily understood harmonies are used, without regard for the harmonic divisions of the phrase, since a restful cadence should not be used at the word *schwer* in the fourth measure, but instead at the word *Sünden* in the seventh and eighth measures.

The second bass is better harmonically with regard to the phrase divisions, because one expects further progression after the second as well as fourth measures. There is also greater variety of chords here than in the first bass, in which only the three primary chords are used; in this one, three additional chords are used in the second, fourth, and seventh measures, which make the melody more noble.

The third bass contains a foreign dominant chord, namely, of D minor in the second measure. This causes the listener to be more attentive, since the main key of B-flat major is weakened and, so to speak, put out of mind by the C-sharp. The same also applies to the subsequent chords in the third,

[d]This remarkable example is mentioned briefly by Putnam Aldrich in his article, "'Rhythmic Harmony' as taught by Johann Philipp Kirnberger," *Studies in Eighteenth-Century Music*, edited by H. C. Robbins Landon in collaboration with Roger E. Chapman (New York, 1970), pp. 37–52. In this article, Aldrich discusses the ways that Kirnberger uses harmony to articulate or to avoid articulation of melodic phrases and phrase divisions. The term "rhythmic harmony" is somewhat misleading, since it can easily be confused with "harmonic rhythm." It is used by Aldrich because the word *Rhythmus* is sometimes used interchangeably with *Einschnitt* by Kirnberger to denote a musical phrase or rhythmic unit. See Volume II, chapter 4, section III.

fourth, and seventh measures, which have thirds other than those determined by the scale of B-flat.

In the second measure of the fourth harmonization there is an A with
the figures $^6_5$ in the bass. This dissonant chord totally negates [the feeling of]
a phrase division (even though the melody here has all the characteristics of a

cadence) and makes further progression even more necessary than a secondary chord from the scale. The chord of the second on the second half of the third measure is closely connected with the following chord, as is suited to the words *wie gross und schwer*.

In the sixth and seventh measures of the fifth harmonization, the bass is

very well suited to the related words *begangne Sünden*.

In the sixth harmonization, as in the third, the word "und" is accompanied by a dissonant chord, which, as above, makes further progres-

EXAMPLE 1.25 (*continued*)

schwer sind   mein be - gang-ne   Sün -   den]

sion necessary.

The following basses more or less express the character of a repentant sinner by means of the accompanying foreign and unexpected harmonies

EXAMPLE 1.25 (*continued*)

[Ach   Gott   und   Herr,   wie   gross   und

and are highly recommended for study to anyone eager to learn.

An illustration where the bass progresses in parallel motion with the vocal part is at no. 14. This is sometimes required by the declamation of the words, particularly at main words or syllables. [31] But this rule applies only to the outer voices. This restriction of melodic progression can seldom occur

EXAMPLE 1.25 (*continued*)

schwer sind mein be - gang-ne Sün — den]

in the inner voices, because of the extraordinary difficulty it entails with regard to strict composition.

Illustrations of contrary motion are at no. 16 and no. 18.

At no. 20 the bass melody is a canonic imitation of the principal melody.

We cannot help being amazed at the variety that harmony offers. The harmonies that could be used with this melody are not at all exhausted by these twenty-six basses. If one now considers that at least as many melodies can be written to each of these basses, that each melody can be changed again in countless ways by florid counterpoint—what wealth, what diversity!

Before we conclude this chapter, we must mention yet another difficulty that occurs when a bass is set to a melody that remains for a long time on one note or repeats the same note many times in succession. Here the bass and harmonies above it must, by themselves, produce the expression that the whole is to communicate. To vary the harmonies that are suited to this note and that are also in conformity with the expression requires some skill in the harmonic arts and particularly in contrapuntal inversions, which will be discussed in the course of this work [Volume II, parts 2 and 3]. Nothing is more repulsive than when a composer is unable to progress with the harmony in such places. One or two chords that alternate as in example 1.26 make a veritable wailing out of the melody, which, taken apart from the harmony, is already rigid in itself. [32] But this melody can acquire great charm and aesthetic force from an accompaniment of well-chosen alternating harmonies.

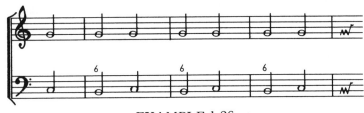

EXAMPLE 1.26

It is not necessary that every beat have a different harmony. Often just the tonic and dominant chords are sufficient; but they must not be of one kind, as above, but must alternate many ways in their different inversions, as in example 1.27.

EXAMPLE 1.27

In addition to these two triads of the tonic and dominant, many others can be used. Indeed, all triads and seventh chords in which the sustained tone occurs can be used, along with their inversions. But one has to pay attention to the following.

1. One must get to the note to which the sustained note progresses, and to the harmony that must accompany it, by means of a natural harmonic progression.

2. With a dissonant chord, the sustained note must either occur again in the following chord of resolution, as in the examples given shortly before, or it must proceed to a note contained in the chord of resolution. Therefore, such a dissonant chord can only be used on the last beat of the sustained note.

3. Except at the beginning of a piece, one must never use the same chord on an accented beat that was just used on the preceding unaccented beat, because the progression to a different chord, which the ear expects, is thereby obstructed, and a faulty monotony is produced. [See example 1.28.]

EXAMPLE 1.28

[33] Here we refer to such passages where the beats of the harmonic progression occur with each note, in this case, every half measure.[e] But if these beats are lengthened so that the harmonic progression occurs at the

---

[e] Here Kirnberger alludes to what is commonly called "harmonic rhythm" today. This term was unknown in Kirnberger's day, which accounts for the rather awkward phrase, "beats of the harmonic progression," to express this concept.

rate of one or two to two or more measures, this rule must also be expanded and observed here. Basically, example 1.29 at (a) is just as faulty and monotonous as at (b), unless the melody were treated so that it was heard as at (c), which is good.

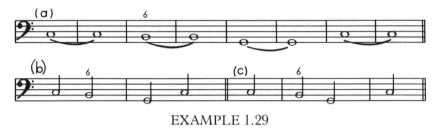

EXAMPLE 1.29

This rule applies not only to such melodies that remain on one tone, but in general. On the other hand, the chord of an accented beat can be used very well on the unaccented beat, as in the last examples, indeed often without any inversions. [34] Thus the first phrase of the song *Ein veste Burg ist unser Gott* is more striking as at (a) in example 1.30 than if the harmony were inverted or changed, as at (b) and (c).

EXAMPLE 1.30

Yet such matters belong with the licenses from strict composition, which are successful only if they serve to intensify the expression.

4. Of the inversions of triads and of the seventh chord, only those in which no leading tone or dissonance would be doubled are permitted, since

otherwise faulty progressions would result. The consonant six-four chord, as the second inversion of the triad, occurs only when it is a dominant chord of the following chord, to which the same note still remains in the melody. It

occurs in place of $\begin{smallmatrix} 6 \\ 4 \\ 3 \end{smallmatrix}$. [see example 1.31].

EXAMPLE 1.31

[35] To clarify this special situation with the fourth, I will present further examples [example 1.32].

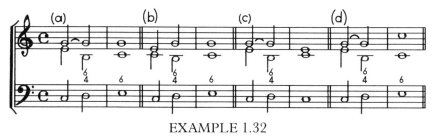

EXAMPLE 1.32

At (a) the example is good, because the fourth is prepared and is sustained. At (b) it is not good, because it enters without preparation. At (c) and (d) it is incorrect, because it is not sustained into the second measure.

5. Even if the harmonic progressions are natural and correct, it must also be observed that they not be extravagant in modulation and not digress too far from the main key. Thus example 1.33 at (a) would be totally wrong in C major, because it digresses too far from the main key; it is better at (b).

[36] Example 1.34 may serve to show beginners how varied the harmony could be to a sustained note, and how the progression to the next note could be accomplished in many ways.

EXAMPLE 1.33

EXAMPLE 1.34 (*to be continued*)

EXAMPLE 1.34 (*continued*)

EXAMPLE 1.34 (*continued*)

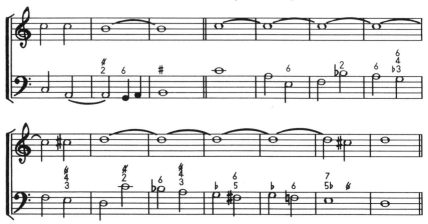

However, it still remains to be noted here that a note in the upper voice will finally tire the listener if it is held too long, even if it is held by the greatest virtuoso or singer. [39] Whoever is free to write what he wants must limit himself in this matter. For it is one thing to write a harmonic accompaniment to a given *cantus firmus*, and another to write one on one's own. Even in the inner voices a note must not be repeated too often or sustained too long; the middle voices in the chorales of the elder Bach are written in such a way that they can pass for a principal voice because of their melody.

However, in pedal points, where the sustained note is in the bass, this note can be held much longer without tiring the listener, because it is the foundation upon which the manifold harmonies that are heard simultaneously with it are built. One can also consider such a sustained bass note as the standard to which all chords above it are compared.

When the sustained note of a *cantus firmus* lasts for very many measures, one must be economical with the changes of harmony and allow each chord to remain for one or even two full measures, since otherwise it would be impossible to use so many harmonies.

Slow changes of harmony generally have far greater impact in the church or serious style than sudden changes, whether they are used with a sustained or progressing *cantus firmus*. The first chorus of Handel's coronation music for the King of England and several other works of this sort by the same composer are the most outstanding models of this.

What is to be observed about modulations in writing a bass can be learned from the seventh chapter of the first volume; therefore we will not repeat it here. We would like to note only that the modulation is often undefined in a *cantus firmus*. Thus the passage at (a) in example 1.35 can conclude in C major as well as in its dominant, depending upon which of the following basses is set to it.

EXAMPLE 1.35

[40] Modulation with respect to the same melody can more or less be prevented by the harmony or can be directed to entirely different keys. Thus the basses in example 1.36 can also be set to (a) in example 1.35, though some of them only in the middle of a piece. Several others can also be used, as can be seen from the chorale example above [example 1.25].

EXAMPLE 1.36

Among the basses set to a melody, some give the whole a quiet indifferent expression, others are pleasantly lively, others sad, and some express the greatest despair. The apprentice must pay attention to this, and always try to select the best bass and best harmony. His sensitivity must serve as a guide, since no definite rules can be given about this matter. It is sufficient that harmony provides him with such diverse means that nothing is left to be desired from this side.

It is clear from this to what extent harmony and strict composition contribute to expression, since they can often give so different an expression to the same melody. But the extent to which the most beautiful melodies can be disfigured by insipid and false harmonies, and by incorrect writing, can be seen by everyone who owns the Telemann chorale book.[f]

[f]Georg Philipp Telemann, *Fast allgemeines Evangelisch-musikalisches Lieder-Buch* (Hamburg, 1730).

CHAPTER 2

The Scale, and the Keys and Modes Derived from It

I. THE OLD MODES

[41] The Greeks are said to have had three principal types of scales, which were differentiated by the terms diatonic, chromatic, and enharmonic.

According to Ptolemy, the diatonic genus was formed by ascending from the principal tone to its fourth, first by a half step and from there by two whole steps in these proportions: 243/256, 8/9, 8/9.[a] These can be represented approximately by the steps B, c, d, e.

Here as well as in the two following examples, these steps are only approximated by the current designation of pitches, since our degrees have different proportions.

The chromatic genus ascended from the principal tone by two half steps and a minor third in these proportions: 27/28, 14/15, 5/6, or roughly B, c, c-sharp, e.

However, the enharmonic genus ascended from the principal tone to the fourth by a quarter step, then a half step and a major third in the proportions 45/46, 23/24, 4/5, or roughly B, B-sharp, c, e.

For many centuries, the chromatic and enharmonic genera of the Greeks were no longer known in music; as far back as we can go uninterrupted in the history of music, at least a thousand years before our time, we find only the diatonic scale. And although progressions that are called

---

[a]Ptolemy's *Harmonics* (second century A.D.) is a major source of information about the musical system of the ancient Greeks, including the tonoi, the three genera, and various tuning systems. Ptolemy did not much favor the system described here.

314

chromatic and enharmonic sometimes occur today in the works of the newer composers, it is generally true that only the diatonic scale has been in use since the decline of ancient Greek music. Our complete system of notes today—C, C-sharp, D, D-sharp, E, etc.—is basically nothing but a system of many diatonic scales joined together, as we shall see in greater detail later on.

[42] The basis of the tone system currently in use throughout Europe is this diatonic scale with the interval proportions written below:[b]

$$\text{C} \quad \text{D} \quad \text{E} \quad\quad \text{F} \quad \text{G} \quad \text{A} \quad \text{B} \quad\quad \text{c}$$
$$\frac{8}{9} \quad \frac{9}{10} \quad \frac{15}{16} \quad \frac{8}{9} \quad \frac{9}{10} \quad \frac{8}{9} \quad \frac{15}{16}$$

We will call this the *basic diatonic scale*. However, this scale is said not to have come into use until Zarlino's time,[c] since before him the steps had these older Greek proportions.[d]

$$\text{C} \quad \text{D} \quad \text{E} \quad\quad \text{F} \quad \text{G} \quad \text{A} \quad \text{B} \quad\quad \text{c}$$
$$\frac{8}{9} \quad \frac{8}{9} \quad \frac{243}{256} \quad \frac{8}{9} \quad \frac{8}{9} \quad \frac{8}{9} \quad \frac{243}{256}$$

It has already been shown in the first volume of this work how five additional scales are contained in this one basic scale. They can also be called diatonic scales and can be used just as well as the basic scale, though each has different intervals.

These six scales are:

1. C, D, E, F, G, A, B, c, etc.
2. D, E, F, G, A, B, c, d, etc.
3. E, F, G, A, B, c, d, e, etc.
4. F, G, A, B, c, d, e, f, etc.
5. G, A, B, c, d, e, f, g, etc.
6. A, B, c, d, e, f, g, a, etc.

We have indicated the exact interval proportions of these six scales in a table in the first volume.[e]

[b] In chapter 1 of Volume I, Kirnberger identified this tuning of the diatonic scale, in which the intervals are just, as the one used by the older composers. See Volume I, chapter 1, note d.

[c] See Volume I, chapter 1, note f.

[d] The proportions given here by Kirnberger are those of Pythagorean tuning.

[e] See Volume I, chapter 2, table 2.1.

In the earliest periods of church music, no other pitches than these were known; and, depending on which of these scales the melody was based, only the notes indicated here could be used. It is apparent that one could not close to the octave through the major seventh or leading tone in most of these scales, which is considered absolutely necessary today.

It has already been mentioned in the first volume that this imperfection was probably too noticeable for singers with a fine ear, and that they made cadences to the octave through the leading tone, even though it was not indicated. [43] This then led to the gradual introduction of the notes C-sharp, D-sharp, F-sharp, and G-sharp. Even though cadences in the Dorian and Aeolian modes were previously notated as at (A) in example 2.1, it is to be presumed that the best singers may have sung them as at (B). We know for sure that they sang the soft B or our B-flat instead of the hard B or our H [B-natural] in certain modes, even though it was not indicated in the notes.

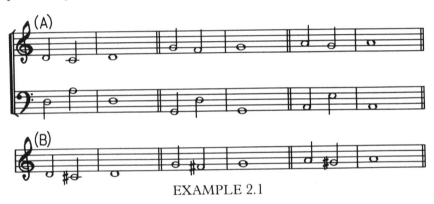

EXAMPLE 2.1

Thus one will scarely err by imagining the old church modes in the following way, as they are still used today:

1. C, D, E, F, G, A, B, c
2. D, E, F, G, A, B, c♯, d
3. E, F, G, A, B, c, d, e
4. F, G, A, B, c, d, e, f
5. G, A, B, c, d, e, f♯, g
6. A, B, c, d, e, f, g♯, a.

Since many compositions are still performed in these scales today, both in the Roman Catholic and Protestant Churches, it appears necessary to me to present sufficient instruction about the nature and treatment of the old church modes before discussing the tone system currently in use.

[44] These six modes are still designated by the names of the former Greek modes:

the first, the Ionian mode
the second, the Dorian mode
the third, the Phrygian mode
the fourth, the Lydian mode
the fifth, the Mixolydian mode
the sixth, the Aeolian mode.

What is called here the first, second mode, etc., refers only to the order adopted by us before. Originally D, or the Dorian mode, was the first; E, or the Phrygian mode, the second; etc. A, or the Aeolian mode, was the fifth, and C, or the Ionian mode, the sixth. Only the original four, namely, D, E,[f] F, and G, were used for the psalms. However, one finds that some of the ancients call the second mode Phrygian and the third Dorian. But today the designations as they have been given here are commonly used.

Each of these six modes was treated in two ways, which were called *authentic* and *plagal*.

The authentic type consisted of taking the range of the melody from the tonic to the dominant, and later up to the octave; but the plagal type took its range from the fifth below up to the tonic, or also to the dominant.

One can guess how this two-fold treatment of one mode originated. In the old times, each melody had only a small range, perhaps of a fifth, which was later expanded to the octave. It was the custom of the earliest churches to set the psalms and hymns for two choirs, which alternated with and responded to each other, so to speak. (Therefore such works were called *antiphona*.) Now if the melody of the first or principal choir had a range from the tonic to approximately the dominant, the other choir had to begin and end differently if its melody were to be distinguished from the first; but it had to remain in the same scale. Furthermore, if the second melody were to maintain the character of the first, it had to ascend and descend by the same steps that were employed in the first melody. [45] Thus the two-fold treatment of one and the same mode came into being, namely, the authentic and the plagal.

A single example will clarify the matter sufficiently.

Suppose one wanted to set a psalm for two alternating choirs in the Dorian mode so that after the first choir has sung a verse or phrase the second were to repeat the same or similar phrase with a different but

[f]C instead of E was mistakenly printed here.

somewhat similar melody. Now to comprehend how both melodies could be similar but sufficiently different, let us imagine the Dorian scale as in example 2.2.

EXAMPLE 2.2

The first melody thus proceeded from the tonic D and ascended up to A or B, or, if you want, possibly to d. Thus the melody got its principal character from the position of the half steps that are found within the octave, and which are designated here by black notes; that is, here the second of the tonic was major, but the third, minor. However, to retain this character, the second melody must not be sung in some other scale, but rather its range must be taken from this scale so that the semitones would be in just the same positions as in the scale of the principal melody. As is evident, this could happen in no other way than by proceeding from the dominant up to its octave above the tonic, as in example 2.3.

EXAMPLE 2.3

In this way the scales of both melodies were given a uniform character and yet were sufficiently without being based on really different scales.

Table 2.1 presents the scales of the twelve church modes all together, the six authentic and six plagal.

[46] If necessary for the sake of singers, each of these modes can be transposed higher or lower according to the current tuning of organs. But one has to pay close attention with these transpositions that the placement of the half steps or so-called mi-fa remains exactly the same as it is in the original mode.

[47] I will note in addition that this two-fold treatment of each mode was originally invented for chants in which one choir answered another. Later, however, sometimes the authentic and sometimes the plagal mode were also chosen for psalms and hymns for a single choir.

For example, the hymn *Jesus Christus unser Heyland* is in the authentic Dorian mode throughout, but *Christ lag in Todesbanden* is in the plagal Dorian mode throughout.

TABLE 2.1.

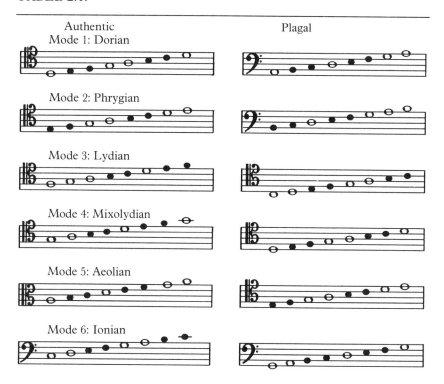

In our current system, where the keys are divided into twelve major and twelve minor ones, we have actually retained only two of the old modes, namely, the Ionian and the Aeolian; the former is the model of all major keys, the latter of all minor keys. However, as we shall see below, each of the twelve major and twelve minor keys has its own character as the result of temperament. But if equal temperament were introduced, as so many insist, the whole wealth of keys would in fact be reduced to only two—namely, C major and A minor—since all major keys would then be mere transpositions of the others, without the slightest individuality of character.

Knowledge of these old church modes and their correct treatment is necessary not only because correct fugue writing cannot be learned without them, as will be clear from what I shall say later about this matter, but also because the old style of writing has real advantages which are missing in the new style.

We have numerous old hymns that are so full of feeling and expression that they cannot be reworked in the new style without noticeably diminishing their value.

Moreover, the old modes have more variety of harmony and modulation than the newer style permits in such simple hymns, where generally only the tonic and its dominant and subdominant chords are used. As an example, I will accompany the chorale melody *Ach Gott, vom Himmel sieh darein* with harmonies suggested by its mode and then present the same melody as it is set or performed by several new composers or organists. Anyone who does not find the first harmonization expressive and admirable, but the second utterly insipid and disgusting, must not have the slightest sensitivity. [See example 2.4.]

[49] I can also state that the finest of the more recent composers, J. S. Bach, considered the technique of composing in the old church modes to be necessary, as is to be seen from his *Catechismus: Gesänge.*[g] Many of these chorale melodies are set in this way.

EXAMPLE 2.4 (*to be continued*)

[g]The work to which Kirnberger refers here is: *Dritter Theil der Clavierübung, bestehend in verschieden Vorspielen über die Catechismus- und andere Gesänge vor die Orgel* (Leipzig, 1739).

EXAMPLE 2.4 (*continued*)

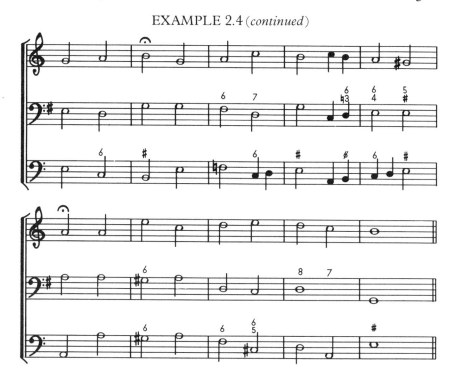

For example:

Christ aller Welt Trost (p. 13) and
Kyrie, Gott heiliger Geist (p. 15), which is Phrygian and transposed to G.
Dies sind die heiligen zehn Gebot (p. 30), Mixolydian; also p. 35, the fugue
    on the same melody.
Wir glauben all' an einen Gott (p. 37), Dorian.
Vater unser im Himmelreich (p. 40), Dorian, but transposed to E.
Christ unser Herr zum Jordan kam (p. 47), Dorian transposed to E.[h]
Aus tiefer Noth, etc. (p. 51), Phrygian.
Jesus Christus, etc. (p. 60), Dorian transposed to E.   Etc.

    What the older composers so often and so universally confirm about the
diversity of character in the old church modes also appears to be no idle
fancy. Without dwelling on what the ancient Greek writers said about the
different effects of the modes (since it is not certain that our church modes

[h] This setting of *Christ unser Herr zum Jordan kam* would appear to be Dorian on C, not E.
The four-part fugue on *Jesus Christus unser Heiland* (p. 60) is Dorian on F, not E.

are the same as those designated by the Greeks with these names),[2] I only want to present the remarks of a few more recent authors.

[50] Generally they derive the individual character of each mode from the position of the half steps, or the mi-fa. To understand the effect that results from this, imagine only the two most contrasting scales:

$$C \quad D \quad \overset{\frown}{E \quad F} \quad G \quad A \quad \overset{\frown}{B \quad c}$$
$$\underset{\smile}{E \quad F} \quad G \quad A \quad \underset{\smile}{B \quad c} \quad d \quad e$$

In the first, the second, third, sixth, and seventh are major, but in the other these intervals are minor. If one also considers how these intervals are approached in both modes by ascending or descending steps, it is easily understood how different the character of a melody would turn out, depending on which of these scales is used. The first is obviously somewhat lively and gay, while the other expresses something sinister and insidious by its small and somewhat peevish and creeping steps.

There are various old church melodies in which the expression of happiness or sadness, of confidence and doubt, and other feelings are so obvious that everyone feels them. That this is accomplished mostly by the judicious choice of mode, however, becomes obvious by the fact that these characters are almost completely lost if one changes the mode.

It may indeed be that some have spoken too pointedly about the specific character of each mode. But some of this is true and perceptible to every sensitive ear. [51] I will present here the characters of the different modes as they have been specified by Printz and Buttstett. Printz says:[i]

2. Everyone knows, for example, that it is said of Timotheus that he incited Alexander irresistibly to war by songs in the Phrygian mode. Today we cannot imagine how such great power could be contained in only one mode. Also we cannot say for sure how the Greek modes were constructed or how they were treated by their composers. However, for those who are still concerned with research into the music of antiquity, I would like to submit for examination the conjecture of one scholar. He believes that what the Greeks called modes is not a special tone system, but a melody especially characterized by such a tone system, like perhaps the national melodies of different peoples today. Thus, he believes that if one finds in antiquity a melody written in the Phrygian, Dorian, or another mode, one must understand it in much the same way as when one says Polish, English, or Sicilian today. National dance melodies do undeniably to have their very well-defined characters of expression.

---

[i] Unfortunately, Kirnberger does not indicate which of Wolfgang Casper Printz's several works is the source of this information. A similar listing of the character of each mode, but for the six plagal as well as six authentic modes, is given in his *Phrynis Mitileneaeus, oder Satyrischer Componist*, Vol. I (Dresden and Leipzig, 1676), pp. 39–40.

The Ionian mode is joyous and gay.
The Dorian mode is moderate and pious.
The Phrygian mode is very sad.
The Lydian mode is hard, unfriendly.
The Mixolydian mode is merry, somewhat temperate.
The Aeolian mode is moderate, tender, somewhat sad.

Buttstett gives the character of both the authentic and plagal modes in this way:[j]

The Dorian—lively, cheerful, and ceremonious.
The Hypodorian[3a]—simple, humble, sad.
The Phrygian—very sad, but also charming and pleasant.
The Hypophrygian—lamenting, lachrymose.
The Lydian—menacing.
The Hypolydian—lamenting.[k]
The Mixolydian—serious.
The Hypomixolydian—modest.
The Aeolian—pleasant, charming.
The Hypoaeolian—sighing, lachrymose, sad, conciliatory.
The Ionian and Hypoionian—lively, joyous, gay.

I shall leave definitions of the different characters of these modes as they are and present here only what I dare to assert confidently about this matter.

Generally every interval that is distinguished from others of the same name has a different effect, since a minor second such as e—f is one thing, and a major or augmented second such as c–d or f–g-sharp is another. The same applies to the other intervals.

Even if the intervals of thirds, fourths, fifths, etc., are identical in their ratios, they become dissimilar in effect because of the different seconds contained in them. With minor thirds, for example, the half step sometimes falls after the first note and sometimes after the second note, as here: e f g; d e f. Furthermore, the effect of the same interval differs according to the harmony on which it is based. [52] For example, e–f–g in the Phrygian mode is entirely different from e–f–g when these notes ascend from the third to

3a. The first is always authentic, the other plagal.

_____

[j]Johann Heinrich Buttstett, *Ut, Re, Mi, Fa, Sol, La, Tota Musica et Harmonia Aeterna* (Leipzig, 1716), chapter 5, pp. 140–68).
[k]This entry is missing in Kirnberger. See Buttstett, p. 160.

the fifth of the final in the Ionian mode; these notes are different again when they ascend from the second to the fourth of the final in the Dorian mode and have yet an entirely different effect when they ascend from the fifth to the seventh in the Aeolian mode. This can generally be stated about all intervals.

From the different position of the half steps in the fourths and fifths, from which the scales that determine the old modes are combined, it is understandable that each mode must have something peculiar to it, and must be more suitable than the others to this or that expression.

The Ionian mode has nothing but euphonious and cheerful progressions from its final: C D, C E, C F, C G, C A. Only the progression from C to B is harsh, and thus is used only when one wants to express something harsh and unpleasant.

The Dorian also has good progressions: D E, D F, D G, D A; only D to B is harsh, and thus is seldom used. In the Ionian mode, each note of the triad on the final has a good fourth: C F, E A, G c. But in the Dorian mode, the third, F, has a harsh fourth, F B. One will easily recognize the distinction between the same melody in these two modes. [See example 2.5]

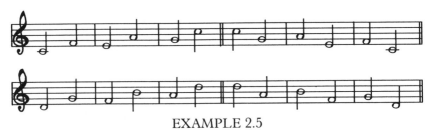

EXAMPLE 2.5

This melodic phrase is as agreeable in the first example as it is harsh and unpleasant in the second.

In the Phrygian mode, the progressions from the final are all good: E F, E G, E A, E B, E c, E d, E e.

The Aeolian mode is identical with the Phrygian except for the second from the final. Yet the minor second E F in the Phrygian mode produces a sadness that extends over the entire mode, but this is not felt in the Aeolian mode.

The Lydian mode, F G A B c d e f, is without doubt the harshest and least pleasant, because the first note does not have a perfect fourth.

[53] The Mixolydian mode is not as perfect by far as the Ionian, because it lacks a leading tone; but it has just as pure intervals from its final. The

progression from the final to the second below it gives this mode a dignity that cannot be obtained in the Ionian. But if this progression is avoided, it is very well suited for lively and cheerful expression.

The chorales in example 2.6 may serve as illustrations of melodies in which the progressions of each mode are rigorously observed.

[57] Each mode is precisely determined in these melodies. The follow-

EXAMPLE 2.6 (*to be continued*)

EXAMPLE 2.6 (*continued*)

Phrygian. Erbarm dich mein, O Herre Gott!

Herzlich thut mich verlangen.

Mixolydian. Komm Gott Schöpfer, Heiliger Geist.

Gelobet seyst du Jesu Christ.

EXAMPLE 2.6 (*continued*)

Aeolian. Allein zu dir, Herr Jesu Christ.

Ich ruf zu dir, Herr Jesu Christ.

This Chorale is transposed down a fifth.

Ionian. Vom Himmel hoch da komm ich her.

EXAMPLE 2.6 (*continued*)

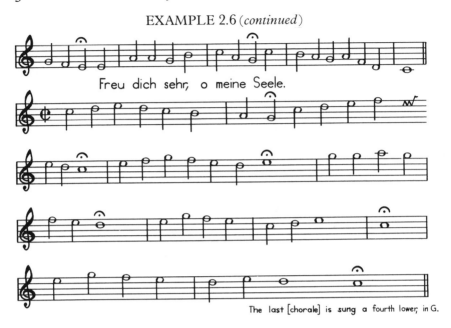

Freu dich sehr, o meine Seele.

The last [chorale] is sung a fourth lower, in G.

ing intervals always occur: The major sixth D B in the Dorian, the minor sixth A F in the Aeolian; the minor second E F in the Phrygian, but the major seconds A B and D E in the Aeolian or Dorian; the major second below or minor seventh above the final (G F) in the Mixolydian, but the minor second below or major seventh above the final (C B) in the Ionian.

For the invention of a good and expressive melody, the first consideration of the composer must be directed at the choice of mode. If he has to write church pieces in the old modes, he cannot ignore the difference of their characters and their peculiarities. After having noted what is necessary regarding this point, I shall now talk about the more precise treatment of all these old modes.

If one were to treat the old modes in an entirely strict way—that is, so that no note not contained in the scale were permitted anywhere, neither in the melody nor in the accompanying harmony—this would result in very constrained and imperfect compositions. [58] Because the older composers sensed the all-too-restricted nature of their scales, they gradually introduced the necessary semitones. Therefore, the best way of treating these modes is to avoid wherever possible in the principal melody as well as in the bass the notes not contained in the common mode; that is, not to use B-flat in D, F-sharp in E, b-flat in F, or f-sharp in G. But these notes are permitted

in the inner voices to avoid a tritone or otherwise to create a more euphonious sound. The leading tone is particularly necessary at all cadences
involving the dominant chord.

However, one cannot close in all modes in the same way; some close
through the chord of the dominant, others through the chord of the subdominant. The Ionian, Dorian, Lydian, and Aeolian modes close through
the chord of the dominant; see (a), (b), (c), and (d) in example 2.7. But the
Phrygian mode closes through the chord of the subdominant to the tonic
chord with the major third, as at (e), or also through the chord a second
below the tonic or its first inversion, as at (f) and (g). The Mixolydian mode
also closes through the chord of the subdominant, since its dominant does
not have a major third in the scale [see (h)].

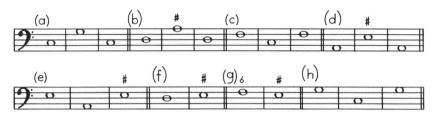

EXAMPLE 2.7

Another favored close in the old modes is the half cadence from the
tonic chord to the dominant chord with the major third. Such cadences in
the Ionian, Dorian, Lydian, and Aeolian modes are shown in example 2.8.

EXAMPLE 2.8

[59] But the Phrygian and Mixolydian modes are excepted, since their
dominants do not have a major third in their scales. If one were to use the
dominant with the major third throughout in the Mixolydian mode, the
mode would instantly become Ionian. However, the major third can be
added to the dominants in the Dorian and Aeolian modes even though they
are not contained in their scales, because they would still be entirely distinct
from the other modes.

Some claim that the major third above the tonic must always be used
with formal cadences, even when the third is minor in the scale. But this

cadence is harsh and objectionable when one closes from the dominant to the tonic in the Dorian and Aeolian modes as at (a) in example 2.9. However, it is euphonious and necessary when the subdominant chord with the minor third proceeds to the tonic, and cadences as at (b).

EXAMPLE 2.9

Among the hymns, there are a few that do not close with the principal note. For example, the chorale melody *Durch Adams Fall*, etc., given in example 2.6 is Dorian but closes on the fifth of the main note. Such cadences must be treated in conformity with the main mode. Thus it would be faulty if one were to conclude the cited chorale in A with a minor third. The cadence must be as shown in example 2.10.

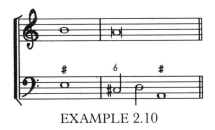

EXAMPLE 2.10

In the case of modulations, the tonic of the new key must retain the third that the scale of the main key indicates. Thus in the Dorian mode, for example, one modulates to the subdominant with the major third; but in the Aeolian mode, which is our minor mode today, one modulates to the subdominant with the minor third. In the Lydian mode, one modulates to the second degree with the major third, but in the Ionian, which is our major mode today, to the second degree with the minor third.

[60] That the old modes are far richer in modulation than ours today is evident from table 2.2, which shows the cadences in each mode to which one can digress from the main mode. By means of longer and shorter note values, it is shown approximately how long one must stay in the secondary modes in such pieces that digress to all the modes indicated. The cadences indicated by quarter notes belong to the more unusual and foreign digressions that are used only in long compositions.

TABLE 2.2.

[61] It must be noted here that among the old hymns there are a few of doubtful mode, so that one cannot immediately tell at first glance from which note they proceed. In such a case one need only look at the digressions to find the main mode and to organize the harmonies accordingly. However, if the modulations are of such a nature that they can belong to two modes, then both modes are valid, and one selects the one that corresponds most closely to the expression of the piece. Thus the melody of the hymn *Nun kommt der Heyden Heyland* is Dorian as well as Aeolian; likewise with the chorale *Auf meinen lieben Gott*. The chorale melodies *Christ lag in*

Todesbanden and *Kyrie Gott Heiliger Geist* can be treated as Phrygian as well
as Aeolian, etc. [62] But in fugal compositions of doubtful mode, the answer
immediately reveals the main mode, as will be shown later.

These are the main points that are to be observed in the treatment of the
old modes. I shall add a few examples here, which can serve to clarify the
preceding remarks. [See examples 2.11 and 2.12.]

EXAMPLE 2.11

EXAMPLE 2.12

Example 2.11 is Dorian, because b, as the major sixth of the main tone,
is used throughout, except for the first b-flat in measure two. [63] In spite of
the fact that the melody in the principal voice is the same, the second
example [example 2.12] is Aeolian, because the minor sixth of the main tone
is used throughout. The result is that the first example is much more
dignified and respectable than the second, and that the second is much more
delicate and tender than the first.

An example of the strictest treatment is the following chorale, *Komm
Gott Schöpfer*, etc., by J. Seb. Bach, which is in the Mixolydian mode.

EXAMPLE 2.13 (*to be continued*)

EXAMPLE 2.13 (*continued*)

[64] In examples 2.14 and 2.15, sometimes the minor and sometimes the major sixth and seventh are used in the harmonic accompaniment for the sake of more pleasant and smoother modulation.

[66] This type of harmonic treatment of the old modes is without doubt the most perfect, since it retains the greatest charm and variety for the ear. The keys unknown to the older composers were not introduced that soon, since only this style of writing was commonly used in polyphonic works for the church. Composers limited themselves in this matter to the most easily intelligible of all modes, the Ionian and Aeolian, the first of which was called the major mode and the second the minor mode. Due to the nature of the tempered organ at that time, these modes could only be transposed to six tones, so that there were only eight keys or modes in total, which are also called church modes by some. In order, these modes were: (1) D minor, (2) G minor, (3) A minor, (4) E minor, (5) C major, (6) F major, (7) G major, and (8) A major. But in choral music, the six old modes were retained. Some treated them in an entirely strict way, that is, without using foreign tones not contained in the scale, while others treated them rather freely. Today the old modes are neglected too much, particularly in Protestant countries, where church music is in a bad state almost everywhere. This is one of the reasons why church music today, even in the Catholic countries, has sunk so low that it can hardly be distinguished any more from theater music. No matter how well such music may be worked out, in church it always has a weak effect, if not one entirely contrary to the sentiments of piety. On the other hand, one should listen to music composed by good masters in the true

Das alte Jahr vergangen ist, by J. S. Bach

EXAMPLE 2.14

church modes, for instance a mass by Prenestini [Palestrina], Leonardo Leo, Lotti, Francesco Gasparini, Frescobaldi, Battiferri, Fux, Handel, J. S. Bach, Froberger, Zelenka, and others. Indeed, one should listen to a simple chorale! What power! What dignity appropriate for church and religion! What nobility of expression! This effect is certainly not produced by the modes alone, but nobody can deny that they contribute to it most forcefully. On this occasion I cannot conceal the righteous indignation that always overcomes me when I think about the new hymns that are written to the

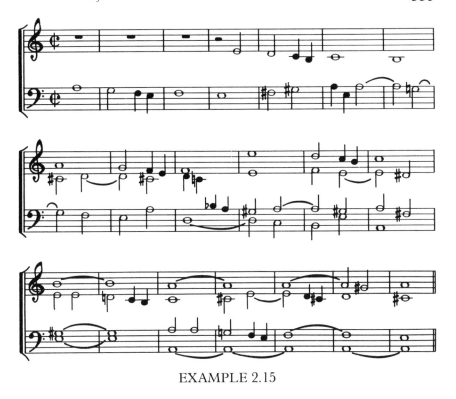

EXAMPLE 2.15

beautiful sacred poems of Gellert, Cramer, and others,[1] and that have already been introduced to some extent in several Protestant countries. Can there be anything more desecrating to religion than chorale settings that have the same mode, melodic features, and modulation as our most vulgar songs; and must not many Christians be stirred more to anger than devotion by them?

[67] The neglect of the old modes will in turn bring about the complete downfall of fugues, or rather has already done so. For rarely does a regular fugue ever appear anywhere. But the extent to which knowledge of these modes is necessary for writing fugues will be discussed later.

[1]Both Gellert and Cramer wrote sacred poems appropriate for use in the Protestant service. Christian Fürchtegott Gellert (1715–69) was one of the most popular poets of the German Enlightenment. He was professor of poetry, rhetoric, and moral philosophy in Leipzig. Johann Andreas Cramer (1723–88), a friend of Gellert, was professor of theology in Kiel.

II. THE KEYS AND MODES OF NEW MUSIC

As is clear from the preceding discussion, the old tone system led to only six different scales, each of which had its special tonic or fundamental note. And since each of these scales was treated in a two-fold way, authentic or plagal, this resulted in a total of twelve modes. In our current tone system—whose nature I have described sufficiently in the first volume and have defined by numbers according to the exact ratio of pitches—each note within the octave can be made the tonic, so that we now have twelve fundamental tones, while the old composers had only six. In addition, our system is constructed in such a way that each tonic has two useful scales, one with the major third, the other with the minor third. Consequently, we have a total of twenty-four different scales, twelve in the large or major mode and twelve in the small or minor mode.

In the first volume I have devised a table from which it can be seen at a glance how each of these twelve major or minor scales is distinguished from the others by various particular intervals.[m] This is now the place where I must discuss the character of these scales with regard to melodic quality, in order to show young composers what they have to consider about choice of key and mode[3b] in specific situations.

[68] The most important distinction results from the two modes. On the one hand the twelve major keys and on the other the twelve minor keys determine two categories that are entirely different in character.

In general, the major keys are distinguished from the minor keys by the following qualities:

Major keys have:	Minor keys have:
the major third,	the minor third,
the major sixth,	the minor sixth,
the major seventh.	the major seventh (ascending),
	the minor seventh (descending).

3b. The terms *key* and *mode* are not always used precisely and are very frequently interchanged. *Key* implies scale insofar as this or that note is its tonic; for example, to write in the key of C means to use the note C as the tonic. Now each note has two scales, namely, major or minor. *Mode* implies scale insofar as it is major or minor for the same tonic.

To speak precisely, one must say that new music has twelve *keys* and each key has two *modes*. However, one must not say either twenty-four keys or twenty-four modes, but rather twenty-four different scales that amount to twelve keys, each of which has two modes.

---

[m] See Volume I, chapter 2, table 2.2.

The reason why the ascending scale is different from the descending scale in minor modes is that the major seventh is necessary in the ascent as the leading tone—or, as the French appropriately call it, the *ton sensible*—in order to be able to close to the octave. Because of this interval, it is also necessary to change the minor sixth into a major sixth in the ascent, so that there will not be a leap of an augmented second from the minor sixth to the major seventh. For example:

$$\begin{array}{cccccccc} & & & & & \star & \star & \\ A & B & c & d & e & f\sharp & g\sharp & a \quad \text{(ascending)} \\ a & g & f & e & d & c & B & A \quad \text{(descending)} \end{array}$$

Since thirds and sixths are the intervals heard most frequently in melody, it can be seen from this that the difference in character between the major and minor keys must be considerable, and that the major modes are generally more pleasant, joyous, harmonious, and fuller sounding than the minor modes, since major thirds and sixths are more consonant than minor ones.

The following remark is for those who want to inquire more deeply into the origin of both modes and want to investigate more closely the reason for their distinction.

The most perfect and most soothing harmony is one that contains the notes produced by bowing a string or by blowing a pipe with increasing force. As is known, they follow the numbers in this order:

$$\begin{array}{cccccccc} 1 & 2 & 3 & 4 & 5 & 6 & 7 & 8 \\ C & c & g & c^1 & e^1 & g^1 & (i)^4 & c^2 \end{array}$$

[69] After these consonant notes, nature provides a dissonant note between two consonances in the fourth octave:

$$\begin{array}{ccccccccc} & \star & & \star & & \star & & \star & & \star \\ 8 & 9 & 10 & 11 & 12 & 13 & 14 & 15 & 16 \\ c & d & e & f & g & a & (i) & b & c^1 \end{array}$$

The notes marked ⋆ are consonant. This is the true *diatonic* scale.

Half steps are produced in the fifth octave:

$$\begin{array}{ccccccc} 16 & 17 & 18 & 19 & 20 & \text{etc.} \\ C & C\sharp & D & D\sharp & E & \text{etc.} \end{array}$$

This is the true *chromatic* scale.

4. See note 24, above (Volume I).

Quarter tones are produced in the sixth octave:

32	33	34	35	36	37	38	39	40	etc.
C	C$^+$	C$\sharp$	C$^{\sharp+}$	D	D$^+$	D$\sharp$	D$^{\sharp+}$	E	etc.

This is the true *enharmonic* scale. Here the quarter tone is marked $+$, the half $\sharp$, and the three-quarter $\sharp+$.

The first three octaves produce only the most perfect consonances, which make up the major triad. But the fourth octave produces the most perfect scale, which is called the major mode. Therefore this mode is the most natural and the most intelligible, and is well suited to the expression of lively sentiments.

There is no doubt that the remaining notes that are dissonant in relation to the fundamental, at whatever distance they occur between 1 and 1024, do not affect the consonant harmony adversely when they are sounded with it; this is confirmed by mixtures on organs. Because of the distance of these notes from the fundamental, the ear cannot compare them to one another or can do so only with difficulty. Moreover, the notes closest to the fundamental are consonant and stronger than the dissonant ones, which are removed from it by many octaves.

[70] The minor mode does not have such a natural origin. This mode differs from the natural generation of notes by the addition of the fifth to the minor third,

5	6	7$\frac{1}{2}$	10
E	G	B	e

and thereby requires more effort of the ear than the major mode. Therefore it is by far not as perfect and soothing as the latter. However, since it is nevertheless easily intelligible to the ear, it has justly been accepted in music, particularly since it is far more suited than is the major mode to the expression of disquieting sentiments and evokes sadness by the minor third from the fundamental tone, while the major third of the major mode arouses joy and liveliness. There is another main feature of these two modes that reinforces their individual character. In the major modes, digressions to the dominant and subdominant lead once again to major keys, but in the minor modes they lead to minor keys.

Thus it can generally be accepted as a true and well-founded rule that major modes are particularly suited to cheerful, lively, and extroverted, carefree melodies; the minor modes, however, are preferable where tenderness, sad and adverse sentiments, caution and indecision are to be expressed.

Of course, the expression or character of a melody does not depend merely on the nature of the scale, as will be shown in more detail in the course of this work. It is possible to produce cheerfulness in a melody composed in a minor key and sadness in one composed in a major key, but this is more forced than if the mode proper to the affection were chosen.

The difference between these two modes is felt most strongly in arias where the sentiment is suddenly changed into an opposite one; for instance, where cheerfulness in the first part of the aria is followed by sadness in the second part because of a change in character. If the first part is composed in the major mode and the second in the minor mode, no ear would be so insensitive not to feel the change of sentiment suddenly and vividly.

Let this suffice regarding the different characters of the major and minor modes in general.

Each major key is also noticeably different from the other major keys, just as each minor key is different from all other minor keys.[n] We also see from the works of the great masters that they have been very careful to select for special effects not only the most suitable mode in general but also the most suitable among the twelve keys of that mode. I want to give only one example to confirm this remark: The well-known chorus, *Mora, mora, Ifigenia*, from Graun's opera *Ifigenia in Aulide* has given rise to terror even in the most insensitive persons.[o] [71] It is written in E-flat major; if it were to be transposed to another major key, for example C major or G major, it would lose much of its power. It is also not difficult to see what causes the almost terrifying power of that major key. From the tonic to the large fourth, there are only progressions by large whole tones ($8/9$); this produces only major thirds of the proportion $64/81$, all of which are larger than the pure major third ($4/5$). In addition, two steps of the small semitone with the proportion $243/256$ occur in this scale, one from the third of the tonic to the fourth (g–a-flat) and the other from the major seventh to the octave (d–e-flat); both are already frightening in themselves, because they are so small and thus so very dissonant.

---

[n] It must be kept in mind that Kirnberger's views concerning the individuality of keys (and his subsequent division of the twelve major and twelve minor keys into three classes each, depending on the purity of their tonic triads) is based on the temperament he proposed in the first chapter of Volume I.

[o] Carl Heinrich Graun's *Ifigenia in Aulide* (dated 16 August 1728) was first performed in Braunschweig in the winter of 1731.

The same can be demonstrated with the keyboard piece by Capellmeister Bach of Hamburg which he entitled *Xenophon*.ᴾ This piece can no more be transposed to another key than can the Graun chorus without losing a great deal of its expression.[5]

Thus it is very important for the composer to know the properties of the different keys precisely and to feel the character of each key. Since so little has been written about so important a matter, I have found it worth my while to discuss it in some detail here.

It can be taken as a basic rule for judging scales that the major keys whose thirds are completely pure possess most strongly the quality of the major mode, and that the greatest roughness and finally even something like ferocity enter into those major keys farthest removed from this purity. The same must also be assumed of minor keys: Those whose thirds are purest have the most gentle and pleasing tenderness and sadness, but those that are farthest removed from this purity blend the most painful and adverse qualities into this character.

[72] It is also very necessary to consider the character of the most closely related keys to which one modulates, and in which one remains the longest after modulation, hence above all the character of the scale of the dominant and subdominant of each tonic.

Having said this, we can divide the major keys into three classes.

The first class contains the keys of C major, D major, F major, and G major.

The second class contains E major, F-sharp major, A major, and B major.

The third class contains D-flat major, E-flat major, A-flat major, and B-flat major.

The first class has the purest triads, whose third has the perfect proportion $4/5$.

The second class has triads that are somewhat less perfect, whose third has the proportion $405/512$.

And the triads of the third class are the least perfect because their third is $64/81$.

5. Incidentally, those who are still and endlessly pressing for equal temperament may learn from these examples what would be gained from this temperament (if it were even possible).

ᴾThe key of "La Xenophon et la Sybille," which was first published in *Musikalisches Allerley von verschiedenen Tonkünstlern* (Berlin, 1761), is C-sharp major.

The keys belonging to one category are further distinguished by the particular features of their secondary keys to which one modulates most frequently. Thus, for example, A-flat major is the most violent key of the third class, because its dominant as well as its subdominant also have this same major third of 64/81; but the dominant of B-flat major has the pure major third of 4/5 in its triad. Therefore, F-sharp major and B major are in the same class as A major and E major, but their modulations make them harsher than the latter.

I want only to mention in addition that the major keys of the first class can become dull more easily than the others, just because they have the purest harmonies and are not as stimulating by far to a trained ear as those of the second and third classes.

The minor keys can also be divided into three classes according to the same basic rule.

I. D minor, E minor, A minor, and B minor are the purest.
II. C-sharp minor, D-sharp minor, F-sharp minor, and G-sharp minor are less pure.
III. C minor, F minor, G minor, and B-flat minor are the least pure, and thus the saddest.

On the basis of these remarks, I have devised two tables for judging keys. The first [table 2.3] shows the three classes of major and minor keys in the order of their diminishing harmonic purity. [73] The five secondary keys to which one can digress from each key are added to it, and next to each of these is listed its dominant chord. The numerals I, II, and III indicate the class to which each key belongs depending on the purity of its triad; that is, the keys designated with I are completely pure, those with II are less pure, and those with III are least pure. Thus, for example, all keys of the C major mode in the top row [sic, left column] are designated with I; this indicates that C major as well as its five neighboring keys—the keys to which one can modulate from it—have completely pure tonic triads and belong to the first class. But among the dominant chords of these keys, three are designated with II, namely, A of D minor, B of E minor, and E of A minor; therefore these chords belong among the less pure of the second class.

The second table [table 2.4] shows at a glance how much harmonic purity each key has in total. The three columns of numbers next to the names of keys are to be understood as follows: The [top] numbers in the first column show to how many keys with completely pure tonic triads one could modulate from the given key. The [top] numbers in the second column show to how many keys one could modulate whose tonic triads are less pure; and the third shows the number of keys whose triads are least pure. But the lower numbers show these same classes of triad purity for the dominants of keys to which one can modulate from the main key. Let us suppose, for example, that we wanted to find out the harmonic purity of the key of E major. It is possible to modulate from this key to six neighboring keys,[q] as is the case with all others. But not one of these, considered as a tonic, has a pure triad. This is indicated by the fact that there is no number in the top row of the first column. However, all neighboring keys of this E major are constituted in such a way that they still have a moderate level of triadic purity. But of the dominant chords of these six neighboring keys, only three are moderately pure and three are in the lowest class of purity. The key of B-flat major can modulate directly to two keys that have a completely pure triad on their tonic; however, the four other neighboring keys have tonic triads only of the lowest level of purity. Of these neighboring keys four have pure dominant chords, one has a dominant chord of moderate purity, and one of the lowest level. These examples will make the tables understandable to everyone.

[q]The six keys include the main key itself.

TABLE 2.3.

First Class of Major Keys with Their Modulations

C major $\frac{4}{5}, \frac{5}{6}, \frac{2}{3}$		G major $\frac{4}{5}, \frac{5}{6}, \frac{2}{3}$		F major $\frac{128}{161}, \frac{5}{6}, \frac{2}{3}$	
Tonic	Dom.	Tonic	Dom.	Tonic	Dom.
C major I	G I	G major I	D I	F major I	C I
D minor I	A II	A minor I	E II	G minor III	D I
E minor I	B II	B minor I	F# II	A minor I	E II
F major I	C I	C major I	G I	B♭ major III	F I
G major I	D I	D major I	A II	C major I	G I
A minor I	E II	E minor I	B II	D minor I	A II

D major $\frac{4}{5}, \frac{135}{161}, \frac{108}{161}$			
Tonic	Dom.		
D Major I	A II		
E minor I	B II		
F# minor II	C# III		
G major I	D I		
A major II	E II		
B minor I	F# II		

Second Class

A major $\frac{13041}{16384}, \frac{1024}{1215}, \frac{161}{240}$		E major $\frac{405}{512}, \frac{1024}{1215}, \frac{2}{3}$		B major $\frac{405}{512}, \frac{1024}{1215}, \frac{2}{3}$		F# major $\frac{405}{512}, \frac{27}{32}, \frac{10935}{16834}$	
Tonic	Dom.	Tonic	Dom.	Tonic	Dom.	Tonic	Dom.
A major II	E II	E major II	B II	B major II	F# II	F# major II	C# III
B minor I	F# II	F# minor II	C# III	C# minor II	G# III	G# minor II	D# III
C# minor II	G# III	G# minor II	D# III	D# minor II	A# III	A# minor III	E II
D major I	A II	A major II	E II	E major II	B II	B major II	F# II
E major II	B II	B major II	F# II	F# major II	C# III	C# major III	G# III
F# minor II	C# III	C# minor II	G# III	G# minor II	D# III	D# minor II	A# III

TABLE 2.3. (*continued*)

Third Class

Bb major $\frac{64}{81}, \frac{27}{32}, \frac{2}{3}$

Tonic	Dom.
Bb major III	F I
C minor III	G I
D minor I	A II
Eb major III	Bb III
F major I	C I
G minor III	D I

Db major $\frac{64}{81}, \frac{27}{32}, \frac{2}{3}$

Tonic	Dom.
Db major III	Ab III
Eb minor II	Bb III
F minor III	C I
Gb major II	Db III
Ab major III	Eb III
Bb minor III	F I

Eb major $\frac{64}{81}, \frac{27}{32}, \frac{2}{3}$

Tonic	Dom.
Eb major III	Bb III
F minor III	C I
G minor III	D I
Ab major III	Eb III
Bb major III	F I
C minor III	G I

Ab major $\frac{64}{81}, \frac{27}{32}, \frac{2}{3}$

Tonic	Dom.
Ab major III	Eb III
Bb minor III	F I
C minor III	G I
Db major III	Ab III
Eb major III	Bb III
F minor III	C I

First Class of Minor Keys with Their Modulations

A minor $\frac{161}{192}, \frac{4}{5}, \frac{161}{240}$

Tonic	Dom.
A minor I	E II
C major I	G I
D minor I	A II
E minor I	B II
F major I	C I
G major I	D I

E minor $\frac{5}{6}, \frac{4}{5}, \frac{2}{3}$

Tonic	Dom.
E minor I	B II
G major I	D I
A minor I	E II
B minor I	F# II
C major I	G I
D major I	A II

B minor $\frac{5}{6}, \frac{4}{5}, \frac{2}{3}$

Tonic	Dom.
B minor I	F# II
D major I	A II
E minor I	B II
F# minor II	C# III
G major I	D I
A major II	E II

D minor $\frac{27}{32}, \frac{128}{161}, \frac{108}{161}$

Tonic	Dom.
D minor I	A II
F major I	C I
G minor III	D I
A minor I	E II
Bb major III	F I
C major I	G I

TABLE 2.3. (*continued*)

Second Class

F# minor $\frac{135}{161}, \frac{13041}{16384}, \frac{10935}{16384}$		C# minor $\frac{1024}{1214}, \frac{405}{512}, \frac{2}{3}$		G# minor $\frac{1024}{1215}, \frac{405}{512}, \frac{2}{3}$		Eb minor $\frac{1024}{1215}, \frac{405}{512}, \frac{2}{3}$	
Tonic	Dom.	Tonic	Dom.	Tonic	Dom.	Tonic	Dom.
F# minor II	C# III	C# minor II	G# III	G# minor II	D# III	Eb minor II	Bb III
A major II	E II	E major II	B II	B major II	F# II	Gb major II	Db III
B minor I	F# II	F# minor II	C# III	C# minor II	G# III	Ab minor II	Eb III
C# minor II	G# III	G# minor II	D# III	D# minor II	A# III	Bb minor III	F I
D major I	A II	A major II	E II	E major II	B II	Cb major II	Gb II
E major II	B II	B major II	F# II	F# major II	C# III	Db major III	Ab III

Third Class

G minor $\frac{27}{32}, \frac{64}{81}, \frac{2}{3}$		C minor $\frac{27}{32}, \frac{64}{81}, \frac{2}{3}$		F minor $\frac{27}{32}, \frac{64}{81}, \frac{2}{3}$		Bb minor $\frac{27}{32}, \frac{64}{81}, \frac{2}{3}$	
Tonic	Dom.	Tonic	Dom.	Tonic	Dom.	Tonic	Dom.
G minor III	D I	C minor III	G I	F minor III	C I	Bb minor III	F I
Bb major III	F I	Eb major III	Bb III	Ab major III	Eb III	Db major III	Ab III
C minor III	G I	F minor III	C I	Bb minor III	F I	Eb minor II	Bb III
D minor I	A II	G minor III	D I	C minor III	G I	F minor III	C I
Eb major III	Bb III	Ab major III	Eb III	Db major III	Ab III	Gb major II	Db III
F major I	C I	Bb major III	F I	Eb major III	Bb III	Ab major III	Eb III

TABLE 2.4.

	Major Keys					Minor Keys		
	I	II	III			I	II	III
C	6	—	—		**C**	—	—	6
	3	3	—			3	—	3
D♭	—	2	4		**C♯**	—	6	—
	2	—	4			—	3	3
D	4	2	—		**D**	4	—	2
	1	4	1			4	2	—
E♭	—	—	6		**E♭**	—	4	2
	4	—	2			1	1	4
E	—	6	—		**E**	6	—	—
	—	3	3			2	4	—
F	4	—	2		**F**	—	—	6
	4	2	—			3	—	3
F♯	—	4	2		**F♯**	2	4	—
	1	1	4			—	4	2
G	6	—	—		**G**	2	—	4
	2	4	—			4	1	1
A♭	—	—	6		**G♯**	—	6	—
	3	—	3			—	2	4
A	2	4	—		**A**	6	—	—
	—	4	2			3	3	—
B♭	2	—	4		**B♭**	—	2	4
	4	1	1			4	1	1
B	—	6	—		**B**	4	2	—
	—	2	4			1	4	1

CHAPTER 3

Melodic Progression and Smoothness of Line

[77] After discussing choice of mode, it is now time to consider melody itself. Melody must have several qualities that, though inseparably linked, need to be considered individually for the purpose of instruction. First one has to be careful that the progression or flow of notes is always smooth and euphonious (unless very special reasons demand the opposite) so that it could be sung or rather comprehended without any objection and with some ease. Just as one generally has to be careful that verses in poetry are euphonious and gently flowing, this euphonious quality must also be sought in melody, even if no accompanying harmony is assumed. Therefore I shall discuss here as precisely as possible what the composer needs to observe in this matter.

The melody of an entire piece is composed of individual melodic phrases in which a caesura or point of rest is felt, as will be shown clearly in the following chapter. Each individual phrase or segment of the melody, which can be considered as a full or half verse, consists of a succession of notes that are taken from a single particular major or minor scale. I shall consider only such phrases here at first, because later I will talk about those that also contain foreign notes taken from other scales.

Even if one were to give the melody only a limited range of an octave and thus allow it to use only eight different notes, an infinite variety of melodic phrases can be invented. But no rules can be made about their invention. If it should occur to a thousand people at the same time to use the C major scale for singing a melodic phrase or a so-called theme, each could do this in his own way. One person begins with this note, another person with another note. Those who begin with the same note can ascend or descend from there, continue by steps or leaps, progress in a faster or slower tempo, make

347

the phrase longer or shorter, etc. Each proceeds as his present mood or feeling leads him.

[78] Thus it is impossible to tell the young composer anything about the invention of such individual phrases. However, several observations can be made about what he must watch for and avoid, so that a phrase invented by him contains nothing harsh, bad sounding, unsingable, and adverse.

Above all, the first phrase of a good melody must have the feature that it allow the scale from which it is taken, namely, the main key of the entire composition, to be felt immediately and without the least ambiguity. For that reason, especially those notes that define the key and mode must be used at the very beginning. No notes other than those that belong to the triad of the main key are more suited to this purpose.

One must begin with one of these three notes. The most perfect beginning, of course, is with the tonic itself, since it conveys the feeling of the main key and its scale immediately. [See example 3.1.]

EXAMPLE 3.1

Next after the tonic, one can begin with the dominant; but the subsequent notes must determine the main key as soon as possible, so that the dominant is not felt as a tonic resulting in an adverse impression on the listener by the destruction of its scale. When a melodic phrase begins on the dominant, the main key is established by progressing to notes of the triad of the main key, or to those notes that belong only to the main key. [See example 3.2.]

EXAMPLE 3.2

At (a), the c following after the first note determines the key of C. True, the same melody could also be harmonized in G major, as in example 3.3. [79] But, in this case, a harmonic accompaniment would already be necessary. However, if the phrase were performed simply as a single line, everyone would feel only C major. Only such phrases are discussed here, since with those that are accompanied the main key is immediately indicated by the harmony. If the phrase were written as in example 3.4, everyone would feel G major, and it would be absurd to begin a piece in C major this way.

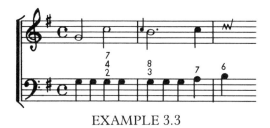

EXAMPLE 3.3

EXAMPLE 3.4

At (b) in example 3.2, the main key is determined by the notes of its triad, which is followed by the dominant; and at (c) it is determined by the f of the first measure, which totally destroys the possibility of feeling it in G major.

If one were to begin a melodic phrase that is to be performed by itself, as in example 3.5, no one would know whether it is written in G major or C major. Anyone who hears nothing beyond these notes will think that the phrase is in G, because the initial note conveys to him the feeling of the scale of this key, which is not destroyed by the subsequent notes. But, if the composer were to have based it on C major, an entirely different effect would result. There is no doubt that the same note has entirely different effects in different keys: G as tonic and G as dominant of C; B as mediant of G and B as the leading tone of C; and all remaining notes in the example above are so different in effect that they do not seem to be the same note. [80] Therefore the principal concern of the composer must be to establish the feeling of the main key right at the beginning so that each note is interpreted correctly.

EXAMPLE 3.5

Thirdly, one can also begin a piece with the mediant, but, as has already been demonstrated, the following notes must determine the main key by their progression. [See example 3.6.]

EXAMPLE 3.6

No other notes of the scale besides these three—the tonic, dominant, and mediant—are suitable to begin a melody, unless one wanted to force them to do so by ingenuity; but this is not to be discussed here. The young composer must first learn to write naturally before he dare try artificial means. But in the middle of a piece, a new phrase can be begun with any note of the scale without being harsh or adverse, as long as the progression is otherwise correct harmonically and melodically.

Thus it is certain that phrases which suggest to us most quickly and clearly the key in which they are written are the best for the beginning of a composition.

Next to be considered are the intervals of the progression. Here it must be stated first that every good melody is based on a proper harmony, and that the melody cannot be smooth where this is not found or felt, no matter how correct or singable their individual progressions may be. [See example 3.7.]

EXAMPLE 3.7

Here each individual progression from note to note is correct and singable; but the phrase as a whole is totally harsh and unpleasant because it does not suggest a natural harmonic succession. I cannot express myself more clearly about this matter; whoever does not feel this will never be able to write a smooth melody.

[81] But it does not follow from this that every melodic phrase that can be based on a correct harmony is smooth. Consider, for instance, the phrase in example 3.8. Despite the correct harmony and the good bass line, the melody of the principal voice is harsh and rigid. Therefore it is to be noted in addition here that phrases which have or give the feeling of a different harmony for each note are not very pleasing or smooth, except in a slower tempo or when required by the character of the composition, as in chorales. Besides, if the melody is to be smooth, the harmony must not change so rapidly, particularly those harmonies that are unexpected to the listener or that are not immediately perceptible from the melody. The tonic triad and the dominant chord with their inversions can often generate a long succession of harmony that can be used as the basis for an infinite number of melodic phrases and that can be altered in countless ways. These chords and the subdominant chord with its inversions are comprehensible to every listener, and there are enough works of considerable length and of the most beautiful and pleasant melody that are based on no other harmonies than the three just mentioned.

EXAMPLE 3.8

Having said this much, various things are still to be considered about the intervals of the progression. These are to be noted here.

If one is concerned only with euphony, ease of singing, or simplicity of line, the best phrases are those whose intervals are taken only from the scale of the given key and in which no notes raised or lowered by a sharp or flat are used, except in a transition to a different key to which one is modulating. That such transitions must happen in a correct way harmonically, and how they can be executed, was sufficiently demonstrated in the seventh chapter of Volume I.

[82] Each interval of the diatonic scale is comprehensible to every ear. However, care has to be taken with the ascending as well as descending progression of the tritone and major seventh [marked by asterisks in ex-

ample 3.9], which are difficult intervals to sing and therefore are not appropriate for use in a smooth melody. However, since there are often reasons why the composer would want to make the melody a bit harsh at some particular place—either for the sake of the expression, or to gain the attention of the listener, or to emphasize the smoothness of his melody by contrast—both progressions can be used to advantage; but, since they are dissonant, their resolutions must be contained in the melody. Therefore, the progressions at (A) in example 3.9 are good, but those at (B) are faulty.

EXAMPLE 3.9

Generally all dissonances that are perceived as such in the melody must also resolve in the melody. Leading tones (*notes sensibles*) belong among these; they must resolve upward if the melody is to be smooth, unless a phrase were to conclude with a leading tone. See example 3.10.

[83] In the second measure of this example, everyone feels the essential seventh chord on g at the f; therefore, the resolution of the seventh is

EXAMPLE 3.10

necessary at the beginning of the third measure. In the fourth measure, the first phrase concludes on the leading tone, that is, the semi tone below c; therefore, it need not resolve upward at the beginning of the fifth measure. But this was absolutely necessary from the fifth to the sixth measure; otherwise the melody would have become unwieldy. One should also note that, since the essential seventh of G is sounded again in the fifth measure, its resolution is also heard in the sixth measure. Likewise, since the g of the sixth measure is still retained by the ear as a seventh of the a in the following measure, it resolves to the following f. Such treatments of dissonance contribute much to the flow and comprehensibility of the melody.

Concerning simplicity and pleasantness of melody, it is to be noted further that the smaller intervals such as the second and third make the melody smoother than leaps by sixth, seventh, octave, etc. Therefore they must occur more often than the latter, and the latter must occur only where the intention is to give the melody an accent or to stress a principal note, or where one digresses from the flow of the melody for the sake of expression. Leaps are most effective for the expression of anger and also joy; but for the expression of tender sentiments, gently flowing progressions are more appropriate than leaps.

When the melody is accompanied harmonically, unharmonic cross relations must be avoided, because they make the melody harsh and the simplest progressions unsingable; this was discussed in detail in the ninth chapter of Volume I. Many useful remarks relevant to this discussion can also be found in that chapter; they will not be repeated here because of their vast scope.

However, even foreign notes, those that are not contained in the scale of the main key, can be used in the melody without reducing its pleasant or light character, if they are used sparingly and in such a way that they are easy to sing or comprehend. The melody can often be enhanced by such a foreign note. Consider, for instance, the beginning of an aria by Graun [example 3.11].[a]

[84] The melody is greatly enhanced by the c-sharp in the third [sic, second] measure and has a far more powerful effect than if c were to have been written instead.

In general, a melody that has no notes other than those in the scale over a long span of time can easily become dull, since there is a short step from smoothness to dullness. To prevent this, there is nothing more effective

[a] Work unidentified.

EXAMPLE 3.11

than to use a note that does not belong to the scale, particularly when it falls on the main accent of the phrase. But the progressions by augmented and diminished intervals shown in example 3.12 must be avoided.

EXAMPLE 3.12

Not that these progressions should never be used; in fact, they can have the greatest power for the expression of disquieting and violent sentiments. But in such a case the composer is not concerned with smoothness in the melody, which we are talking about here.

It may be well worth the trouble to consider in greater detail the effect of each interval by which one can progress and the different types of uniform progressions that continue for a while by intervals of the same name (seconds, thirds, fourths, etc.) from the standpoint of melodic simplicity and pleasantness.

[85] Progression by diatonic steps makes the melody most comprehensible and is agreeable to any ear. [See example 3.13.]

EXAMPLE 3.13

Although all of the passages in example 3.14 are simple and flowing, everyone feels that those at (b) and (d) are smoother and more pleasant than those at (a) and (c).

EXAMPLE 3.14

However, the rushing from a note up to its octave and back down to the prime [example 3.15], in which many seem to seek beauty, becomes sickening. But octave runs that are repeated by steps or even by leaps, as in example 3.16, are pleasant.

EXAMPLE 3.15

EXAMPLE 3.16

[86] Stepwise progression in which the second step is repeated, as in example 3.17, is also agreeable to every listener.

EXAMPLE 3.17

Such stepwise progressions, which can be altered in numerous ways, give rise to many kinds of pleasant melodic passages, like those in example 3.18.

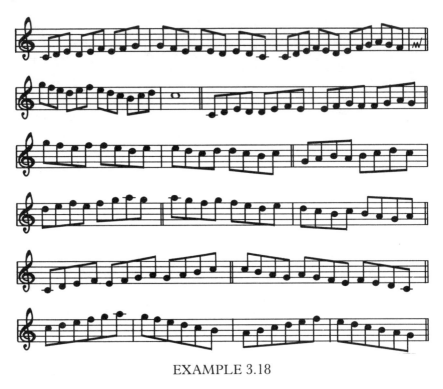

EXAMPLE 3.18

Many minor seconds and augmented primes can follow one another in a slow tempo and in the expression of sad feelings; but they are comprehensible only to trained ears. [See example 3.19.]

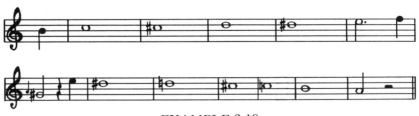

EXAMPLE 3.19

[87] Three major seconds can follow one another, both ascending and descending. [See example 3.20.]

EXAMPLE 3.20

In the minor mode even four ascending as well as descending major seconds can follow one another, but only when the entire ascending or descending scale is used, as in example 3.21. Yet both types are not very pleasant, and the second even less than the first.

EXAMPLE 3.21

The augmented second does not belong among the pleasant progressions. Thus it must be used only rarely and only where the melody is to be enhanced by an unexpected progression. It occurs only in the minor mode from the minor sixth to the major seventh of the principal tone, for instance as in example 3.22 in A minor.

EXAMPLE 3.22

[88] We note here in general that neither two augmented nor two diminished intervals can be written consecutively.

Next to seconds, progressions by third are pleasant and light. A whole series of leaps by thirds that ascend or descend by step can be used, as in example 3.23.

EXAMPLE 3.23

However, two ascending major thirds in succession are not only un-pleasant but also barely singable because of the tritone, particularly if the tempo is rather lively. [See example 3.24.] But descending they are good, as in example 3.25. The ascending tritone is tolerable in the way shown in example 3.26.

EXAMPLE 3.24

EXAMPLE 3.25   EXAMPLE 3.26

Four consecutive ascending as well as descending minor thirds can be written as in example 3.27.

EXAMPLE 3.27

Leaps by thirds that gradually descend in the manner shown in example 3.28 are very unpleasant and very uncomfortable to sing.

EXAMPLE 3.28

[89] I have found this unusual progression only in the second volume of *Pièces pour le Clavecin*, p. 8, by a certain Domenico Scarlatti.[b]

[b] Work unidentified.

However, this progression is pleasant and agreeable in the way shown in example 3.29. Here the tritone indicated by a bracket is scarcely noticeable, whereas in the preceding example it has a most disagreeable effect.

EXAMPLE 3.29

A series of successive thirds is also pleasant and light. Yet only four thirds at the most can follow one another in succession. These thirds are then arpeggiations of an underlying seventh chord, whose seventh must resolve. [See example 3.30.]

EXAMPLE 3.30

Two successive major thirds up or down cannot be written as at (a) in example 3.31. But they can be written as at (b).

EXAMPLE 3.31

However, successive minor thirds up or down can be written in various ways, as in example 3.32.

EXAMPLE 3.32

The diminished third occurs in the affective style only descending, but not ascending. [See example 3.33.]

EXAMPLE 3.33

[90] In general, progressions by thirds can be counted among the lightest and most pleasant progressions.

There are pieces with beautiful and gentle melodies in which no intervals larger than seconds and thirds appear, yet which still have variety and diversity. However, these characteristics can be attained to a greater degree if progressions by larger intervals are mingled with the smaller ones. Moreover, as was mentioned above, a single leap often highlights the whole phrase and gives the melodic phrase a primary accent. They are effective for the expression of volatile sentiments, but if too many of them are used in succession, they exhaust the attention of the listener, just as smaller progressions finally lull the attention to sleep when they are used throughout entire pieces without alternating with larger intervals. The expression must determine the more frequent or more infrequent use of larger intervals among the smaller ones, which must always be the most numerous if the melody as a whole is to be smooth.

Individual leaps by fourths are easy from each degree of the scale, except from the degree where the fourth becomes a tritone. However, a succession of falling fourths that moves up or down by step is awkward. [See example 3.34.] But a succession of ascending fourths, as in example 3.35, is good.

EXAMPLE 3.34

EXAMPLE 3.35

[91] Two pure fourths can be used ascending without interruption, but not descending. [See example 3.36.]

The augmented fourth or tritone is difficult to sing but is very expres-

EXAMPLE 3.36

sive in intense passages. It is often used in recitatives, ascending as well as descending. One must not confuse the tritone with the large fourth, which, in the minor mode, is located from the sixth to the ninth of the main note. The former is difficult to sing, is rarely written, and, since it is dissonant, must also resolve in the melody, as at (A) in example 3.37. However, the latter (B) is consonant, easier to sing, and thus can be used more frequently.

EXAMPLE 3.37

The diminished fourth belongs among the more unusual progressions but can be used both ascending and descending at the proper time and place. [See example 3.38]

EXAMPLE 3.38

[92] All pure fifths that occur in the diatonic scale are easy to sing, except in the major mode from the third of the main note to its seventh, that is,

when the third is treated as the mediant and the seventh as the leading tone. [See example 3.39.]

EXAMPLE 3.39

Many pure falling fifths in succession that proceed downward by step, as at (A) in example 3.40, are good. But they are not as good ascending, as at (B), and even less in the manner shown at (C).

EXAMPLE 3.40

Two consecutive ascending fifths are good only in the situation shown at (A) in example 3.41; and descending they are good only in bass melodies, as at (B).

EXAMPLE 3.41

[93] The false fifth, which is an inversion of the tritone, belongs among the unusual progressions but is easier to sing than the tritone. In pieces where the melody is supposed to be exotic, the two can alternate, as in example 3.42.

EXAMPLE 3.42

The small or diminished fifth, which is an inversion of the large fourth and occurs only in minor keys, can be used without hesitation because it is easy to sing.

The augmented fifth can only occur ascending; however, in bass melodies, it can also occur descending, as in example 3.43.

EXAMPLE 3.43

Sixths that are contained in the scale are all easy to sing and comprehensible; however, many successive sixths must not be written in a smooth melody, because the leap is quite large. At most, two minor sixths can occur in succession, and then only in the way shown in example 3.44.

EXAMPLE 3.44

Several major sixths can occur in succession because they are inversions of the minor third, but they are not as pleasant as those shown in example 3.45.

EXAMPLE 3.45

Such passages are really to be considered as consisting of two parts, each of which progresses by seconds, as in example 3.46.

EXAMPLE 3.46

[94] In such cases, progressions can occur that in other situations would be harsh and difficult to sing, such as the descending progression of the augmented fifth from the sixth to the seventh note in example 3.45.

However, the progression of successive sixths in example 3.47 would be unsingable.

EXAMPLE 3.47

The progression of sixths alternating with seconds, as in example 3.48, is simple and smooth.

EXAMPLE 3.48

The progression by augmented sixth never occurs in a good melody, except in arpeggiations such as those just mentioned. [See example 3.49.]

EXAMPLE 3.49

Of the progressions by seventh, the minor seventh of the dominant chord is very easy to sing and is beautiful in the smoothest melodies, as in example 3.50.

EXAMPLE 3.50

The progression by diminished seventh is also easy to sing ascending as well as descending, as in example 3.51.

EXAMPLE 3.51

[95] Only the progression by major seventh is harsh, and previously it was counted among the forbidden augmented progressions. However, it can occur by chance where it is not difficult to sing, as, for instance, in the sixth-progression at (a) in example 3.52.

EXAMPLE 3.52

It can also have a powerful effect in an accompanying bass melody, as in example 3.53 where (a) is better than (b).

EXAMPLE 3.53

The octave progression is very easy to sing and is used in many ways.

Progression by minor as well as major ninth is also not difficult to sing, because it is so close to the octave. But it can only occur ascending, and in that case the lowest note must be the dominant. Such a ninth-progression has the greatest power in melody and thus must occur only infrequently. [See example 3.54.]

EXAMPLE 3.54

The remaining progressions by leap—by tenth, eleventh, twelfth, etc.—can also be used, though infrequently. However, both intervals [*sic*, notes of the intervals] must belong to the same harmony, as in example 3.55.

EXAMPLE 3.55

[96] Where this is not the case, such progressions by leap are difficult to sing and to comprehend. [See example 3.56.]

EXAMPLE 3.56

The register of the instrument or voice for which the melody is written must also be considered with regard to larger or smaller progressions. It is obvious and in conformity with the nature of sound that larger intervals are preferable to smaller ones in a melody for the bass, and the latter to the former for the soprano. Not that a bass melody should progress only by leaps and a soprano melody only by seconds, but the large intervals are generally more natural in the low register and can occur more often without inhibiting the flow of the bass melody than in the high register, which, on the other hand, tolerates more small progressions than leaps in its melody. To convince oneself of this, one need only play a smooth soprano melody a few octaves lower and a good bass line a few octaves higher. Therein lies the difference between the smoothness of a melody in the low register and one in a high register; a smooth bass aria is one thing and a smooth soprano aria another. The young composer must observe this and try to become familiar with both types. The difference in cadences alone does not produce this. The main difference lies in the manner of their progressions. That tempo also influences this, in that higher melodies progress most naturally by shorter notes and lower melodies by longer notes, will be shown in the following chapter.

Moreover, there is a difference between a smooth melody for voice and a smooth melody for an instrument. In the latter, progressions can be used that cannot be dared in the former. Thus, for example, arpeggiations of chords and generally many leaps in succession are not contrary to the smooth line for an instrument, as long as they are easy to produce. On the other hand, a phrase made up of the easiest and most singable progressions can lose all its ease and smoothness and can be performed only with effort if it is written contrary to the fingering of the instrument. [97] Thus it is necessary that the composer know the instrument for which he is writing. Each instrument has something peculiar to it that, independent of the melodic progressions, contributes to the smoothness of the melody. The composer must feel this, and even if he does not play the instrument himself, he must at least know exactly what is produced easily or with difficulty on that instrument. If he does not know this, he should not be surprised frequently to hear in performance an entirely different type of melody than he had conceived.

The same is true of the human voice. The composer who wants to write for it must be a singer himself. If nature has not provided him with a voice, he must at least be able to sing in his mind; otherwise he will not capture the essence of vocal melody and will often be rigid and harsh where he intends to be smooth.

In a vocal melody, particular care has to be taken that the progressions coincide exactly with the declamation of the words, i.e., that unimportant progressions are not used at principal words and accented syllables, or that significant leaps or striking progressions are not used at short syllables and unimportant words. By the same token, if the voice rises in the declamation of words, it must not fall in the melody, and, vice versa, must not ascend when it falls in the declamation. The vocal composer must be a perfect orator at the same time. He must be so familiar with the language of the poet that he is in complete command of the power of each word, the level of height or depth of various accents, and the character of expressions, so that he may organize the progressions of his melody accordingly. Without this quality he will make mistakes that are noticeable to everyone, and he is well-advised to devote himself to instrumental composition, since he lacks what is most essential to a vocal composer.

The natural range of each voice—which should not be exceeded in choral works by a composer who writes for average human voices—is a tenth or at most an eleventh in all voices, as can be seen from example 3.57.

EXAMPLE 3.57

[98] In arias, the composer is allowed to go a step higher or lower, since only one singer who has the voice range is needed. For all voices are limited to the given range of a tenth or eleventh; some go higher by one or several notes, others lower. Some have voices that encompass three octaves and a half. There are soprano voices that go up to the three-line d and even higher; there are also high or low alto voices. However, the composer writes for such voices only in special situations.

Moreover, in vocal or instrumental pieces, a certain uniformity must also be observed in the progressions; that is, when the melody progresses by step or by small intervals at the beginning, phrases involving just leaps must not be used all of a sudden, since in that way the unity of expression can easily be destroyed and generally the cohesion of the melody can be completely disrupted. Only in the expression of such passions that at times move the spirit gently and at others storm violently through the soul can such an alternation of melodic phrases that move by step or by leap have a good effect. But in such cases, change of tempo or meter is far more powerful, as will be shown in the following chapter.

Likewise, if the melody proceeds for a while in notes from the diatonic scale, one must not suddenly use many foreign or chromatic progressions, since this can easily make the whole mottled and can completely destroy the unity of expression. In general, one must proceed carefully with the use of foreign notes, since they are more difficult than the diatonic ones to sing or comprehend. They must always occur as leading tones of the notes a half step above or below them,[c] and at the same time must suggest the harmony from which they are taken. [See example 3.58.]

---

[c] It is worth noting that Kirnberger identifies two types of leading tones, one ascending and the other descending. In his *Grundsätze des Generalbasses* (Berlin, 1781), p. 43, Kirnberger explains the origin of both types as follows. The ascending leading tone (*note sensible*) is the

EXAMPLE 3.58

[99] Therefore, since the progression by augmented third does not suggest a definite harmony, it is an absurdity in the melody and must be abandoned as such. Who could sing the progression in example 3.59, no matter what key it were in?

EXAMPLE 3.59

The progression by augmented sixth is also unusable for this reason; however, it can be more useful than the augmented third when the harmony is arranged as in example 3.60.

EXAMPLE 3.60

semitone below the tonic, to which it must lead. As the third of the dominant harmony, it is not dissonant; yet it must resolve upward to the tonic at the subsequent harmony. The descending leading tone, however, is dissonant. As the seventh of the dominant harmony, it is an essential dissonance and thus must resolve to the third scale degree at the subsequent harmony. These, then, are the two leading tones of the diatonic scale, and notes foreign to the scale can be considered as leading tones of the diatonic steps. Thus in C major, for example, f-sharp is the ascending leading tone of g, and b-flat is the descending leading tone of a.

Kirnberger's definition of ascending and descending leading tones is comparable to Rameau's definition of major and minor dissonance, as stated in Book II, chapter 16, article 2 (pp. 100–04) [Gossett translation, pp. 114–18] of his *Traité de l'harmonie* (Paris, 1722).

If, this [procedure] is observed, a melodic phrase can contain many foreign notes, yet remain intelligible. Consider the melody in example 3.61.

EXAMPLE 3.61

[100] A not entirely untrained ear will find this melody strange but not incomprehensible.

The same can be said about chromatic motions that ascend or descend by half steps. Each foreign note must be a leading tone of the following note of the diatonic scale and must suggest a definite harmony. Therefore, the motion through a-sharp in example 3.62 is incorrect in C major, since no harmony can be conceived for the a-sharp of the fourth measure without destroying the key of C major. Instead, b-flat must be written, as in example 3.63.

EXAMPLE 3.62

EXAMPLE 3.63

Here b-flat is really leading tone of a, which should follow; the F major harmony would have been used with this a, but this harmony has been omitted here. Such harmonic omissions have been discussed in detail in the first volume of this work, particularly in the appendix. Therefore, we will not repeat the explanation of this here.

It still remains to be noted in reference to such chromatic motions that, when ascending, the notes outside of the scale must fall on a weak beat, but those within the scale on a strong beat. The reverse is true in falling chromatic motions. Therefore the progressions (A) in example 3.64 are good, but those at (B) are incorrect.

EXAMPLE 3.64

[101] More than five semitones ascending or descending cannot follow one another in succession without either producing a phrase division or leaving the key.

On this occasion, we would still like to note regarding the chromatic progression by diminished third that it is most natural in major keys when digressing to the mediant, and in minor keys when digressing to the fifth. Thus in C major, for example, the phrase at (a) in example 3.65, which modulates to E minor, is more natural than the one at (b), which modulates to A minor, because the key of C major is not destroyed as much in the first example as in the second.

EXAMPLE 3.65

For the same reason, the phrase in A minor at (a) in example 3.66, which modulates to E minor, is more natural than the one at (b), which modulates to D minor.

EXAMPLE 3.66

[102] Enharmonic progressions, about which so much ado is made in some textbooks despite the fact that there is really no enharmonic genus in our music, are possible only in the unique situation where a so-called enharmonic modulation is brought about by means of the diminished seventh chord. The singer who has to hold the note at which the enharmonic change occurs adjusts the pitch higher or lower unnoticed and without knowing it, in order to agree with the harmony used with it. Let us assume that the singer had a-flat as the minor third of F, and the composer were to lead the harmony to E major and make the a-flat a g-sharp. Without knowing it, the singer would lower the pitch as much as necessary to sing the pure third of E. And if the g-sharp were to be made an a-flat again, he would raise the pitch by just as much. [See example 3.67.]

EXAMPLE 3.67

On keyboard instruments, where the notes c-sharp and d-flat, d-sharp and e-flat, etc., are not at all differentiated from one another, the ear raises or lowers the pitch in such passages, as does the singer in the situation above. Thus enharmonic progressions are not to be considered melodically, but, since they are established only by the harmony, they cannot be separated from it. But how powerful enharmonic progressions can be if they are used sparingly and with deliberation has already been discussed in the first chapter.

The melody that progresses without purpose, now by leaps and now by steps, sometimes by diatonic notes and sometimes by chromatic and enharmonic notes, cannot possibly have a good effect nor be expressive. Therefore, the young composer must take great pains to observe unity of progression in the melodic phrases of his work, so that the whole does not become shapeless.

That expression in melody depends to a large extent on the progressions surely requires no proof. However, it is impossible to specify precisely which progressions are to be used for a melody that is to have this or that expression. To a certain extent each interval has its own expression, which, however, can be greatly changed or completely lost through the harmony or through the different manner of using the harmony. [103] Nevertheless, if one considers only the progressions of a melody without regard for the remaining secondary circumstances, the intervals can be characterized approximately as follows:

Ascending

The *augmented prime*—anxious.

The *minor second*—sad; the *major*—pleasant, but also pathetic; the *augmented*—yearning.

The *minor third*—sad, melancholy; the *major*—joyful.

The *diminished fourth*—melancholy, plaintive; the *small*—happy; the *large*—sad; the *augmented* or *tritone*—intense.

The *small fifth*—tender; the *false*—graceful, imploring; the *perfect*—happy, courageous; the *augmented*—anxious.

The *minor sixth*—melancholy, imploring, caressing; the *major*—merry, vehement, intense; the *augmented* does not occur in melody.

The *diminished seventh*—painful; the *minor*—tender, sad, also indecisive; the *major*—intense, raving, in the expression of desperation.

The *octave*—happy, courageous, encouraging.

Descending

The *augmented prime*—extremely sad.

The *minor second*—pleasant; the *major*—serious, soothing; the *augmented* —plaintive, tender, caressing.

The *diminished third*—very melancholy, tender; the *minor*—calm, moderately cheerful; the *major*—pathetic, also melancholy.

The *diminished fourth*—melancoly, anxious; the *small*—calm, content; the
   large—very depressed; the *augmented* or the *tritone*—desperately sad.
The *small fifth*—tenderly sad; the *false*—imploring; the *perfect*—content,
   soothing; the *augmented* (occurs only in the bass)—timid.
[104] The *minor sixth*—depressed; the *major*—rather timid; the *augmented*
   does not occur in melody.
The *diminished seventh*—lamenting; the *minor*—rather frightful; the *major*
   —tremendously frightful.
The *octave*—very soothing.

   I do not mean to imply that these melodic progressions have only the
effects indicated and cannot be changed in any way. Rather, I mean only
that these effects seem to me to be most appropriate to them. Much depends
here on what precedes and follows and, in general, on the totality of the
melodic phrase in which these progressions occur; it also depends on the
position of the intermingled minor and major seconds of the scale or mode,
and above all on the beat of the measure on which they are used and on the
harmony that is placed under them. Every melodic progression can acquire
a different shade of expression from the harmony. Nevertheless it is certain
that the effect must be all the greater when the melodic progression in itself
is well chosen and is supported by a powerful harmony. This good choice of
melodic progression is necessary above all in compositions whose greatest
expressive power must lie in the melody, and in which no harmonic accompaniment is necessary, as in arias and songs. Great men have always
been very careful in this choice. Consider, for example, the first phrase of an
aria by the famous Benedetto Marcello in example 3.68.[d] Can one imagine a
progression that is more striking and better suited to the words?

As - pra   e   cru-da quel-la pe-na

EXAMPLE 3.68

[d] Work unidentified.

CHAPTER 4

Tempo, Meter, and Rhythm

[105] A succession of notes that mean nothing by themselves and are differentiated from one another only by pitch can be transformed into a real melody—one that has a definite character and depicts a passion or a particular sentiment—by means of tempo, meter, and rhythm, which give the melody its character and expression. It is immediately apparent to everyone that the most moving melody would be completely stripped of all its power and expression if one note after another were performed without precise regulation of speed, without accents, and without rest points, even if performed with the strictest observance of pitch. Even common speech would become partly incomprehensible and completely disagreeable if a proper measure of speed were not observed in the delivery, if the words were not separated from one another by the accents associated with the length and brevity of the syllables, and finally if the phrases and sentences were not differentiated by rest points. Such a lifeless delivery would make the most beautiful speech sound no better than the letter-by-letter reading of children.

Thus tempo, meter, and rhythm give melody its life and power. *Tempo* defines the rate of speed, which by itself is already important since it designates a lively or quiet character. *Meter* determines the accents in addition to the length and brevity of the notes and the lighter or more emphatic delivery; and it shapes the notes into words, so to speak. But *rhythm* establishes for the ear the individual phrases formed by the words and the periods composed of several phrases. Melody is transformed into a comprehensible and stimulating speech by the proper combination of these three things.

But it must be kept in mind that none of these elements is sufficient by

375

itself to give the melody a precise character; the true expression of the melody is determined only by their synthesis and their interaction. Two compositions may have the same rate of allegro or largo, yet still have an entirely different effect; according to the type of meter, the motion is more hurried or emphatic, lighter or heavier, even while the speed remains the same. From this it is clear that tempo and meter must combine their forces. [106] The same is also true of rhythm: the components from which a melody is formed can assume an entirely different expression depending on meter and tempo.

Thus, whoever wants to write a melody must pay attention to the combined effect of tempo, meter, and rhythm and must consider none of these without regard to the other two. Nevertheless, it is unavoidable for me to discuss each of them separately here and to tell the aspiring composer what he needs to know about each individual point.

I. TEMPO

The composer must never forget that every melody is supposed to be a natural and faithful illustration or portrayal of a mood or sentiment, insofar as it can be represented by a succession of notes. The term *Gemüthsbewegung*, which we Germans give to passions or affections, already indicates their analogy to tempo.[a] In fact, every passion and every sentiment—in its intrinsic effect as well as in the words by which it is expressed—has its faster or slower, more violent or more passive tempo. This tempo must be correctly captured by the composer to conform with the type of sentiment he has to express.

Thus I must admonish the aspiring composer above all that he study diligently the nature of every passion and sentiment with regard to tempo, so that he does not make the terrible mistake of giving the melody a slow tempo where it should be fast, or a fast tempo where it should be slow. However, this is a field that is not limited to music, and that the composer has in common with the orator and poet.

Furthermore, he must have acquired a correct feeling for the natural tempo of every meter, or for what is called *tempo giusto*. This is attained by diligent study of all kinds of dance pieces. Every dance piece has its definite tempo, determined by the meter and the note values that are employed in it.

---

[a] The German words used by Kirnberger for tempo are *Bewegung* and *Taktbewegung*. The former also has a more general meaning that has been translated throughout as "motion."

Regarding meter, those having larger values, like alla breve, 3/2, and 6/4 meter, have a heavier and slower tempo than those of smaller values, like 2/4, 3/4, and 6/8 meter, and these in turn are less lively than 3/8 or 6/16 meter. Thus, for example, a loure in 3/2 meter has a slower tempo than a minuet in 3/4 meter, and the latter is in turn slower than a passepied in 3/8 meter. [107] Regarding note values, dance pieces involving sixteenth and thirty-second notes have a slower tempo than those that tolerate only eighth and at most sixteenth notes as the fastest note values in the same meter. Thus, for example, a sarabande in 3/4 meter has a slower tempo than a minuet, even though both are written in the same meter.

Thus the *tempo giusto* is determined by the meter and by the longer and shorter note values of a composition. Once the young composer has a feeling for this, he will soon understand to what degree the adjectives *largo, adagio, andante, allegro, presto,* and their modifications *larghetto, andantino, allegretto,* and *prestissimo* add to or take away from the fast or slow motion of the natural tempo. He will soon be able not only to write in every type of tempo, but also in such a way that this tempo is captured quickly and correctly by the performers.

However, tempo in music is not limited just to the different degrees of slow and fast motion. There are passions "in which the images flow monotonously like a gentle brook; others where they flow faster with a moderate stir, but without delay; some in which the succession of images is similar to wild brooks swollen by heavy rains, which rush violently along and sweep with them everything that stands in their way; and again others in which the images are similar to the wild sea, which violently beats against the shore and then recedes to crash again with new force."[6] Similarly, tempo in melody can also be violent or tender, skipping or monotonous, fiery or bland even when the degree of fast or slow motion is the same, depending upon the type of note values chosen for the melody. Consider example 4.1.

EXAMPLE 4.1 (*to be continued*)

6. See the article "Ausdruck" in Sulzer's [*Allgemeine*] *Theorie der schönen Künste* [Leipzig, 1771–74].

EXAMPLE 4.1 (*continued*)

EXAMPLE 4.1 (*continued*)

[111] Each of these examples is distinguished from the others by a characteristic motion that is felt first of all through the differences of tempo and meter, and in those that have the same tempo and meter through the difference of note values from which the melody is composed. The young composer must pay particular attention to this and must, by diligent study of the works of excellent masters, gain sufficient experience in the particular effect of each type of note value in every meter. Assuming he has a correct feeling for this, he will thereby obtain control over the means by which he incorporates into his melody exactly that type of motion which allows the mood of the chosen passion to be perceived most clearly.

Thus the composer, in constructing a piece, has to consider two things regarding tempo: (1) the slow or fast pace of the tempo; and (2) the characteristic motion of the parts of the measure, or the type of rhythmic changes. Lively sentiments generally require a fast tempo; but the expression can become playful, or flirtatious, or happy, or tender, or pathetic by means of the type of characteristic motion of the parts of the measure, or the rhythmic steps. Likewise, a slower tempo generally is appropriate to the expression of sad sentiments, but through the second type of motion the expression can become more or less agitated, tender or violent, gentle or painful. Of course, it is not the motion alone that has this effect; the remaining good qualities of an expressive melody must be united with it, but then it contributes most forcefully to the expression.

This may be sufficient to draw the prospective composer's attention to the effect of motion in general. In the following two sections of this chapter we will have the opportunity to discuss in greater detail the particular effects of metric and rhythmic motion. [112] Therefore, it may suffice here to add a couple of remarks for the young composer regarding motion in general.

He must be careful in writing a piece not to make it hurry or drag. Although these words are common only in the theory of performance, they can also be applied to composition. It can easily happen that a composer, without noticing it, rushes the tempo in writing a fiery allegro, or lets it drag in a sad largo; or, out of fondness for a phrase, he may unwittingly become lax about the tempo, so that the phrase becomes vague because of its fast rate of rhythmic motion or dull because of its slowness. The composer suffers in the performance of such pieces, but through his own fault.

He must not overstep the limits of fast or slow tempo. What is too fast cannot be performed clearly, and what is too slow cannot be comprehended. This applies mainly to pieces where the composer himself indicates the tempo.

Because of the long period of vibration of low notes, all short note values must be avoided in the low register; but in the high register they are more effective than long sustained notes. The progression of the bass generally relates to that of the highest part like the walk of a mature man to that of a young girl. Where she takes two or three steps, he takes only one, yet both cover the same distance. Not that a young girl could not go slowly and a mature man quickly, but it is not as natural. Similarly, the voices in the middle registers can be considered as gaits of boys and young adults by analogy to the shorter or longer note values of their rhythmic steps.

Finally, the composer must not neglect to designate the tempo of his piece as precisely as possible whenever it cannot be determined from the features given above. He must use the terms *allegro assai, allegro moderato, poco allegro,* etc., wherever the word *allegro* would indicate a tempo that is too fast or not fast enough. The same is true of slow pieces. The words that refer to characteristic motion, such as *maestoso, scherzando, vivo, mesto,* etc., are often of the greatest significance in expressive pieces, and not meaningless for those who want to perform a piece well. Hasse is so precise in the designation of his tempi that he often makes lengthy descriptions of how the piece is to be performed: *Andantino grazioso, ma non patetico, non languente; Allegro vivo, e con spirito,* or *allegro vivo, che arrivi quasi all'allegro intiero; un poco lento, e maestoso, ma che non languisca, e abbia il dovuto suo moto.*

II. METER

[113] If one imagines a melody in which all the notes are presented with the same intensity or stress, and in which they have the same length or duration (as if, for example, the melody were to consist only of whole notes), it would be comparable to a monotonously flowing stream. What distinguishes one melody from another is the faster or slower current: one is comparable to a thundering stream, another to a gentle, somewhat faster or slower flowing river, and a third to a gently rippling brook. If a more or less full and consonant harmony is imagined along with such a melody, one has everything that could distinguish one melody from another.

The entire power or expression of such a melody would consist only of a gentle and light or a lively and strong current, which would lull us to sleep or wake us up. If melody is to become similar to speech and adapted to the expression of various emotions and sentiments, individual notes must be turned into meaningful words and several words into comprehensible phrases. This transformation of a mere stream of notes into a melody resembling speech is accomplished in part by accents that are given to a few notes, and partly by the difference of their durations. It is just the same as with common speech, where we distinguish words and sentences only by means of the accents and durations of syllables.

Meter actually consists of the precise uniformity of accents that are given to a few notes and of the completely regular distribution of long and short syllables. That is, when these heavier or lighter accents recur at regular intervals, the melody acquires a meter or a measure. If these accents were not distributed regularly, so that no precise periodic recurrence occurred, the melody would be similar only to common prosaic speech; but with this periodic return it is comparable to poetic speech, which has its precise meter.

[114] This matter can also be conceived by picturing a simple motion. A melody that just flows along without accents resembles a continuous motion, like that created when a body falls or is thrown through the air; but an accented melody is similar to a motion divided into steps or to walking. Just as walking receives its particular character from the type as well as the speed of the steps, melody receives its character and expression in quite a similar way.

A regular walk has steps of equal length, each of which represents a measure of the melody. However, the steps can consist of more or fewer little movements or *beats*, and these movements or beats, all of which are of the same duration, can have smaller divisions or parts; they can also be distinguished by other modifications—by gradations of heavy and light, flowing or leaping, etc. If a precise uniformity is observed in the steps and small movements, this results in the measured walk which we call dance, and this is precisely analogous to measured melody. In just the same way as dance expresses or portrays various sentiments merely by motion, melody does it merely by notes.

Whoever considers this closely will easily understand how much the character of a melody depends on tempo and meter. The clearest examples of this can be found in the various dance melodies. However, it is not possible to give definite rules that would specify the most suitable tempo and meter for every type of sentiment. For the most part, it depends on a refined and accurate sensitivity.

Everything that can be said to a composer about this subject beyond what I have already stated about tempo is contained in the following main topics: (1) that all types of meters invented and in use up to now be described to him, each according to its true structure and its precise execution; (2) that the spirit or character of each meter be defined as precisely as possible; (3) finally, for the situation where the melody is to be written to a given text, that directions be given how the best or at least a suitable type of meter is to be chosen for it. I will have to discuss these three points here.

1. If one hears a succession of equal pulses that are repeated at the same time interval, as in example 4.2, experience teaches us that we immediately divide them metrically in our minds by arranging them in groups containing an equal number of pulses; and we do this in such a way that we put an accent on the first pulse of each group or imagine hearing it stronger than the others. [115] This division can occur in three ways, as shown in example 4.3.

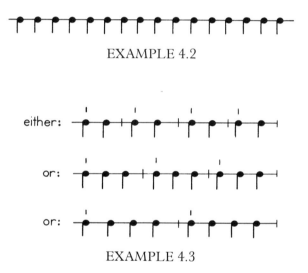

EXAMPLE 4.2

EXAMPLE 4.3

That is, we divide the pulses into groups of two, three, or four. We do not arrive at any other division in a natural way. No one can repeat groups of five and even less of seven equal pulses in succession without wearisome strain. It can be done more easily with six, especially when the pulses go rather quickly; however, one will notice that groups of six or more pulses are not easily comprehended without thinking of a subdivision, in which case they once again resemble the above-mentioned groups of two, three, and four. [See example 4.4.]

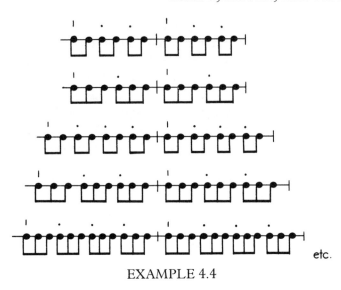

EXAMPLE 4.4

[116] Here many kinds of pulses are used in one group. The dots indicate the main pulses to which the others are subordinate, since they are not felt as strongly as the former; thus these groups become similar again to those mentioned above, or rather they are the same. With fast pulses, even many more can be subsumed under one principal pulse, but the arrangement of the groups is always the same.

It is easy to apply this. Instead of the word "pulse," one uses *beat*, and *measure* instead of "group"; in this way one gets an idea of what the measure is and of its many varieties. The measure consists of two, three, or four equal beats; besides these, there is no other natural type of measure.

To all appearances, only three time signatures would be required to indicate these meters, namely, one that indicates a measure of two, another that indicates a measure of three, and a third that indicates a measure of four beats. However, from what we have stated already in the preceding section of this chapter about *tempo giusto* and the natural motion of longer and shorter note values, it becomes clear, for example, that a measure of two quarter notes and another of two half notes, and likewise a measure of three quarter notes and anotther of three eighth notes, indicate a different tempo, even though they have the same number of beats. In addition, longer note values are always performed with more weight and emphasis than shorter ones; consequently, a composition that is to be performed with weight and emphasis can only be notated with long note values, and another that is to be performed in a light and playful manner can only be notated with short note values.

From this the necessity of different meters with the same number of beats becomes apparent, which we shall now consider in greater detail. In general, meters are divided into even and odd: *even* are those of two and four beats; and *odd*, those of three beats, which are also called triple meters. Furthermore, a distinction is made between simple and compound meters: *simple* meters are constituted in such a way that each measure amounts to only one foot, which cannot be divided in the middle; however, *compound* meters can be divided in the middle of each measure, since they are composed of two simple meters, as will be shown in greater detail below.

[117] Before we list the meters in order, it must still be noted that it is just as easy to divide each beat of a meter into three parts or to triple it as it is to perceive triple meter; this is already obvious from [the existence of] triplets. This gives rise to meters of *triple beats*, where three pulses fall on one beat. We shall indicate these now, along with the meters from which they are derived, and shall note what is necessary regarding their true structure, their usefulness or unusefulness, and their exact execution. [See table 4.1.[b]]

TABLE 4.1.

Simple Even Meters of Two Beats
1. 2/1 meter or Φ: tripled—6/2 meter.
2. 2/2 meter or ¢: tripled—6/4 meter.
3. 2/4 meter: tripled—6/8 meter.
4. 2/8 meter: tripled—6/16 meter.
Simple Even Meters of Four beats
1. 4/2 meter or O: tripled—12/4 meter.
2. 4/4 meter or C: tripled—12/8 meter.
3. 4/8 meter: tripled—12/16 meter.
Simple Odd Meters of Three Beats
1. 3/1 meter or 3: tripled—9/2 meter.
2. 3/2 meter: tripled—9/4 meter.
3. 3/4 meter: tripled—9/8 meter.
4. 3/8 meter: tripled—9/16 meter.
5. 3/16 meter: tripled—9/32 meter.

[b] It is clear from this table that Kirnberger's conception of the distinction between simple and compound meter is not consistent with the commonly accepted definition of these terms.

OBSERVATIONS ABOUT SIMPLE EVEN METERS OF TWO BEATS

[118] (A) 2/1 meter, which is also called *large alla breve* by some, consists of two whole notes or semibreves [per measure]. However, as is the case with the 6/2 meter of two triple beats that is derived from it, it is no longer used because of the confusion caused by the rests, since the same rest has a value of half a measure at one time and a whole measure at another. In place of these, it is better to use 2/2 and 6/4 with the adjective *grave* to indicate the emphatic and weighty performance required by these meters. I know of only one Credo by the elder Bach in the large alla breve meter of two beats, which he designated, however, with C to show that the rests have the same value as in ordinary alla breve time.[c] Telemann, however, has even written church pieces in 6/1 and other similar meters; one can easily see that these are only eccentricities.

(B) 2/2 meter, or rather *alla breve*, which is always designated by ¢ or 2̸, is most often used in church pieces, fugues, and elaborate choruses. It is to be noted about this meter that it is very serious and emphatic, yet is performed twice as fast as its note values indicate, unless a slower tempo is specified by the adjectives *grave*, *adagio*, etc. The same is true of the 6/4 meter of two triple beats that is derived from 2/2 meter, but the *tempo giusto* of this meter is somewhat more moderate. Both meters tolerate no shorter note values than eighths.

(C) 2/4 meter has the same tempo as alla breve but is performed much

---

(Footnote b continued)

The meters listed in the right column, those that are derived from the simple meters in the left column by multiples of three, are normally considered as compound meters; Kirnberger, however, considers them among the simple meters. According to Kirnberger, compound meters, the most useful of which are listed in table 4.2, are derived from simple meters by multiples of two. This definition leads to certain inconsistencies: no meter of nine (three triple beats), for example, can be considered as compound, since it cannot be divided in the middle. Other meters, like 6/8, can be simple (derived from 3/4) or compound (derived from 3/8); but in both cases, the measure is divided into two triple beats.

Kirnberger's views on meter are reflected in the writings of Heinrich Christoph Koch. See the article "Taktart" in his *Musikalisches Lexikon* (Frankfurt, 1802) or his *Versuch einer Anleitung zur Composition*, vol. II, part II, chapter 2 (Leipzig, 1782–93). The only significant difference is that Koch lists the meters derived from simple meters by multiples of three, which Kirnberger considers under the heading of simple, as among the "mixed" meters.

A different classification of meters was given by Johann Adolph Scheibe in his treatise, *Über die musikalische Composition*, vol. I, chapter 5 (Leipzig, 1773). Scheibe divides meter into four categories: (1) simple even (duple or quadruple) meters; (2) simple odd (triple) meters; (3) compound even meters; and (4) compound odd meters. This corresponds to the commonly accepted classification of meter today.

[c] The work to which Kirnberger refers is the Credo from the *Mass in B minor* (*BWV* 232).

more lightly. The difference in performance between the two meters is too noticeable for anyone to believe that it makes no difference whether a piece is written in C or in 2/4. Consider, for example, the following melodic phrase in both meters [example 4.5].

EXAMPLE 4.5

[119] If this phrase is performed correctly, everyone will notice that it is much more serious and emphatic in *alla breve* (A) than in 2/4 (B) meter, where it comes close to being playful. This is the difference between meters having the same number of beats, as was noted above.

2/4 meter as well as the 6/8 meter that is derived from it are most often used in chamber and theater pieces. In their natural tempi, sixteenth notes and a few thirty-second notes in succession are their shortest note values. But if the tempo is modified by the adjectives *andante*, *largo*, *allegro*, etc., more or none of these note values can be used, depending on the rate of speed.

(D) 2/8 meter would be appropriate only for short amusing dance pieces because of its fast tempo and its all too great lightness of execution. However, it is not in use, and we would not have mentioned it if 6/16 meter —which is derived from it and in which many pieces have been written— did not have to be listed. It differs greatly from 6/8 meter in the hurried nature of its tempo and the lightness of its execution. J. S. Bach and Couperin[7] have written some of their pieces in 6/16 meter, not without good reason. Who does not know the Bach fugue at (A) in example 4.6?[d] [120] If this theme is rewritten as at (B), the tempo is no longer the same, the gait is much more ponderous, and the notes, particularly the passing notes, are

7. Former court organist in Paris. He has published many pieces engraved in copper under the title, *Pièces de Clavecin*, which in all respects are models of good keyboard pieces.

---

[d] Fugue in F major (*BWV* 880) from *Das wohltemperierte Klavier II*.

emphasized too much; in short, the expression of the piece as a whole suffers
and is no longer the one given to it by Bach. If this fugue is to be performed
correctly on the keyboard, the notes must be played lightly and without the
least pressure in a fast tempo; this is what 6/16 meter requires. On the violin,
pieces in this and other similarly light meters are to be played just with the
point of the bow; however, weightier meters require a longer stroke and
more bow pressure. The fact that these and several other meters that we
shall list are considered superfluous and obsolete today indicates either that
good and correct execution has been lost or that an aspect of expression
which is easy to obtain only in these meters is entirely unknown to us. Both
[of these conclusions] do little credit to the art, which supposedly has
reached its peak in our time.

EXAMPLE 4.6

It is now to be noted in particular about these duple meters that each
measure amounts to one foot of two parts, the first of which is accented and
the second unaccented,[e] and that each main note of a melodic phrase must
fall on the first beat of the measure, or, as is said, on the downbeat. To clarify
this for the aspiring composer, let us divide the words *Dank und Lob und
Preis und Macht* musically and metrically. They cannot be divided naturally
other than as at (A) in example 4.7. It would be most clumsy and unnatural if
the nouns of this example were to be placed on the unaccented beats, as at
(B). The same applies to melody without words. All principal notes must fall
on the downbeat, because the first beat of the measure has the greatest
weight and is accented. What I mean by the principal notes here are those at
which even a crude peasant nods his head or stamps his foot when expressing the feeling of the meter. Therefore the inexperienced composer is
advised first to sing or play the melody that he has in his head and wants to

---

[e] Here Kirnberger uses the adjectives *lang* and *kurz*, which refer to the long and short
syllables of poetic feet, to indicate the accented or unaccented parts of the measure. They do not
imply a difference of duration, but of stress. He also uses the expressions *gute Zeit* (strong beat)
and *schlechte* or *leichte Zeit* (weak or light beat).

write down, and to beat the time with his hand or foot. [121] In this way he will not miss the principal notes that fall on the downbeat, provided that the melody is metric. And he will not write down the idea at (A) in example 4.8 so that the weight of the first beat falls on the second beat, as at (B).

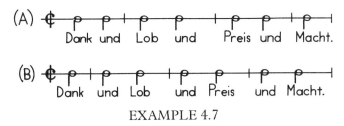

EXAMPLE 4.7

EXAMPLE 4.8

This is the most blatant error that can be committed, although it has been and still is made by composers whom one would at least have credited with a sensitivity to metric stress, since they have written so much. Among other [examples], I know of a long aria in alla breve time by one Perez, who has written many operas. It begins with the words, *Invano il tuo furore*, etc.[f] Shortly after the beginning of the vocal part, a rhythmic error occurs whereby the entire remaining part of the aria is displaced by half a measure. It is unbelievable how difficult it is to perform or to accompany such a confusingly notated piece.

Regarding unaccented or accented beats of the measure, it is to be noted that no nonessential dissonance can be used on the unaccented beat but must be prepared on the accented beat and resolved on the unaccented,[g] as in example 4.9.

[f] Work unidentified.

[g] Here Kirnberger is not very precise in his definition. What he means is that a nonessential dissonance must occur on an accented beat but is prepared and resolved on an unaccented beat.

EXAMPLE 4.9

[122] The unaccented beat may not be treated in passing in these meters, but, like the accented beat, must have a perceptible fundamental harmony.

The concluding note must always fall on the downbeat of the measure. If this does not happen, it indicates that somewhere in the melody there is an extra or missing half measure. The concluding note in music is always accented; therefore, it is a mistake if the poet provides the composer with verses in which the last syllable is feminine, that is, ends with a short syllable.

OBSERVATIONS ABOUT SIMPLE EVEN METERS OF FOUR BEATS

(A) 4/2 meter, or ○, like 2/1 time, is no longer in use; it also is objectionable because of the confusion caused by its rests, as is the 12/3 meter of four triple beats derived from it. They are mentioned here only because one now and then comes across old pieces in these meters. Instead of these, it is better to use 4/4 and 12/8 meter with the adjective *grave* to designate the weighty tempo and emphatic performance appropriate to the former meters. If young composers should come across church pieces in *alla breve* time where there are four half notes between two barlines, they must not let themselves be misled and conclude that the meter is 4/2. This occurs only as a convenience for the composer to avoid an excess of barlines and ties, and he is free to do so. But this does not change the nature of the ¢ measure, which always has the same stress every other half note; and the upbeat and downbeat of the measure is fixed even when four, six, and more measures are joined without barline, as Handel, among others, has frequently done in his oratorios. Furthermore, this does not cause confusion regarding the rests, whose value always remains the same in such situations.

(B) 4/4 meter, which is designated by C, is of two types: either it is used with the adjective *grave* in place of the 4/2 meter just mentioned, in which case it is called large 4/4 time; or it is the so-called common even meter, which is also called small 4/4 time.

[123] Large 4/4 time is of extremely weighty tempo and execution and, because of its emphatic nature, is suited primarily to church piece, choruses, and fugues. Eighth and a few sixteenth notes in succession are its fastest note values. To distinguish it from small 4/4 time, it should be designated by 4/4 instead of C. The two meters have nothing in common except for their signatures.

Small 4/4 time has a more lively tempo and a far lighter execution. It tolerates all note values up to sixteenth notes and is used very often in all styles.

The same is true of 12/8 meter of [four] triple beats that is derived from 4/4 meter. A few older composers who were very sensitive about the manner in which their pieces were performed often designated pieces consisting only of sixteenth notes by 24/16 instead of 12/8 to indicate that the sixteenth notes should be performed lightly, quickly, and without the slightest pressure on the first note of each beat. Composers and performers today seem to know so little about these subtleties that they believe, on the contrary, that such meter designations were only an eccentricity of the older composers.

(C) 4/8 is the lightest of the quadruple meters in execution and tempo. It is distinguished from 2/4 meter by the weight of its beats, all of which are equally stressed; but in 2/4 meter the first and third beats are emphasized. [See example 4.10.] Therefore, it has a somewhat slower tempo than 2/4 meter. Yet, since the liveliness of the tempo makes the stress of the beats less noticeable in both meters, the two are not as different from one another as are 4/4 meter and *alla breve*. Furthermore, today's composers no longer designate pieces with 4/8, but always with 2/4 instead.

EXAMPLE 4.10

Although 12/16 meter of [four] triple beats, which is derived from 4/8 meter, is presently neglected and 12/8 meter is always written instead, it is completely different from the latter in its greater lightness of execution. The elder Bach has certainly not written the fugue at (A) in example 4.11 in 12/8 and the other at (B) in 12/16 without good reason.[h]

[124] Everyone will easily perceive the distinction between the two meters in these examples. The one at (A) designates a slower tempo and a

---

[h] The first is the subject of the Fughetta in c minor (*BWV* 961); the second is the subject of the Fugue in C-sharp minor (*BWV* 873) from *Das wohltemperierte Klavier* II.

EXAMPLE 4.11

more emphatic performance; furthermore, many sixteenth notes can be used in this meter. However, no shorter note values can be used in the one at (B), and the sixteenth notes are performed quickly and plainly, without any emphasis. Handel, Bach, and Couperin have written many pieces in 12/16 meter.

In quadruple meter, the first and third beats are accented, but the second and fourth unaccented. The former are also called strong and the latter weak beats. Of the accented beats, the first is in turn stressed more than the third, as can be seen from example 4.12, where ___ means accented, and ⌣ unaccented.

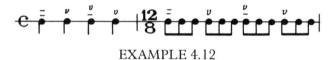

EXAMPLE 4.12

Therefore the principal notes of the melody must always fall on the first beat; the other notes receive more or less weight depending on the intrinsic stress of the other beats. In these meters, the closing note always falls on the first beat and must last four beats, except in pieces where the phrase begins on the upbeat, because the cadence is felt only up to the point where a new phrase can begin. [See example 4.13.]

[125] In the melody at (A), the concluding note cannot be shortened, or, if it were to be sounded only briefly for reasons of performance, at least no new phrase can be begun until the four beats of the last measure are over. This applies not only to the last note of a piece, but to all concluding notes of a musical period. In the melody at (B) the concluding note is felt for only three beats because the phrase begins on the upbeat; and in the melody at (C) it is felt for only two beats. The young composer has to pay careful attention to this so that he acquires a proper feeling for meter and learns to write correctly. It is very unpleasant for the listener to hear a new period

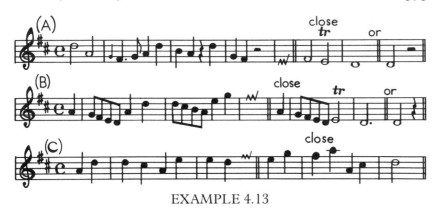

EXAMPLE 4.13

begin before the preceding one has ended, and even more troublesome for
the performer of such a piece, particularly if the accents of the melody fall on
the incorrect beat through such an error.

[126] It is generally difficult for beginners to feel clearly the difference
between quadruple and duple meters, and they often write in duple meter
where they should have chosen a quadruple meter, and vice versa. To avoid
this error when writing a piece in even meter, they must carefully consider
whether four equal pulses can be counted without a break or comma being
felt between the second and third beats, as at (A) in example 4.14. In this
case, the meter is always quadruple. But in the other case, that is, when a
clear break—which has the effect of a comma in speech—is felt between the
second and third pulse, that is, so that the first and third pulses are of equal
weight, as at (B), then the meter of the piece is duple. Thus, if (A) in example
4.13 were written as at (A) in example 4.15, it would be notated totally
contrary to the meter contained in the melody. Here this manner of notating
would have the same effect as misplaced commas in speech, which would
sever inseparable little phrases by a clumsy break and divide them into two
sentences. Of course, this same melody can very well be written in 2/4 if a

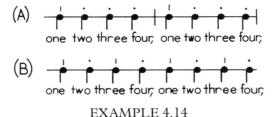

EXAMPLE 4.14

EXAMPLE 4.15

more lively and lighter tempo and performance are desired, but only as at
(B) in example 4.15.

Here the division of the melody into measures is as correct as above in C.
However, here 4/8 meter is really felt; as was mentioned above, it is always
notated in 2/4 in contemporary music.

OBSERVATIONS ABOUT ODD METER OF THREE BEATS

[127] (A) 3/1 meter, which consists of three whole notes [per measure],
and the 9/2 meter of three triple beats that is derived from it are of no use
whatsoever. The weighty and emphatic performance that would be specified by both is achieved by means of the two following meters, particularly if
the adjective *grave* is added; furthermore, [in the latter] the eye is not
exhausted by the many large notes and rests that cause only ambiguity and
confusion in the former meters.

(B) 3/2 meter is used very often, especially in church pieces, because of
the ponderous and slow performance indicated by its note values. In this
style, quarter and, at most, eighth notes are its fastest note values. In the
chamber style, sixteenth notes can also be used in 3/2 meter; C. P. E. Bach
has even begun a symphony in this meter with many thirty-second notes in a
row.[i] With such note values, the three beats of this meter must be indicated
most clearly in the other voices; otherwise the melody would remain fuzzy
and incomprehensible to the listener.

Because of the different weights of their beats, 3/2 meter has no other
similarity with 6/4 meter except that both contain six quarter notes. Yet it is
to be noted as something special that good composers of old have treated the

---

[i]Wotquenne lists a symphony in E-flat for two horns, two oboes, two violins, viola, and
bass (1757) that begins with continuous sixteenth-note (but not thirty-second-note) motion in
3/2 meter. See Alfred Wotquenne, *C. Ph. Em. Bach: Thematisches Verzeichnis seiner Werke*
(Leipzig, 1905), no. 179 (p. 61).

courante, which is generally written in 3/2, in such a way that both meters were often combined in it. Consider, for example, the first part of a courante for keyboard by Couperin in example 4.16.[j]

EXAMPLE 4.16

[128] The second and sixth measures and the bass melody of the seventh measure of this courante are in 3/2 meter, but the other measures are written in 6/4. In the works of J. S. Bach there are a number of courantes treated in this same way.

The 9/4 meter of [three] triple beats that is derived from 3/2 occurs rarely, since 9/8 is used instead. But it is easily understood that the two meters are very different with respect to the performance and tempo that they specify. [129] In the church style, where a ponderous and emphatic execution is generally combined with a subdued and slow tempo, 9/4 meter is preferable by far to 9/8, since a melody that assumes a serious expression in the former meter can easily appear playful in the latter. [See example 4.17.]

[j] François Couperin. *Pièces de Clavecin*, Book 1 (Paris, 1713), first order, first courante.

EXAMPLE 4.17

(C) Because of its lighter execution, 3/4 meter is not as common in the church style as 3/2; but it is used very often in the chamber and theatrical styles.

Its natural tempo is that of a minuet, and in this tempo it does not tolerate many sixteenth notes, even less thirty-second notes, in succession. However, since it assumes all degrees of tempo from the adjectives *adagio*, *allegro*, etc., all note values that fit this tempo can be used, depending on the rate of speed.

The 9/8 meter of three triple beats that is derived from 3/4 has the same tempo as 3/4, but the eighth notes are performed more lightly than in 3/4.

It is a mistake to consider this meter as a 3/4 meter whose beats consist of triplets. He who has only a moderate command of performance knows that triplets in 3/4 meter are played differently from eighths in 9/8 meter. The former are played very lightly and without the slightest pressure on the last note, but the latter heavier and with some weight on the last note. The former never or only rarely permit a harmony to be sounded with the last note, but the latter do very often. The former do not permit any arpeggiations in sixteenth notes, but the latter do very easily. If the two meters were not distinguished by special qualities, all gigues in 6/8 could also be written in 2/4; 12/8 would be a C meter, and 6/8 a 2/4 meter. How senseless this is can easily be discovered by anyone who rewrites, for example, a gigue in 12/8 or 6/8 meter in C or 2/4 meter.

[130] 3/4 and 9/8 meter gave the older composers the opportunity to use an 18/16 meter of three sextuplet beats when they wanted to indicate that the piece should be performed lightly, swiftly, and without the slightest pressure on the first note of each beat. [See example 4.18.]

EXAMPLE 4.18

However, since such subtleties of performance have been lost to such a degree that even many who are called virtuosos perform six beamed sixteenths like two compounded triplets, 18/16 meter belongs among the meters that are lost and highly dispensable today.

(D) 3/8 meter has the lively tempo of a passepied; it is performed in a light but not an entirely playful manner and is widely used in chamber and theatrical music.

9/16 meter of three triple beats that is derived from 3/8 was used in many ways by the older composers for gigue-like pieces that are to be performed extremely quickly and lightly. But it no longer occurs in contemporary music; 9/8 meter appears in its place.

(E) 3/16 meter, which indicates the truly light performance of hasty pieces and dances that are commonly written in 3/8, where only one beat can be heard for each measure because of the very fast tempo, has been used rarely. In Handel's keyboard suites there is a gigue in 3/16 meter that begins as shown in example 4.19. That this is nothing other than 3/16 meter—even though the signature is 12/8 instead of 3/16 in the edition by John Walsh[k]— is evident from the concluding note, which falls on the downbeat and lasts for just three sixteenths. This is not possible in 12/16 meter but is possible in compound 6/16 meter, as will be shown in greater detail when we discuss compound meters.

EXAMPLE 4.19

9/32 meter of three triple beats that is derived from 3/16 is of no use at all and, furthermore, has never been used.

[131] These triple meters have the common element that, in each, three beats are felt per measure, the first of which is always accented, the third unaccented. The second can be accented or unaccented, depending on the nature of the piece. That is, it is usually accented in ponderous meters and in serious pieces, as in chaconnes and many sarabandes; but in light meters this second beat is weak. This two-fold treatment of the second beat in triple meter is clarified by example 4.20.

[k] In the Walsh edition of the second volume of these suites (London, 1736?), the meter signature is given as 12/8 but the piece is notated in 12/16. Kirnberger, however, insists that the meter is really 3/16 but notated in 12/16 to avoid writing so many barlines.

EXAMPLE 4.20

In the first example, a nonessential dissonance, which can only appear on a strong beat, falls on the second quarter. In the second, the cadence falls on the same beat; consequently it is also accented here. But in the third example it is weak.

What I have stated previously about the treatment of even meters with regard to the different weights of the beats can easily be applied to triple meter as well. Suspensions or nonessential dissonances, principal notes, and cadences can fall only on accented beats. However, cadences on the second strong beat of the triple measure are less common than those on the first, or downbeat. Many English and, particularly, Scottish dances deviate from this rule and conclude on the upbeat; but in this way they acquire a somewhat strange flavor, which is noticeable even to an untrained ear.

When eighth notes occur in 3/4 meter and sixteenths in 3/8, the first of these eighths or sixteenths is accented.

OBSERVATIONS ABOUT COMPOUND METER

In duple as well as in triple meter, there are melodies in which it is obvious that whole measures are alternately strong and weak, so that a whole measure is heard as only one beat. If the melody is of such a nature that the entire measure is felt as only one beat, two measures must be grouped together to form just one, whose first part is accented and the other unaccented. If this contraction were not to occur, the result would be a melody consisting only of accented beats, because of the necessary weight of the downbeat. This would be as unpleasant as a sentence in speech consisting entirely of one-syllable words, each of which had an accent.

[132] This resulted in compound meters, namely, compound 4/4 from two combined measures of 2/4, compound 6/8 from two combined measures of 3/8, etc.

This combining [of measures] actually occurs only so that the player can arrive at the proper performance and play the second half of such a measure more lightly than the first. These meters—for example, the compound 4/4 and the simple common 4/4—can easily be distinguished, since, in the former, the cadences fall naturally on the second part of the measure and last only half a measure, which would not be possible in simple 4/4 meter. Likewise, in compound 6/4 meter the close can occur on the fourth quarter, which is not possible in simple 6/4 meter.

Otherwise, compound meters are no different from the simple ones with regard to weighty and light performance and tempo. That is, compound 4/4 or 6/4 meter has the same character as simple 4/4 or 6/4 meter in tempo and performance.

The most useful compound meters are given in table 4.2.

TABLE 4.2.

---

1. Compound 4/4 meter, combined from two 2/4 measures,
2. Compound 12/8 meter, combined from two 6/8 measures,
3. Compound 12/16 meter, combined from two 6/16 measures,
4. Compound 6/4 meter, combined from two 3/4 measures,
5. Compound 6/8 meter, combined from two 3/8 measures,
6. Compound 6/16 meter, combined from two 3/16 measures.

These compound meters are not to be confused with [those found in] pieces where only one barline is written every two measures simply to avoid an excess of barlines, but which in other respects completely retain the nature of simple meters. Most largos in Graun's operas were written in this way; they are actually in true 2/4 meter but always have a barline after four quarters simply for the sake of abbreviation.

Let this now suffice concerning knowledge of the mechanical nature of all common meters. According to the outline presented on p. 383, above, I now have to consider:

2. the spirit or actual character of each of these meters from the standpoint of their power to express sentiments and passions.

[133] Here it is not so much the even or odd number of beats in a measure that matters as the slower or faster tempo and the heavier or lighter gait of the measure. One meter can be used for contrasting passions, depending upon the tempo and other factors. However, since each meter has a treatment that is most suitable and natural to it, or, if one wants, most common, then it also has to this extent a special character that can, of course, be taken away from it by a strange and unusual treatment.

Thus, what I have to say here concerns the special ease with which this or that meter can assume a certain character.

It is to be noted in general that, among the meters which have the same number of beats, the one that has larger or longer beats is naturally a bit more serious than the one of shorter beats. Thus 4/4 meter is less lively than

4/8 meter; 3/2 meter is more ponderous than 3/4, and the latter is not as lively as 3/8.

For solemn and pathetic pieces, *alla breve* is especially appropriate and is therefore used in motets and other solemn church pieces. Large 4/4 meter has a very emphatic and serious motion and is suited to stately choruses, to fugues in church pieces, and generally to pieces where pomp and gravity is required. 3/2 meter is emphatic and very serious as long as not too many short notes are used. 4/4 meter is best suited for a lively and exhilarating expression that is still somewhat emphatic. 2/4 is also lively but certainly combined with more lightness and, for that reason, can be used well to express playfulness. 4/8 meter is definitely totally fleeting, and its liveliness no longer contains any of the emphasis of 4/4 meter. The character of 3/4 appears to be gentle and noble, particularly when it consists only, or at least mostly, of quarter notes. But 3/8 meter has a liveliness that is somewhat frolicsome.

These general characters are defined even more specifically by the particular note value that prevails and by rules that determine progression by larger or smaller intervals. The character of 3/4 meter is entirely different when quarter notes are used almost exclusively throughout than when many eighths and even smaller notes occur, and when it progresses mostly by small intervals than when leaps occur more often. Since many dances receive their peculiar character from such special determining features within the same meter, and since I plan to discuss this matter in a special chapter, I will have the opportunity to speak there about the character of such pieces that are bound to specific rules.

[134] From the few remarks that I have made here about the different characters of the meters, it is evident that this difference of meters is very well suited to express particular nuances of the passions.

Each passion has its own degrees of strength and, if I may say so, its own deeper or shallower character. Joy, for example, can be solemn and almost exalted; it can be overwhelming, but also leaping and frolicsome. Joy can have these and even more levels and nuances, and such is the case with the other passions as well. Above all, the composer must have a definite impression of the particular passion that he has to portray and then choose a more ponderous or lighter meter depending upon whether the affect in its particular nuance requires one or the other.

3. How is one to approach vocal pieces with regard to meter? First of all, one must pay attention to the sentiment contained in the words, and, depending upon its nature, select one of the more serious or lively types of meter. Everything that is sung in *alla breve* time, for example, can also be

sung in 2/4 meter, but in performance such a piece would sound far more serious in the first meter and far more lively in the second.

Second, one must investigate whether the text requires a meter of two, three, or four beats. That is, each long syllable must fall on an accented beat, and each short syllable on an unaccented beat. The key word of a verse must fall on the first beat. [See example 4.21.]

> Weiser Damon, dessen Haupt
> Lorbeer um und um belaubt.

EXAMPLE 4.21

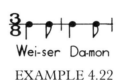

EXAMPLE 4.22

Here a weak syllable always follows a long one, and [the verse] could also be set in 3/8, as in example 4.22. [135] But, since the verse has a serious character, 2/4 is preferable to 3/8. However, the following verses have a lively character, although long and short syllables alternate just as above.

> Ein kleines Kind mit Flügeln,
> Das ich noch nie gesehen etc.

These [words] must be set in 6/8, as in example 4.23, but they must not be written in 3/8, because then the last syllable of the word "Flügeln," which is weak, would fall on the first beat and therefore would be accented. Since the close always falls in the middle during the course of these verses, this is indicative of compound 6/8 meter.

EXAMPLE 4.23

The situation is different in example 4.24, where the meter is simple 6/8 because of the close. If this example were to be written in 3/8, a false phrase of three measures would result at the end, disregarding the fact that the last syllable of the word "Freude" would be accented. [See example 4.25.]

EXAMPLE 4.24

EXAMPLE 4.25

Here follow a few additional examples [examples 4.26 and 4.27] that need no further explanation at this point.

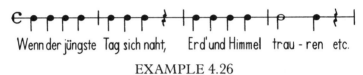

EXAMPLE 4.26

or: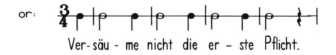

or:

or:

Ver - säu-me nicht die er - ste Pflicht.

EXAMPLE 4.27

[136] Depending upon the content of the words, one or the other type is suited to the expression. [See example 4.28.]

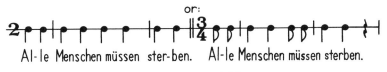

Al-le Menschen müssen ster-ben.   Al-le Menschen müssen sterben.

EXAMPLE 4.28

It can be seen from these few examples that different meters and rhythmic progressions can be chosen for the same words, and yet the long and short syllables always be treated correctly. Here we are talking only about those melodies where each syllable is set to one note. However, since many notes and even whole passages can be written to one syllable in an embellished melody, it becomes clear that almost all meters can fit the same words. Therefore, when writing large vocal compositions involving an embellished melody, one must have a feeling for the special effect of each meter and choose the one that best represents the expression to be portrayed. Graun and Hasse have often set the same arias in very different meters; however, this certainly does not result from indifference toward meter, but rather because they perceived the affection contained in the words from different points of view. One presents jealousy, for example, in a more lamenting way, and the other in a more violent way; both can be correct. Frequently they also had before them words with no trace of sentiment, to which, naturally, every meter that was not contrary to the prosody of the words was suited.

III. RHYTHM[8]

[137] Melody receives its character from tempo and meter, through which a gentle or violent, a sad or joyful sentiment is expressed. The flow of the melody is divided into larger or smaller phrases by the rhythm, without which the melody would progress monotonously; each of these phrases has its special meaning, like phrases in speech. Melody becomes diversified in

8. This word has two meanings: sometimes it means what the ancients called "rhythmoponie," that is, the rhythmic character of a piece; at other times it means a phrase or segment. It has the first meaning when one says, "This piece is incorrect rhythmically, or the rhythm is no good." It is used in its other meaning when one says, "a rhythmic unit (phrase) of four measures."

this way and, with its other amenities, becomes a speech that entertains the ear and senses with numerous phrases, some of which taken together form a complete sentence.

Anyone with an average ear will have noticed that the greatest power of melody comes from rhythm. It unites both the melody and the harmony of several measures into a single phrase that is immediately grasped by the ear; and several small phrases are again combined as a larger unit to form a complete sentence with a rest point at its end, which allows us to comprehend these individual phrases as a unit.

The rhythm of a composition is very similar to the versification of a lyric poem. Individual melodic phrases represent the lines, and larger sections of several phrases are musical strophes. Just as the lyric poem depends greatly on a good versification, rhythm is also a very important ingredient in melody. For that reason, I have resolved to discuss this matter very thoroughly here.

There are melodies whose rhythm is organized precisely throughout according to certain rules that may not be broken. However, other pieces are not bound by such definite rules; rather, the composer is free to select a rhythm or a musical verse form. [138] In the first category belong melodies written for dancing, in the second the other types of muscial compositions. But even in the latter situation certain rules must be observed, so that one does not interfere with the rhythmic euphony.

Since I have resolved to talk in particular about the most common dance melodies in one of the following chapters, I shall say nothing of their rhythmic quality here but shall present only the general rules that have to do with the rhythmic character of all pieces in general.

In speech one comprehends the meaning only at the end of a sentence and is more or less satisfied by it depending on whether this meaning establishes a more or less complete statement. The same is true in music. Not until a succession of connected notes reaches a point of rest at which the ear is somewhat satisfied does it comprehend these notes as a small unit; before this, the ear perceives no meaning and is anxious to understand what this succession of notes really wants to say. However, if a noticeable break does occur after a moderately long succession of connected notes, which provides the ear with a small rest point and concludes the meaning of the phrase, then the ear combines all these notes into a comprehensible unit.

This break or rest point can be achieved either by a complete cadence or simply by a melodic close with a restful harmony, without a close in the bass. In the first case, we have a complete musical statement that is equivalent to a full sentence in speech, after which a period is placed. But in the other case, we have a phrase that is indeed comprehensible, yet after which another or several more phrases are expected to complete the meaning of the period. The musical statement that is complete and ends with a formal cadence we will call a *section* or *period*; but the incomplete one that ends only with a melodic break or a satisfying harmony we will call a *phrase* or a *rhythmic unit*.[1]

One can easily understand that every good melody must consist of various periods and these in turn of several phrases. I first want to discuss here what is to be observed regarding these periods and phrases so that the ear is never offended or loses interest.

[139] A musical period, then, is a succession of connected notes that concludes with a complete or formal cadence. The effect of this cadence is so satisfying to the ear that it permits it to comprehend the entire succession of notes combined in this period as a unit, without being disturbed in this sensation by the expectation of what might follow. If this close occurs in the principal tonic of the piece, the satisfaction is complete and nothing further is expected, since the entire musical speech has reached its goal. But if it occurs in a key other than the main key, the satisfaction is incomplete,[m] since the ear wants to hear the main key again.

A series of such periods, none of which but the last closes in the main

[1]The following are the terms used by Kirnberger to describe the formal divisions in a musical composition. The composition itself is divided into principal sections (*Haupttheile*) and each of these into several periods or smaller sections (*Perioden* or *Abschnitte*), which end with a formal cadence. The latter, which in speech are equivalent to complete sentences, are also called *Hauptsätze*. Each period is divided into two or more phrases (*Einschnitte* or *Sätze*), which are articulated by less conclusive rest points. The phrase is also called a rhythmic unit (*Rhythmus*), which reflects the eighteenth-century conception of rhythmic organization at that level; the norm is given as the four-measure unit.

Kirnberger's use of terminology is not consistent. The term *Einschnitt*, for example, is most often used to mean phrase; but at other times it is used synonymously with *Glied*, which denotes an articulated segment of the phrase. And at other places in this work it means phrase division and is thus equivalent to *Cäsur* (caesura).

It should also be noted that the terminology used by theorists of the eighteenth century to describe formal divisions in music was not standard. Heinrich Christoph Koch, for example, used more precise terminology than Kirnberger in his *Versuch einer Anleitung zur Composition* (Leipzig, 1782–93); he was also more consistent than Kirnberger in applying them to music. The main source for Koch's ideas on this subject was Joseph Riepel's *Anfangsgründe zur musikalischen Setzkunst* (Regensburg, 1752–68). Despite the difference in terminology, it would seem likely from the contents of this section that Kirnberger was also strongly influenced by Riepel's ideas.

[m]Although Kirnberger states that the satisfaction would be complete under these circumstances, it is clear that he means the opposite.

key, forms a single composition. However, if one or more periods were to conclude with a cadence in the main key before the end of a composition, one would no longer have a single melody, but a composition that is made up of two or more similar melodies.

Therefore, it should be a principal rule not to conclude any period but the last in an entire piece with the principal tonic. For when this happens, the entire piece really comes to an end. However, this natural rule is often broken. In concerti and arias, the tutti and ritornelli normally close in the main key and are thus complete independent pieces, since the ear is already completely satisfied after such a close and perceives nothing at all that arouses the expectation of a new succession of notes.

However, the style of some composers—who at the very beginning of a piece close again in the principal tonic after two or four measures, and hence stand again exactly where they began—is entirely bad. To avoid this and to connect the ritornello closely with the following material, the solo or vocal part could begin directly at the close of the ritornello, whereby the smoothest connection between the principal sections of the composition would be achieved. The following keyboard concerto [example 4.29] by J. S. Bach can serve as an example of this type of connection.[n]

EXAMPLE 4.29

[140] The separation of the first ritornello from the following solo part can also be avoided by closing the ritornello on the dominant of the main key. [See example 4.30.]

Otherwise the unity of the melody requires that all periods begin on the same beat throughout the piece. It would completely disrupt the feeling of

[n] Concerto in d minor (*BWV* 1052).

EXAMPLE 4.30

unity if they were sometimes to begin on the upbeat and at other times on the downbeat.

The length of periods is not bound to any definite rule except in dance melodies, where they always have a definite number of measures. Nevertheless, one cannot be entirely arbitrary in this matter, since periods can be too short and too long. A series of very short periods consisting of a few measures would soon become unpleasant, because the ear would feel points of rest too close in succession. The ear wants to be somewhat satiated by the key of each period and not to be thrown into new suspense at each moment. [141] However, a period can also be too long. If one has been entertained for a long time by one key, he desires to hear another key as well. Moreover, a period can be so long that the ear completely loses track of its beginning before the end is perceived. In this case a period can no longer be comprehended as a single unit.

From this it is clear that certain limits are set for periods, limits that one cannot overstep without detriment to the euphony. The shortest periods are from six to eight measures; the longest extend not much over thirty-two measures. I am referring here only to what is most common and sounds best, because it sometimes happens that shorter periods occur for special reasons, particularly if required by a text; and sometimes they can also be extended beyond the mentioned limits without becoming boring.

One must avoid periods that are too short, particularly at the beginning of pieces. The ear must be so imbued with the main key that it never completely loses its feeling throughout the entire piece. Moreover, the attention is still at its full strength at the beginning of a composition, and the ear can comprehend more at this point than when it has already become somewhat exhausted.

According to the rules of modulation, a period must be all the shorter the more distant is its key from the main key. If one remains for too long in such a key, the feeling for the main key would be completely lost.

It has been noted that periods consisting of a number of measures that can be divided by four are most pleasing. Those that can be divided by three are less pleasing. However, they must always be divisible by two, since a period consisting of an odd number of measures has something disagreeable about it. However, if the break at the last phrase is made by the dominant chord in such a way that the close to the tonic absolutely requires an additional measure, the final period acquires an odd number of measures— thirty-three instead of thirty-two, forty-nine instead of forty-eight— without offending the ear. This is also the case in the situation I mentioned before, where the end of a ritornello coincides with the beginning of the vocal or solo part.

[142] Each period generally consists of a larger or smaller number of phrases that are not completely cut off or separated from one another yet are somewhat detached by smaller rest points than those produced by cadences. These smaller rest points are created in melody either by melodic closes or by rests, but in harmony by restful chords, particularly dominant chords; a new consonant harmony must at least be heard where the small rest point is supposed to be. Cadential chords can also be used for this, but they must be weakened by inversions or dissonances so that the feeling of rest is not too strong and the ear is kept in close anticipation of what follows.

A phrase is articulated most forcefully by the half cadence; its inversions produce weaker breaks. Inversions of full cadences can also be used for this, and even the cadence itself if it falls on a weak beat, as happens most commonly in gavottes. Finally, each new consonant harmony produces a small break or rest point. Thus the break or end of a phrase can be made perceptible in all these different ways.

Such phrases, also called rhythmic units, can be of different lengths; they can be of one to four, five, and even more measures in length, just as there are long and short lines in poetry. But the longer ones, particularly when they are longer than four measures, are usually divided into two or even more smaller segments that are articulated by very small rest points, which are comparable to the caesura in verses and are thus also called *caesuras*.

Just as the ear soon perceives the meter in every composition and wants it to be retained for the entire piece, the ear is also soon influenced by the rhythmic organization and is always inclined to count the same number of measures for each phrase; it is actually somewhat offended if this uniformity is broken. There are, of course, situations where individual phrases of more or fewer measures than the others are very appropriate for the sake of a particular expression. But this must be considered as an exception to the rule. As long as one is concerned only with euphony and a comprehensible, pleasing melody, the best effect is without doubt achieved by having the same length of phrases throughout. [143] An example of a phrase that does not have the same length as the others and that has a very good effect just because it is so unique can be seen in an aria that begins as in example 4.31.

Par-to qual na-vi-gan - te qual na-vi - gan - te

EXAMPLE 4.31

Here the meter is compound 4/4, where half a measure is already as much as a whole measure. The segments are two measures in length, but the very first is only half a measure, and in this way the important word "Parto," with which the aria begins, is greatly stressed.

There are also cases where a short segment of one measure can even be inserted among longer ones without disrupting the grouping of the remaining units of equal length; it is not counted, since it is heard as something foreign that attracts the attention in a very special way, as in example 4.32.

Mi par ch'io sen - to la dol - ce spe - me

EXAMPLE 4.32

Here the third measure is inserted between the first and second segments and is like an echo of the preceding measure, which, because of the text, is very effective. There are also examples of such repetitions of two measures after rhythmic units of four measures. However, such insertions must be used with careful consideration, and must either be given to a secondary part or especially be distinguished from the preceding by *piano* or *forte*. In addition, one must take good care that the continuation does not fall on the wrong beats as a result of such insertions.

A complete melody consisting of only one-measure segments would amount to a childish song; even segments of two measures in succession become annoying after a while unless something very fleeting or playful is being expressed. The best melodies are always those whose phrases have four measures. A few of two measures may enter in among them, but they must occur in pairs, since they are then heard as phrases of four measures with a caesura in the middle. [144] In the succession of four-measure phrases, two of one measure and then one of two measures can be written in place of one of four measures. But it is necessary that the two of one measure be similar. See example 4.33. If one tries to omit the small segment indicated by (b), he will soon notice how unnatural and unpleasant the melody becomes. Here the first phrase is four measures long; the second is just as long, but it consists of three segments of which two are one measure long and the third is two measures long. In this way rhythmic variety is given to a succession of equally long phrases. However, a four-measure phrase cannot be formed by two segments of one and three measures [respectively]; but one can repeat the last measure of a three-measure phrase as an echo and thus form from them a rhythmic unit of four measures, as in example 4.34.

EXAMPLE 4.33

EXAMPLE 4.34

Phrases of three measures cannot be used throughout an entire melody, except in very short pieces that are supposed to have a somewhat burlesque character, like the small dance pieces that are called *Bayerisch*. Thus this three-measure phrase, which is perceived as something foreign and unusual, can only be used at the beginning of a composition, or also here and there in the middle where the intention is to surprise the ear by something strange.

This phrase is more comprehensible in triple meter than in even meter. If it is simple and without caesura, it cannot easily occur by itself but must be written in pairs and, indeed, in such a way that the two are similar, as I have noted about segments of one measure. [145] Example 4.35 can serve as an illustration. If one were to write another phrase of two or four measures after the first phrase in these examples, perhaps in the way shown in example 4.36, the melody would become, if not completely unpleasant, at least very unusual.

Such irregularities could be used in situations where the intention is to surprise the listener by something unusual and irrational.

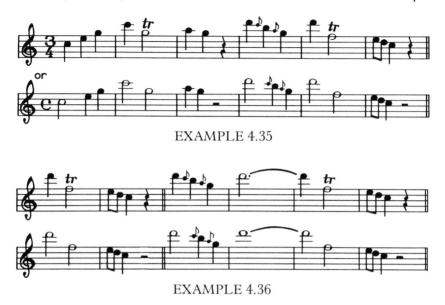

EXAMPLE 4.35

EXAMPLE 4.36

It deserves to be noted here as something special that there are situations where a phrase of four measures can be transformed into rhythmic units of five measures by extension of certain principal notes that are to be given a special emphasis. The ear is not only not offended by it, but the excessive length of such a phrase often has great impact. [146] Thus the four-measure phrase at (A) in example 4.37 can be changed into the five-measure phrase at (B), which is considered only as four measures.

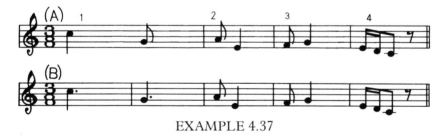

EXAMPLE 4.37

Phrases of five, seven, and nine measures must be divided into smaller segments by appropriate caesuras if they are not to sound unpleasant. However, such long phrases in succession can make the melody somewhat confusing; therefore, they can be used only with great care and particularly in situations where perhaps a violent or very solemn expression is sought.

There is an excellent aria by Graun that consists almost entirely of five-measure phrases, some even without caesuras. But the words require something extraordinary and almost frantic. The beginning of the aria is given in example 4.38.[o]

Non v'é la   nell'a - re - ne del cau-ca-so crude-le non

EXAMPLE 4.38

There are also phrases of seven, nine, and more measures that contain nothing unpleasant or unclear; but they must be made comprehensible by caesuras and, besides, can occur only in short meters. Example 4.39 can serve to illustrate this.

EXAMPLE 4.39

[147] If such long phrases of five or seven measures occur in a piece in which units of four measures prevail, these longer phrases usually result from the above-mentioned extension of a few notes and are perceived as units of four measures, as in example 4.40, where the first two measures of the phrase always represent a single measure.

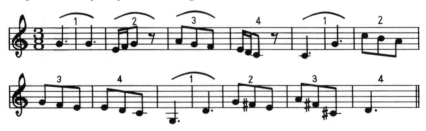

EXAMPLE 4.40

[o] Work unidentified.

This is as much as I have found necessary to note about the length of phrases.

The beginning of a phrase, and hence its end as well, is not restricted to any point within the measure; not only can they fall on any beat but also on any small part of the beat. However, to compose in the easiest and most comprehensible way, one begins either on the downbeat or upbeat.

However, this restriction must be observed: When the phrase division is articulated by a half cadence or a cadential pattern of some kind, the end, namely, this break, must fall on a strong beat, since by its nature such an ending must be accented. Example 4.41 can serve as clarification of this rule.

EXAMPLE 4.41

[148] In the first version the end of the phrase falls in the wrong place; this error has been rectified in the second one.

Smaller rest points, however, can fall on any beat, and likewise caesuras can fall anywhere in the measure and on any chord, except those containing nonessential dissonances or suspensions. Consequently, what some teach— that the caesura is restricted to certain beats—is erroneous. Consider the well-known keyboard sonata by Bach, the beginning of which is given in example 4.42.[P] [149] If one plays all the way through it, he will find that caesuras fall on any eighth note of the measure.

When the first phrase begins on the downbeat, the following phrases

[P]C. P. E. Bach, *Sechs Sonaten für Clavier mit veränderten Reprisen* (Berlin, 1760), first sonata (Wotquenne 50, no. 1).

EXAMPLE 4.42

can nevertheless begin on the upbeat. But if the composition begins on the upbeat, the following phrases must also regularly begin on the upbeat, as can be seen in passepieds, gavottes, loures, and the like.

Still, when a composition begins in a somewhat unusual way—for example with the second, third, or fifth eighth in 4/4 meter or the second or third eighth in 3/4 meter—it is not appropriate in short pieces to begin the following rhythmic units in a different way. In longer pieces this is possible, but the rhythmic unit as stated at the beginning must be repeated most often, just as the principal key must frequently be brought to the attention of the ear in modulation. An example and model of such treatment is the keyboard sonata by Bach, the beginning of which is given in example 4.43.[q]

When a segment that begins on the downbeat is followed by another

EXAMPLE 4.43

[q]C. P. E. Bach, *Fortsetzung von Sechs Sonaten fürs Clavier* (Berlin, 1761), fifth sonata (Wotquenne 51, no. 5), third movement. There are a number of discrepancies (mostly registral) between Kirnberger's example and the following, which is quoted from the edition of 1761.

that begins on the upbeat, the first must be somewhat shorter than its full length. Consider example 4.44.

EXAMPLE 4.44

[150] Since the piece begins on the downbeat, the first segment should last throughout the first two measures. However, the second segment begins on the third quarter of the second measure, and consequently the first segment seems to be short by this quarter. Yet this is not only not objectionable but is pleasing, no doubt because the ear perceives the first segment as continuing after the beginning of the second one and thus intertwines the two. Such overlapping segments occur frequently in arias and are often most effective in making the expression more forceful.

In pieces with two and more parts the rhythmic organization may be different in each part. Consider examples 4.45 and 4.46.

[151] In the first, the rhythmic unit in the upper voice begins on the

EXAMPLE 4.45

EXAMPLE 4.46 (*to be continued*)

EXAMPLE 4.46 (*continued*)

pie - no   og ———————   gi spe-rar   per

— nel tu - o   bel   se - no   og ———————

te,   og ———————   gi spe-rar   per te.

— gi spe-rar   per - te   spe-rar   per-te.

fourth eighth, but in the bass on the second eighth. In the the other, the phrase endings of one part overlap with the beginning of those of the other part. One would think that such irregularities might confuse the ear. Instead it finds them pleasant, probably because one is aware that it is more perfect to comprehend two different rhythmic patterns simultaneously than just one. But when many parts, each with its own rhythmic pattern, are heard simultaneously, the trained ear of a connoisseur is required if the composition is not to be perceived as a confusing clamour. Perhaps it is awareness of the great difficulty of comprehending everything clearly in such situations that makes great composers take immense pleasure in writing fugues for many voices, which become unpleasant to untrained ears.

Everything that I have said to this point about rhythm concerns its external and somewhat mechanical nature. Now I must also say something about its internal nature.

[152] The invention of a single melodic unit or phrase which is an intelligible statement from the language of sentiments and which produces in the sensitive listener the frame of mind that has generated it is simply a work of genius and cannot be taught by rules. Thus I can say nothing about the invention of rhythmic patterns appropriate for the expression of specific sentiments.

Only this can be noted in general—that short phrases are best suited for gentle, tender, agreeable, and particularly for fleeting, frivolous, and playful pieces. But long phrases are suited for emphatic and very serious sentiments, particularly for the expression of something quite pathetic.

But expression is certainly not determined just be length and brevity; the real spirit of each sentiment must still be drawn into it, to which tempo, meter, note values, intervals, and harmony contribute the most.

The entire spirit of a piece must be contained immediately in its initial period, and all the following periods must have some similarity with the first one so that the unity of sentiment is preserved throughout. Thus, whatever rhythmic patterns occur in the first period, similar ones must be heard in the other periods. I do not mean to imply that they should be the same in another key—that is, transposed higher or lower—but only that they should be in the same spirit and above all that they should not stray too far from the patterns of the first period in their note values or metric division, since this would give an entirely different turn to the expression. If, for example, mostly eighth notes were to be used in the rhythmic patterns of the first period, dotted eighth notes followed by sixteenths ($\sqcap$) cannot be written frequently in the following period without erasing the character of the initial rhythms. One very often hears pieces in the new Italian style these days in which there are places having note values that do not appear anywhere else in the entire piece. This completely disrupts the unity of expression and results in the fact that one does not at all understand what he has heard at the end of a piece.

However, since the entire rhythmic character of a piece is generally more the result of a refined sensitivity than a definite theory, I advise young composers to play diligently through the works of the greatest masters in order to acquire the feeling for this important aspect of composition. [153] He who has listened to many well-chosen and rhythmically perfect pieces for a long time will then notice with fair ease every error that is committed against the correctness and the character of the rhythm.

Melodies that are written to texts must conform to the text in their phrases and caesuras. Nothing is more unpleasant than a melodic phrase division which falls at a place in the text that does not permit a resting point. This frequently occurs in odes and songs, but in such pieces it generally results from mistakes made by the poet. However, in arias and other melodies that are based only on a single strophe of the text, such errors committed by the composer against the meaning of the text are inexcusable. It may not be entirely unnecessary to recommend to young composers that they carefully read the ninth chapter of the second part of Mattheson's *Der vollkommene Capellmeister*.[r]

---

[r] Johann Mattheson, *Der vollkommene Capellmeister*, part 2, chapter 9 ("Von den Ab- und Einschnitten der Klang-Rede") (Hamburg, 1739), pp. 180–95.

Index

Page numbers in italics refer to commentaries of the translator.

419